About the author

Alix Fano is a New York-based writer and activist who, for the past ten years, has written about health, animal advocacy and environmental issues. She has had opinion pieces published in *The New York Times* and other US-based newspapers and magazines. She holds a master's degree in urban and environmental policy from Tufts University in Medford, Massachusetts. Formerly the media director for the London-based group Doctors and Lawyers for Responsible Medicine, she is currently co-ordinator for the Medical Research Modernization Committee in New York City. This is her first book.

What people say about this book

'A thoroughly documented, scientific indictment of the current addiction to animal testing. It makes a compelling case for companies to wake up to the non-animal technologies that already exist, and get off the animal-testing treadmill.' *David Phillips, Executive Director, Earth Island Institute, San Francisco, California*

'Cogently argued and well researched, Ms Fano's analysis is a "must read" for anyone involved in environmental policy or public health. Her description of non-animal methods for toxicological testing is comprehensive and invaluable.' *Andrew Kimbrell, Executive Director, International Center for Technology Assessment, Washington, DC*

'A grand synthesis of ideas and science that critically reviews a central dogma in toxicological research. At a time when there is criticism of animal toxicological studies from several directions, Ms Fano has broken new ground, specifically on the question of the use of animals in toxicological testing of chemicals. Her book may prove to be the best intellectual treatise for the critical position she puts forward.' *Sheldon Krimsky, Professor of Urban and Environmental Policy, Tufts University, Medford, Massachusetts*

'It is the accumulation of millions of "safe doses" of the chemicals we are exposed to that is one of the main causes of many diseases, including cancer. But is it possible to establish *really* safe doses for the 75,000 chemicals in commercial use, let alone the 1,500 new ones introduced every year on the basis of animal tests? The answer is "no". What we must do is use far less chemicals. This is the thesis of Alix Fano's highly documented new book—and it is very convincingly argued.' *Edward Goldsmith, author of* The Way

'A powerful, well documented indictment of how violence against animals has become a basis of scientific research and how this violence eventually harms the human species. It helps reawaken the ancient idea that other species are not merely objects for human exploitation and experimentation, they are members of the Earth Family.' *Vandana Shiva, author of* Staying Alive

'A scientific and well documented critique of current animal-based methodologies still being used today as the baseline standard in toxicity testing. Recent developments in the field of molecular toxicology, coupled with advances in vitro techniques, have clearly surpassed the traditional animal tests in all respects. *Lethal Laws* should give added impetus to those health agencies in search of the scientific data necessary to overcome the barriers to regulatory acceptance of these new methods.' *Dr Andre Menache BVSc, MRCVS, President, Doctors and Lawyers for Responsible Medicine*

LETHAL LAWS
Animal testing, human health and environmental policy

Alix Fano

Zed Books Ltd
LONDON & NEW YORK

Lethal Laws: Animal testing, human health and environmental policy
was first published by Zed Books Ltd, 7 Cynthia Street,
London N1 9JF, UK and Room 400, 175 Fifth Avenue,
New York, NY 10010, USA in 1997.

Distributed exclusively in the USA by St Martin's Press, Inc.,
175 Fifth Avenue, New York, NY 10010, USA.

Published in Burma, Cambodia, Laos and Thailand by
White Lotus Co. Ltd, GPO Box 1141, Bangkok 10501,
Thailand in 1997

Cover photos: Rat in EPA toxicology study © Charles
Gupton/Uniphoto; Industrial smokestack © Matthew McVay/
Tony Stone Images/PNI; Newborn baby © J. Pickerell/FPG
International

Cover designed by Guido Caroti
Set in Baskerville and Univers by Ewan Smith
Printed and bound in the United Kingdom
by Biddles Ltd, Guildford and King's Lynn

A catalogue record for this book is available from the British
Library

Library of Congress Cataloging-in-Publication Data

Fano, Alix, 1965–
    Lethal laws: animal testing, human health and environ-
    mental policy / Alix Fano
            p. cm.
        ISBN 1-85649-497-7. — ISBN 1-85649-498-5 (pbk.)
        1. Animal experimentation. 2. Toxicity testing–In vivo.
    3. Environmental policy. I. Title.
    R853.A53F36 1997
    179'.4–dc21   97–98182
                                                   CIP

ISBN 1 85649 497 7 cased
ISBN 1 85649 498 5 limp

Contents

Preface

'Whatever happens to the animals will happen soon also to human beings ...
Continue to soil your bed and one night you will suffocate in your own waste.'
Chief Seattle of the Dwamish Tribe, Washington territory, at the signing of the
Port Elliott Treaty (USA) 1855

'One does not exploit a nature with which one identifies.' Hans Peter Duerr in
Rudolf Bahro, *Building the Green Movement* (Philadelphia: New Society Publishers,
1986), p. 206

For more than a decade, I have been an activist working in the areas
of health/preventive medicine, anti-vivisection and environmental
advocacy. Through the years, I have come to understand that our
personal health, which has both a physical and a spiritual component,
is intimately dependent on the way we treat our bodies, each other,
our environment, and non-human animals. Just as all living things are
interdependent, so have I seen the themes in all my areas of interest
converge. Today, I firmly believe that our personal health and the
health of our environment is linked to what is done to animals in
toxicology laboratories throughout the world.

I wrote *Lethal Laws* to expose these links to the public and to
advocacy groups who may want to take up the battle to abolish animal
testing. I also wrote it because I am outraged that an allegedly advanced
society, which has invented countless sophisticated computer, space,
and medical technologies, is still burning, gassing, blinding and poisoning millions of animals in archaic tests with the excuse that they are
the only reliable means available to protect human health. The closed-
mindedness and entrenched attitude of the scientists and regulators
who continue to favor these outdated methodologies over modern and
humane technologies is equally shocking and needs to be exposed. It is
the hypocrisy of a system which willingly destroys one life form under
the pretense of protecting another; which dominates nature and yet
expects to live in harmony with it.

Such behaviors and attitudes are based on a profound disrespect for life, and can only perpetuate violence, illness, and unhappiness. The various heinous forms of environmental destruction, and human and animal experimentation we are witnessing in the twentieth century, are a product of those attitudes.

Unfortunately, the practice of animal testing may soon spread to developing countries (particularly in Eastern Europe and Latin America) as they race to attract foreign investment dollars and move further into chemical manufacturing. Given the trend towards an international standardization of regulatory controls, they will inevitably be drawn into regulatory bureaucracies that are replete with animal testing requirements. Moreover, because of its enormous political and economic power, the United States has the ability to shape research agendas, not only in developing countries, but in industrialized Europe and Asia; it does this through organizations in which it is a major participant and financial supporter, such as the Organization for Economic Cooperation and Development (OECD), the United Nations which includes the United Nations Educational, Scientific and Cultural Organization (UNESCO), the World Health Organization (WHO) and the International Agency for Research on Cancer (IARC), and the USA's own National Institute for Environmental Health Sciences (NIEHS) which funds one third of all toxicology studies worldwide.

A majority of laypeople are ignorant about what goes on in federally funded toxicology laboratories, how many and what kinds of animals are used in toxicity tests, what these tests are costing individual nations, and how the test results directly impact on their lives. This is understandable because the public rarely asks about what it is not told and what it cannot see. Animal experimentation has relied and continues to rely on secrecy to survive. It is hidden from view in highly guarded laboratories purposely designed to prevent public access. The secrecy surrounding animal testing (and much scientific research) makes it difficult for the public to scrutinize the research. As a result, few question federal regulatory agencies' lack of accountability to the public about the decision to use animals in toxicity tests; fewer question the necessity or validity of the research that is done; and fewer still question whether there is a better way of doing things.

In *Lethal Laws*, the reader will not only gain an understanding of what toxicity testing on animals is about and how it's done, but he or she will come to know the regulatory system that sustains it, the 'science' of risk assessment that relies on it, the arguments used to justify it, the arguments against it, and the prospects for a future without animal testing. In this sense, *Lethal Laws* is unabashedly an advocacy piece. Although I have devoted several pages to an examination of pro-animal testing arguments, I have done so to lay the groundwork for my rebuttal. Indeed the bulk of this work is dedicated to highlighting the thoughts and ideas of those who oppose animal testing on scientific grounds. To this end I have compiled disconnected testimonials, spanning several decades, that have not been brought together in one document before. Because the toxicology literature has historically favored the pro-animal-testing perspective, I felt that it was time to provide some balance, and create a comprehensive, well-documented book against animal testing.

The public has historically been exposed to unbalanced debates about animal testing which have typically pitted scientific arguments against ethical ones, and left the public with the impression that animal testing is a necessary evil. While a recent Associated Press poll revealed that two-thirds of Americans believe it is seldom or never right to test cosmetics on animals, 70 percent are prepared to accept the need for animal research, at least under some circumstances.[1] In 1996, however, a National Science Foundation survey found that over two-thirds of Americans sampled lacked fundamental knowledge of basic science; only 9 percent knew what a molecule was and only 21 percent could define DNA,[2] indicating that the public is making decisions based on insufficient information, and has perhaps been unduly influenced by proponents of animal research.

Confronting the problem of animal testing on ethical grounds *is* important, and this tactic may have brought about a collective shift in consciousness, but it has not succeeded in eradicating the practice, or challenged citizens to think critically about the need for it. A more pragmatic approach is necessary to confront animal testing proponents on their own grounds. *Lethal Laws* approaches the animal testing debate from a scientific rather than an ethical perspective. It also establishes a link that is long overdue between the fields of health, animal advocacy and environmentalism, uniting different interest groups in what could potentially be a common cause.

I hope *Lethal Laws* will accomplish several things: provide a document which presents arguments against animal testing in a way that satisfies the needs of scientists and yet is clear and understandable to a layperson; motivate health, animal, and environmental advocacy groups to raise public awareness on this issue; hold government accountable for failing to protect human health; encourage the fight for truly effective environmental health science policies, and help to change legislation, thereby radically transforming the way science is currently practiced.

Many people helped me through this process, both directly and indirectly, by providing me with research materials, advice, feedback, inspiration, and encouragement. Though I cannot thank them all, I would especially like to cite the following people: Sara Amundson of the Doris Day Animal League in Washington, DC; Thomas Atherholt of the New Jersey Department of Environmental Protection in Trenton; Rudolf Bahro at the University of Berlin, Germany; Professor Frank Barile at York College in Jamaica, New York; David Basketter at Unilever UK; Diane Birely of In Vitro International in Irvine, California; Professor Phil Brown at Brown University in Providence, Rhode Island; Phil Casterton at Amway in Michigan; Dr Murry Cohen of the Medical Research Modernization Committee in New York City; Dr Pietro Croce and Sylvia Croce of Vicenza, Italy; Professor Anne Marie Desmarais of the Department of Civil and Environmental Engineering at Tufts University in Medford, Massachusetts; my friend Robin Desser for her editorial input; Dr Eric Dunayer (DVM), in Rockville, Maryland; author Edith Efron; Dr Björn Ekwall, of the Department of Toxicology at the University of Uppsala, Sweden; Professor Sheldon Krimsky of the Department of Urban and Environmental Policy at Tufts University; Pam Logemann at Advanced Tissue Sciences in La Jolla, California; Dr Carlton H. Nadolney at the US Environmental Protection Agency; Dr Dennis V. Parke in Surrey, UK; the Physicians Committee for Responsible Medicine in Washington, DC; my friend and fellow activist Bina Robinson; Hans Ruesch, without whose writings I would never have had the courage or inspiration to become an activist in this field to begin with; Dr Robert Sharpe in Sheffield, UK; Dr William Stokes of the National Institute of Environmental Health Sciences in Research Triangle Park, North Carolina; and Guido for his love, patience, and invaluable computer assistance. Last but not least, I dedicate this work to the loving memories of my parents and grandparents, whose deaths from cancer and other degenerative illnesses gave me the courage of my convictions.

Notes

1. David Foster, 'Animal Rights Tenets Are Gaining Support in US, Poll Shows,' *The Seattle Times*, 3 December 1995, p. A4.

2. Anon, 'Americans Flunk Science, A Study Finds,' *The New York Times*, 24 May 1996; see also Anon, 'Poll Finds Americans Ignorant of Science,' *The New York Times*, 25 October 1988.

Abbreviations

AAVS	American Anti Vivisection Society
ACS	American Cancer Society
ADA	American Dental Association
ADI	Acceptable Daily Intake
AFAAR	American Fund for Alternatives to Animal Research
ATS	Advanced Tissue Sciences
ATSDR	Agency for Toxic Substances and Disease Registry
CAAT	Center for Alternatives to Animal Testing
CAMVA	Chorio-Allantoic Membrane Vascular Assay
CDC	Centers for Disease Control and Prevention
CERCLA	Comprehensive Environmental Response, Compensation and Liability Act
CFR	Code of Federal Regulations
CMA	Chemical Manufacturers Association
COLIPA	Perfume Cosmetics Products and Toiletries Industries
COMPACT	Computer-Optimized Molecular Parametric Analysis of Chemical Toxicity
CPF	Carcinogen Potency Factor
CPSC	Consumer Product Safety Commission
CRBL	Charles River Breeding Laboratories
CTFA	Cosmetic, Toiletry and Fragrance Association
DDAL	Doris Day Animal League
DDT	Dichloro-Diphenyl-Trichloro-Ethane
DHHS	Department of Health and Human Services
DNA	Deoxyribonucleic Acid
DOD	Department of Defense
DOE	Department of Energy
DOL	Department of Labor
DOT	Department of Transportation
ECETOC	European Center for the Ecotoxicology and Toxicology of Chemicals
EDIT	Evaluation-Guided Development of New In Vitro Toxicity and Kinetic Tests

ECU	European Currency Unit
ECVAM	European Center for the Validation of Alternative Methods
EDF	Environmental Defense Fund
EEC	European Economic Community
EFPIA	European Federation of Pharmaceutical Industries Association
EPA	Environmental Protection Agency
ERF	Environmental Research Foundation
FDA	Food and Drug Administration
FDCA	Food, Drug and Cosmetic Act
FETAX	Frog Embryo Teratogenesis Assay-Xenopus
FHSA	Federal Hazardous Substances Act
FIFRA	Federal Insecticide, Fungicide, and Rodenticide Act
FRAME	Fund for the Replacement of Animals in Medical Experiments
FTC	Federal Trade Commission
GATT	General Agreement on Tariffs and Trade
HCS	Hazard Communication Standard
HEAST	Health Effects Assessment Summary Tables
HETCAM	Hen Egg Test Chorio-Allantoic Membrane
IARC	International Agency for Research on Cancer
ICCVAM	Interagency Coordinating Committee on the Validation of Alternative Methods
IRAG	Interagency Regulatory Alternatives Group
IRIS	Integrated Risk Information System
IRLG	Interagency Regulatory Liaison Group
IRPTC	International Register of Potentially Toxic Chemicals
LAPS	Light Addressable Potentiometric Sensor
LD50/LC50	Lethal Dose/Lethal Concentration
MBT	Mechanism-Based Toxicology
MCL	Maximum Contamination Level
MCS	Multiple Chemical Sensitivity
MEDLARS	Medical Literature and Analysis Retrieval System
MEIC	Multi Center for the Evaluation of In Vitro Cytotoxicity
MIT	Massachusetts Institute of Technology
MRI/MRS	Magnetic Resonance Imaging/Spectroscopy
MSDS	Material Safety Data Sheet
MTD	Maximum Tolerated Dose
NCI	National Cancer Institute
NCTR	National Center for Toxicological Research

NGO	Non-Governmental Organization
NIEHS	National Institute of Environmental Health Sciences
NIH	National Institutes of Health
NIOSH	National Institute for Occupational Safety and Health
NRDC	Natural Resources Defense Council
NJDEP	New Jersey Department of Environmental Protection
NTP	National Toxicology Program
OECD	Organisation for Economic Cooperation and Development
OSHA	Occupational Safety and Health Administration
OTA	Office of Technology Assessment
PAH	Polycyclic Aromatic Hydrocarbon(s)
PBBK	Physiologically Based Bio Kinetic (Models)
PCB(s)	Polychlorinated Biphenyl(s)
PEL	Permissible Exposure Limit
PET	Positron Emission Tomography
PETA	People for the Ethical Treatment of Animals
RfD	Reference Dose
SAR	Structure-Activity Relationship
SCAAT	Steering Committee on Alternatives to Animal Testing
TCE	Trichloroethylene
TDRC	Toxicology Design Review Committee
TNC	Transnational Corporation
TSCA	Toxic Substances Control Act
UK	United Kingdom
UN	United Nations
UNEP	United Nations Environment Program
UNESCO	United Nations Educational, Scientific and Cultural Organization
US	United States
USDA	United States Department of Agriculture
WEDO	Women's Environment and Development Organization
WHO	World Health Organization
WRI	World Resources Institute
WTO	World Trade Organization
WWF	Worldwide Fund for Nature

Introduction

'Animal experiments have an extremely important role in underpinning, facilitating and justifying the machinery of progress with which we are working on our own annihilation ... As far as I can see, animal experiments are one of the most political questions we have ever had to deal with. To become a radical in this area means to slaughter one of the holiest cows in modern Western idolatry, the "freedom of science" ... ' Rudolf Bahro, *Building the Green Movement* (Philadelphia: New Society Publishers, 1986), p. 202

For the last 150 years, industrial, agricultural, and household chemicals have been tested on animals for the alleged purpose of protecting the public from their dangerous effects. Scientists say that performing toxicity tests on live animals and transferring the results to humans allows them to predict cancer, and signs of poisoning, in advance.[1] Though accompanied by warning labels about their toxicity, millions of chemicals in common use have been deemed to be 'safe' by federal regulatory agencies based on lethal dose, skin and eye irritancy, reproductive, neurotoxicity, and cancer tests on numerous species of animals. Scientists and federal regulatory agencies allege that no other reliable technologies currently exist to replace animals in toxicity tests.

Because the arguments in favor of animal testing have been widely disseminated to the public by its proponents through media reports about chemicals causing cancer in 'laboratory animals,' people have been misled into believing that what causes cancer (and other toxic effects) in 'laboratory animals' will cause the same or similar effects in humans. And because most citizens know little, if anything, about federal animal testing programs or about developments in new testing technologies, a majority now believe that animal safety tests are necessary and effective in protecting them from the toxic chemicals in the air they breathe, the water they drink, and the food they eat. In addition, while many environmentalists and health advocates say that the real answer lies in using fewer toxic chemicals, most still join the general public in supporting animal testing for those reasons.[2]

Adding fuel to a controversy which began in the 1970s and has continued unabated since, opponents of animal testing say that animal tests are unreliable, and that better, less costly and more humane technologies exist which could predict toxic effects in less time. These scientists, animal advocates and manufacturers of advanced testing technologies say it is the regulatory bureaucracy, and lack of vision in the scientific community, that is stalling the acceptance of non-animal methods in toxicology research, not the inadequate technology cited by animal testing proponents. Moreover, they contend that the full potential of epidemiology (the study of diseases in populations, which often forges the links between human disease and chemical pollution) has not been explored due to a historical bias in federal funding which favors animal rather than human-based research.[3]

Lethal Laws goes further by demonstrating that governments' current reliance on animal tests to prove the safety of a toxic product is an illusory farce; in reality, human beings have become the ultimate 'guinea pigs' in an increasingly polluted world. Rather than being instrumental in safeguarding our health, animal testing programs have legitimized the continued production and use of millions of toxic chemicals. Federal scientists—and those within the chemical, pharmaceutical and petroleum industries—have relied on animal testing programs to make chemicals acceptable to regulators, attractive to consumers, and to protect themselves from costly litigation. The endless controversies within the scientific and regulatory communities over the staggering amounts of ambiguous animal test data have stalled the removal of dangerous substances from the market. Furthermore, even when a chemical has caused cancer and other effects in animals, cost–benefit decisions play a key role in federal agencies' decisions to leave a chemical on the market, regardless of the danger it could pose to millions of people. Hence animal testing is a principal component of a regulatory system which, in making concessions to industry, has lost sight of its mandate to protect human health.

There is clear evidence today that the piling up of millions of 'safe doses' of chemicals in our food, air and water, is causing the steady deterioration of our health and our environment. Studies are showing that certain cancers, infectious diseases and immune system disorders are on the rise;[4] numerous reports have been issued about the declining quality of our soil, water and food.[5] It is apparent that our society's endorsement of inhumane and ineffectual toxicity tests, in which live animals are essentially poisoned to death, has fostered a lack of respect for life—in science, government and industry—which has predictably boomeranged.

Although an array of modern non-animal technologies exist which could screen toxic substances quickly, accurately, and cheaply, thereby preventing their production and distribution, scientists continue to try to 'improve' the animal tests: by devising new testing regimes, varying the dosages of a test substance, and making use of countless statistical models to extrapolate animal data to humans—all in the hope of creating the perfect human surrogate. This 'band-aid' approach has led to ever more complex testing protocols and regulations, but not more effective or humane environmental health science policies.

Hence *Lethal Laws* is a call to action; in it I will argue that federal governments ought to abandon animal-based toxicological research in favor of modern, non-animal technologies which already exist. Examples will be used to illustrate the unreliability of animal test results, and their ineffectiveness in protecting humans and the environment from poisons. The notion that the use of animal test data has led to the establishment of effective environmental policies will be challenged. Non-animal testing methods, and the prospects for their acceptance and implementation will be discussed. By argument along these lines, the unyielding positions of regulators and pro-animal-testing scientists that are responsible for slowing down progress in this area will be exposed. I will argue that a move away from animal tests will better serve the goal of protecting human health and the environment. It will also do much to restore integrity and compassion to science.

A good deal of the literature I rely on for my critique of animal testing predates the 1980s. Today, though libraries are filled with books, journals and promotional materials which embrace animal-based toxicity testing, literature critical of the practice is scant and hard to find. If and when critiques of animal testing do appear, they are accompanied by commentaries which dilute the criticism and reinforce outmoded ways of thinking.

Surprisingly, the 1970s was a period in history unlike any other with respect to the issue of animal testing for commercial and consumer products. During this time, scientists argued vigorously—often behind the scenes, at conferences, and in the pages of scientific journals—about the validity and morality of animal testing. Critiques of animal testing, and of weak federal environmental health science programs, could readily be found in the scientific literature. Non-scientists have not been privy to this information, and have rarely heard scientific arguments against animal testing. *Lethal Laws* not only resuscitates earlier scientific critiques but also expands on them, using updated sources from books, scientific journals, media reports, and excerpts from interviews with American and foreign toxicologists.

Because of the acknowledged suffering endured by animals in toxicity tests, animal testing is an emotional issue for animal advocates and others who have written about the practice and campaigned against it. As ethical considerations are important and should be heard, they have been given some space in this work. But *Lethal Laws* fills a void in the literature against animal testing by presenting primarily *scientific* arguments against it, as opposed to the ethical arguments which have been dominant for decades. By taking a rational as opposed to an emotional approach, I hope to convince skeptics to think critically about this issue. I hope that activists interested in making concrete changes in this area will read *Lethal Laws* and become informed and empowered by it. In addition, I intend to show that commonalities do indeed exist between environmental, health, and animal advocacy, and that these different interest groups can work together towards the common goal of reforming ineffective and inhumane regulatory policies.

The analysis is broken down into six chapters. Chapter 1 introduces the reader to the debate over the causes of cancer and the role of animal tests in that debate; it also recounts the historical roots of animal testing for cosmetic, household, agricultural and industrial chemicals. Chapter 2 provides an overview of the US National Toxicology Program's federal cancer prevention/animal testing program, and the various ways in which animal data are used by regulatory agencies. (It should be noted here that, although this book focuses primarily on American policies and practices, the basic issues discussed transcend national boundaries. Because of the US's formidable influence abroad, however, and because US health science policies and programs are often held up as models in much of the world, the reader may assume that most industrialized countries have toxicity testing programs similar to those of the US). Chapter 2 also offers descriptions of the species and numbers of animals used in toxicity tests, and the ways in which the tests are performed.

Chapter 3 presents the arguments advanced by proponents of animal-based toxicity tests, and provides a detailed rebuttal of those arguments. Several areas of uncertainty plaguing the inter-species extrapolation process will be discussed. A compendium of critiques by toxicologists, statisticians, regulators, animal advocates and others is used to support this scientific and socio-ethical analysis.

Chapter 4 provides the evidence that animal tests do not protect humans from harmful toxins in the marketplace and the environment. Several examples of specific products, from pesticides to shampoos, which the EPA has failed to regulate despite evidence of harm from animal tests, are given. An overview of the federal regulatory system and the laws governing animal testing, as well as an examination of who profits from the practice, is provided.

Chapter 5 highlights several non-animal testing methods and their uses, and examines the barriers to their adoption. Given that, in many cases, invertebrates and small mammals are considered to be valid replacements or 'alternatives' to larger mammals in toxicity tests, the question of what constitutes a true non-animal method will be explored. The belief, held by some scientists and animal advocates, that the goal to validate alternatives is slowing down their implementation will also be addressed.

Chapter 6 concludes by calling for a radical change in federal toxicity testing policies which would bring forth new regulatory standards based on the acceptance of data from (human) clinical and epidemiological studies, and non-animal testing technologies. The role that animal advocates, toxicologists and others must play in this regard is emphasized.

Notes

1. Toxicity is defined as 'the production of any type of damage, permanent or impermanent, to the structure or functioning of any part of the body.' Joseph V. Rodricks, *Calculated Risks* (UK: Cambridge University Press, 1992), p. 15.

2. Jim Motavalli, 'Our Agony Over Animals,' *E Magazine*, September/October 1995, p.37.

3. Pietro Croce, *Vivisection or Science: A Choice to Make* (Switzerland: Civis Publications, 1991), pp. 139–52. In 1979, epidemiologist Irving Kessler expressed his conviction that information about occupational cancer would come only from serious epidemiological studies of human beings, not from feeding rodents massive amounts of chemicals. He argued that epidemiology would never become an important discipline 'if it degenerated into mindless statistical manipulation.' He expressed his concern about the political implications of announcing cancer risks based on speculative animal tests with little empirical evidence. 'Needed: Better Studies of Links to Cancer,' *Chemical Week*, 14 February 1979, p. 39.

4. Eric Chivian, et al., eds, *Critical Condition: Human Health and the Environment* (Cambridge, MA: MIT Press, 1993); National Center for Infectious Diseases, *Addressing Emerging Infectious Disease Threats: A Prevention Strategy for the United States* (Atlanta: Centers for Disease Control and Prevention, 1994); Joshua Lederberg, et al., eds, Institute of Medicine, National Academy of Sciences, *Emerging Infectious Microbial Threats to Health in the United States* (Washington, DC: National Academy Press, 1992); Ann Misch, 'Assessing Environmental Health Risks,' in Lester R. Brown, et al., *State of the World 1994: A Worldwatch Institute Report* ... (New York: W. W. Norton & Co.), pp. 117–36.

5. Lester R. Brown, et al., *State of the World: A Worldwatch Institute Report* ... (New York: W. W. Norton & Co., 1984–present).

1. Fatal connection: cancer and animal testing

During the 1970s, regulatory agencies' and scientists' statements about this or that chemical causing cancer in 'laboratory animals' (which have appeared in the media on a regular basis for decades), may have contributed a great deal to the public's fear of cancer. It may be argued that this fear, whether real or heightened by media reports, has fueled the regulatory science called risk assessment which has come to embody federal cancer prevention policies. The American public's fear of cancer has been used by researchers and health advocates (who lobby Congress for the appropriation of funds), to justify enormous expenditures for federal cancer prevention programs. The goal of these programs in the United States (US) is to protect—in advance—all 280,000,000 citizens from the real or potential effects of carcinogens, particularly the most sensitive individuals in the population: children, the elderly, pregnant women and individuals with chemical sensitivities.[1]

But, as author Edith Efron asks in *The Apocalyptics: Cancer and the Big Lie* (1984, p. 337), 'who will be the most sensitive to a disease that has not yet occurred and whose mechanisms are not understood?'

The politics of cancer

'If anyone pronounces that they know the mechanism of a carcinogenic agent, my guess is that they will be proven wrong, because most, if not all, carcinogens will operate through multiple mechanisms.' Carl Barrett, Chief of the National Institute for Environmental Health Sciences Laboratory of Molecular Carcinogenesis, quoted in *Environmental Health Perspectives* 101, no. 5 (October 1993): 399

Theories about the causes of human cancer remain controversial because, despite years of research (much of it carried out with non-human animals), it remains a disease with many causes, treatments and outcomes.[2] Cancer appears to be triggered by a malfunctioning of the body's mechanisms that control cell division. Cancer cells are essentially renegade cells: they begin multiplying rapidly, invade surrounding tissues, and can metastasize, form lumps or tumors, and overwhelm their host.[3]

Cancer researchers have developed several theories about the mechanisms of cancer or the way it develops. The 'initiation and promotion' theory holds that some chemical agents initiate a pattern of uncontrolled cell divisions (mutations) and subsequent exposures to a different chemical cause the cells to become cancerous.[4] The so-called 'one-hit' hypothesis advances the theory that cancer can be caused by a single mutation of a cell—caused by exposure to a chemical, for example.[5] The 'mutation theory' of cancer hypothesizes that cell divisions are caused by a change, rearrangement or deletion of the primary structure of DNA. Many scientists believe that these mutations are caused by low, rather than high, doses of mutagens like radiation and chemicals.[6]

The 'no-threshold theory' holds that even a single molecule of a cancer-causing agent or 'carcinogen' might give someone cancer and consequently the only safe dose of, or exposure to, a chemical is zero.[7] To confuse matters further, William Lijinsky, a prominent cancer researcher, has said that while it is unlikely that just *one* molecule of a carcinogen will present a risk to humans, no one knows how many molecules do represent a risk. Some researchers assume that there is a 'threshold of action' for a carcinogen—a point below which carcinogens will *not* cause an effect—but it is not possible to determine what that threshold is.[8] Still other scientists believe that cancer is simply a natural result of the human body's aging process and its susceptibility to a host of naturally occurring chemicals (such as those found in foods for example), the metabolized by-products of which become carcinogenic.[9]

Despite all these theories, there is general agreement that carcinogens in the environment increase the likelihood of cancer-initiating cell mutations; hence most carcinogens have been dubbed genetic toxins or 'mutagens,' in that they can cause genetic damage to the DNA in human cells.[10]

The debate over the causes of cancer

Although the precise mechanisms of carcinogenicity in humans are still not understood, numerous sources claim to know what causes cancer and/or how it can be prevented. The US National Research Council determined that 60–90 percent of all human cancers are attributable to diet and lifestyle factors, and are thus preventable.[11] The National Cancer Institute (NCI) and American Cancer Society (ACS) estimate that diet accounts for 35–60 percent, smoking for 30 percent, radiation and alcohol for 3 percent respectively, medication for 2 percent and environmental exposures (air and water pollution) for 1–5 percent of cancers.[12]

In their book *The Causes of Cancer* (1981), noted British epidemiologists Richard Doll and Richard Peto similarly conclude that only 1–2 percent of cancers are attributable to chemical pollution. Biochemist Bruce Ames, who postulates that naturally occurring chemicals found in common foods may be causing cancer, has gone even further by saying that pesticides actually *lower* the cancer rate.[13] Some scientists claim that, as a result of under-reporting in the past, age-adjusted deaths from many types of cancers (except lung cancer) have been declining significantly for decades and, hence, there is no epidemic of human cancer in the United States.[14]

Environmentalists on the other hand, and others like Samuel Epstein, author of *The Politics of Cancer* (1978), and Philip Landrigan, co-author of *Raising Children Toxic-Free* (1994), assert that 70–90 percent of cancers are induced by environmental carcinogens such as chemicals, radiation, and probably viruses.[15] Some scientists and health advocacy organizations claim that cancer rates are rising. The Women's Environment and Development Organization (WEDO), an international non-profit organization, recently stated that the incidence rates of kidney, liver, breast, brain and testicular cancers are rising. While the causes remain unknown, WEDO cited a recent report by the NCI which revealed a possible link between increased cancer rates and environmental exposures to solvents, fuels and pesticides.[16] A New York State Department of Health report from 1994 concluded that women who lived within one kilometer of chemical, rubber or plastic manufacturing plants had a 62 percent elevated risk of breast cancer.[17] And on 24 May 1994 (p.C3) *The New York Times* reported that non-Hodgkin's lymphoma, a cancer of the immune system which causes fever, fatigue and weight loss, is one of the fastest growing cancers in the United States.

Turning to animal testing for answers

Amid the debate over the mechanisms and causes of human cancer, scientists have increasingly turned to animal testing to quantify their various theories, and to try to understand which factors contribute the greatest risk. Though many scientists believe that rodent tumors are substantially different from human tumors, both in origin and in the way they metastasize,[18] the 'rodent carcinogen bioassay,' which involves exposing rats and mice of both sexes to chemicals and monitoring the animals for tumor development, has become the standard test for identifying possible human carcinogens.

The government's decision to adopt the rodent bioassay as the standard testing vehicle has divided the scientific community, and has created conflicts among environmental, health, and animal advocates, heads of industry, and federal regulators. The scientific community is split between those who question the validity and necessity of animal tests (both on scientific and ethical grounds) and those who support them. Samuel Epstein has said that: 'there is overwhelming agreement by most qualified scientists that if a chemical causes cancer in well-diagnosed animal tests, there is a strong likelihood that it will also cause cancer in exposed humans.'[19] Federal regulators and scientists who defend the tests say they are a necessary evil and the best predictive tools we have at the present time. The chemical products industry argues that animal tests are expensive and greatly overestimate risks, while health advocates argue that the tests vastly underestimate risks. Animal advocates and some manufacturers of advanced testing technologies claim that the animal tests are not only crude and inhumane but produce results which are not applicable to humans.

While acknowledging that the results of animal tests are difficult to extrapolate to humans, American environmental groups point out that a host of US environmental laws, and health and safety regulations— the Clean Air Act, Safe Drinking Water Act, Occupational Health and Safety Act—were formulated using animal test data.[20] In essence, animal tests have allowed environmentalists to convict certain chemicals of attempted murder. And so, in pressing for stricter laws and standards, environmentalists and public figures like Epstein frequently cite data from animal cancer tests to justify their demands.

All scientists are not in agreement with Epstein about the alleged benefits of animal testing, however, and criticisms of his point of view can be found throughout the scientific literature;[21] indeed, as early as 1954, D. A. Long of the World Health Organization stated, 'it must never be forgotten that the results of animal tests may be of little value in forecasting the effects of substances on man.'[22]

In addition, scientists like Gio Batta Gori, formerly in the Division of Cancer Cause and Prevention at the National Cancer Institute, believe that using animals to test carcinogens has its roots in basic research where the emphasis is on pure experimentation for its own sake, rather than on the assessment of real-life risk.[23] Gori believes this has introduced various forms of bias into the design of animal cancer tests. For example, researchers are encouraged to obtain positive results in animal tests because negative results are 'unfruitful.' Hence the use of exaggerated dosing strategies using susceptible animal species, sexes, and strains; this will be discussed in subsequent chapters.

In order to gain a better understanding of the debate over the validity of animal testing, it is useful to become familiar with the history of toxicity testing on animals, and to learn when, how, and why animal tests became a fixture in toxicology labs throughout the United States and the world.

A brief history of toxicological testing on animals

In the sixteenth century, the Swiss physician and alchemist Paracelsus declared that every substance could be a poison depending on the dose,[24] and this idea has become the fundamental principle of modern toxicology.

From the mid-1870s onward, after the birth of the synthetic dye industry, the science of toxicology grew in response to the need to understand how the tens of thousands of new industrial chemicals might affect the health of the workers and consumers involved in their production and use. Pharmacologists were also seeking a better understanding of the biological action of drugs.

In the mid- to late-1800s, animals began to be used in laboratories to study the effects of countless variations and doses of drugs and poisons in basic research.[25] German physiological chemists like Baumann administered purified chemicals like benzene and toluene to dogs to study their metabolism and effect on the body.[26] The work of vitamin researcher Philip B. Hawk during the First World War, followed by research in experimental nutrition, led to the development of animal models to study the effects of both natural and man-made chemicals.[27] In 1915, Japanese scientists K. Yamagiwa and K. Ichikawa were the first to produce (skin) tumors in animals using chemicals or chemical mixtures. They painted rabbits' ears with coal tar for months in an attempt to verify the correlation between soot and scrotal cancer in humans, established by the physician Percival Pott in 1775.[28] Experiments like these were repeated in laboratories around the world.

The phenomenon of using live, unanesthetized non-human animals to study the potentially toxic effects of an increasing array of drugs, pesticides and food additives began in earnest in the early 1920s. It was then that cancer researcher Isaac Berenblum painted mice, rabbits and other animals' sometimes punctured skin with tars and chemicals, in an attempt to understand the mechanisms of cancer induction, and to see how many of the animals would simply die.[29] During that time,

British scientists E. L. Kennaway and I. Heiger applied components of coal tar to the skin of shaved mice, to demonstrate that a single chemical compound could produce tumors.[30]

Eye irritancy tests in animals began in the 1920s. Following soldiers' exposure to mustard gas in the First World War, scientists studied the effects of mustard gas in rabbits' eyes to compare them with the effects observed in humans.[31]

The Lethal Dose 50 or LD50 test—designed to kill 50 percent of the test animals in an experiment—was introduced by British pharmacologist J. W. Trevan in 1927, to measure the toxicity of drugs and thus establish health precautions. By segregating mice or rats into subsets and graphing the different dosages of a chemical the animal received against the time it took each group to die, Trevan was able to determine the theoretical amount of a compound needed to kill half the animals in the group. The test was crude and often involved at least 100 animals per test; but, as author Robert Sharpe explains in his book *The Cruel Deception* (1988, p. 95), because it was simple and replaced biological complexity with 'a single numerical index of toxicity,' it appealed to government bureaucrats, despite the fact that it gave wildly varying results depending on the substance and species being tested. Sharpe writes that it soon became standard procedure in toxicology laboratories, and part of government requirements for the testing of 'a wide range of substances including drugs, pesticides, [cosmetics and] industrial products.'[32] (It was ultimately adopted in 1981 by the Council of the Organisation for Economic Cooperation and Development (OECD) under the OECD Guidelines for the Testing of Chemicals, and became a component of 51 international guidelines to rank hazards in the workplace and label internationally traded goods according to their toxicity.)[33] A more in-depth discussion about federal regulations governing animal testing will be presented in Chapter 4.

Though researchers had successfully learned how to poison animals for the determination of crude LD50 values, attempts to extrapolate decades worth of animal test data to humans had been haphazard and fruitless; it was not until the 1930s that scientists and statisticians began to devise ways to 'predict' the occurrence of human cancer using animal data.[34] Epidemiological studies in the 1930s and 1940s which linked occupational cancer and other ailments to chemical exposures, propelled toxicologists to explore the chemical–cancer connection further. For example, it was found that a special group of hydrocarbons, the chlorinated naphthalenes, caused hepatitis and a rare fatal liver disease in humans exposed to them in occupational settings, particularly in electrical industries. Attention ironically turned away from epidemiology and to this new breed of animal experiments which were being performed with increasing fervor.[35]

After the US Congress passed the Food, Drug and Cosmetic Act (FDCA) in 1938, which required the safety testing of drugs, food additives and cosmetics to ensure that they were not contaminated and thus illegal,[36] an array of testing procedures and standards emerged which were eventually incorporated into federal regulatory guidelines for toxicity testing.

Wild rats became experimental animals of choice in India in the 1940s as a result of Gandhi's desire to protect his citizens from human experimentation in the early days of drug safety evaluation. During this period, clinical pharmacologists tested low doses of therapeutic preparations on each other before expanding the pool of human volunteers.[37] In 1944, John Draize, a scientist with the US Food and Drug Administration (FDA), standardized eye irritancy testing in albino rabbits by developing an irritation scoring system dubbed the Draize test. Though many modern technologies exist today which could replace rabbits, the Draize test is still used to meet product labelling and classification requirements.

After the Second World War, the number of new chemicals being produced increased rapidly; petroleum-based products were introduced, as were solvents for degreasing machinery parts and dry-cleaning clothes. Animal testing efforts simultaneously intensified. In the late 1940s, cancer researcher William Hueper, expanding on his previous work with dogs, established an Environmental Cancer Section at the National Cancer Institute (NCI), a program which used animals in tests aimed at identifying chemical carcinogens.

Animal testing programs gradually expanded and became increasingly complex. British biochemist Dennis V. Parke writes that acute studies which once lasted a week or two, were lengthened to three months, then six, then were extended to last the entire life span of the animal as researchers experimented with different dosages of countless compounds. Parke says, 'a single dose level became three ... a group of three rats became six,' and when statisticians became involved, the number of animals grew to 50; and 'because of the increasingly observed differences in species metabolism, and in mechanisms of toxicity, the variety of animals used grew to include rodents, rabbits, dogs, monkeys, and baboons, in the hope that no aspect of toxicity would be missed.'[38] In the 1950s, the statistical methods for extrapolating animal data to humans grew in number and complexity. Some involved mathematical formulas that were pages long.[39] The late 1950s saw an increase in the use of animals for drug and product safety evaluations since studies in human volunteers, which up until that point had been routine, exposed companies to the possibility of expensive litigation.[40] In the US, the Delaney Clause (enacted in 1958 under the Food Drug and Cosmetic Act) forbade the addition of substances in foods that caused cancer in animals.

In the 1960s and 1970s, analytical chemists became able to detect synthetic chemicals in water, air, and food at parts per billion and parts per trillion. Environmentalists' concerns about the cancer-causing potential of these chemicals, and their impact on the environment, led to a host of federal laws and programs aimed at regulating those chemicals. Consumer advocates' demands for safe products also helped to initiate expanded testing programs.[41] In Japan, the Ministry of Health and Welfare enacted the Pharmaceutical Affairs Law in 1961, which included animal testing guidelines for new drugs; these are also distributed to cosmetics manufacturers.[42] Soon after the introduction of the Medicines Act of 1968 in the UK (enacted to ensure the safety of drugs), the Health and Safety Executive was created in the early 1970s to monitor and evaluate environmental hazards. The US Environmental Protection Agency was established in 1970 and issued a host of environmental laws shortly thereafter. In 1977, the OECD enacted its Chemicals Testing Programme, with the aim of developing internationally recognized toxicity testing guidelines. Since that time, the OECD Council, composed of representatives of 26 member countries (with the recent addition of Poland in late 1996),[43] has promulgated dozens of guidelines for toxicity testing requirements.

It was during the 1970s that formal procedures for performing toxicity tests on animals used in qualitative risk assessment were standardized and incorporated into federal regulatory policies and guidelines. Testing requirements were imposed on chemical companies as part of detailed product notification procedures under laws like the US Toxic Substances Control Act (TSCA) of 1976. Today, although human studies are required prior to the marketing of a new drug, animal data are considered sufficient for the introduction of pesticides, food additives and industrial chemicals.

The use of animals as surrogates for humans in risk assessment research has become a vast scientific enterprise. Well over a dozen US (and international) regulatory agencies are currently involved in some form of risk assessment research focusing on the identification of carcinogens and their effects. Most toxicity testing in the US, which was formerly carried out by the NCI, is currently carried out under the auspices of the federal National Toxicology Program (NTP). NTP coordinates toxicology testing for the National Institute of Environmental Health Sciences (NIEHS), the National Institutes of Health (NIH), FDA's National Center for Toxicological Research (NCTR), and the Centers for Disease Control and Prevention's National Institute for Occupational Safety and Health (NIOSH).[44] The NIEHS currently funds approximately one-third of toxicology studies worldwide[45] which undoubtedly enables this US agency to influence other countries' research agendas. The US has a close relationship with the OECD, which regularly consults the scientific community of its member states and regulatory agencies in North America and Japan. Similarly, US regulators meet annually with their counterparts in Europe and Canada to exchange views about requirements for toxicological testing and risk assessment. Indeed, toxicity tests for American and Japanese companies are often conducted in France, the UK and Germany.[46] Contact is also maintained with Nordic countries and developing countries; the World Health Organization (which receives substantial support from the US) provides developing countries with risk assessment data.[47]

It is important to understand just how pervasive animal testing in the federal government is, and to what extent it shapes federal policies in the area of environmental and human health. It is also important to understand how the risk assessment process works in order better to judge the claims made by animal testing proponents. Chapter 2 will examine the NTP's animal testing program and its connection to risk assessment research. Examples of the way animal data are used by federal regulatory agencies in risk assessments will be provided. The species and numbers of animals used in toxicity tests, the ways in which the tests themselves are performed, and the way the data are extrapolated to humans, will be explained.

Notes

1. In the United States, the Clean Air Act and the Occupational Safety and Health Act require the Environmental Protection Agency (EPA) and the Occupational Safety and Health Administration (OSHA) to set ambient air quality and workplace exposure standards to protect even the most susceptible subgroup in the population.

2. In 1981, scientists John Weisburger and Gary Williams wrote, 'the mechanisms of cancer's evolution in the human body are poorly understood and are probably distinct for different classes of carcinogens; for example, they may involve long-term tissue injury, immunosuppressive effects, hormonal imbalances, stimulation of cell proliferation, or other processes not yet known.' J. H. Weisburger and G. M. Williams, 'Carcinogen Testing: Current Problems and New Approaches,' *Science* 214 (23 October 1981).

3. James B. Wyngaarden and L. H. Smith Jr., *Cecil Textbook of Medicine*, 16th Edition (Philadelphia: W. B. Saunders, 1982).

4. Ruth Hubbard and Elijah Wald, *Exploding the Gene Myth* (Boston: Beacon Press, 1993), p. 83.

5. Eric Dunayer, 'Testing Chemicals: Animal Testing Impedes Regulatory Action,' 1992, Unpublished paper courtesy of the Physicians Committee for Responsible Medicine, Washington, DC.

6. T. F. Mancuso, et al., 'Radiation Exposures of Hanford Workers Dying from Cancer and Other Causes,' *Health Phys.* 33 (November 1977): 369–85. See also K. Messing, et al., 'Mutant Frequency of Radiotherapy Technicians Appears to be Associated with Recent Dose of Ionizing Radiation,' *Health Phys.* 57, no. 4 (October 1989): 537–44; G. S. Wilkinson, 'Leukemia among Nuclear Workers with Protracted Exposure to Low-dose Ionizing Radiation,' *Epidemiology* 2, no. 4 (July 1991): 305–9; Irwin D. Bross and D. Driscoll, 'Direct Estimates of Low-Level Radiation Risks of Lung Cancer at Two NRC-Compliant Nuclear Installations …,' *Yale Journal of Biology and Medicine* 54 (1981): 317–28; Theodore Puck, et al., 'Caffeine Enhanced Measurement of Mutagenesis by Low Levels of Gamma-Irradiation in Human Lymphocytes,' *Somatic Cell and Molecular Genetics* 19, no. 5 (1993): 423–9; Charles Waldren, et al., 'Measurement of Low Levels of X-Ray Mutagenesis in Relation to Human Disease,' *Proc. Natl. Acad. Sci. USA* 83 (July 1986): 4839–43.

7. Marvin Schneiderman, *Urban Environment Conference* Proceedings (Washington, DC: National Cancer Institute, 1977), p. 10.

8. William Lijinsky, Statement before the United States Department of Labor, OSHA, 1980, OSHA Docket No. 090, pp. 30–1. For scientific or regulatory purposes, 'threshold' is the dose below which a toxic effect will *not* occur. The threshold principle is contentious since it requires proof of a negative, which is logically impossible.

9. Gio Batta Gori, 'Whither Risk Assessment?,' *Regulatory Toxicology & Pharmacology* 17 (1993): 227.

10. Ruth Hubbard and Elijah Wald (1993), p. 83.

11. Neal Barnard, 'Getting Chemicals Out of Our Environment,' *PCRM Update*, newsletter of the Physicians Committee for Responsible Medicine, Washington, DC (January–February 1990): 1.

12. Oliver Alabaster, *The Power of Prevention: A Personal Plan to Reduce Your Cancer Risk By as Much as 70%* (Washington, DC: Saville Books, 1988); American Cancer Society, 'Cancer Facts and Figures,' brochure (New York: 1995).

13. Jane E. Brody, 'Scientist at Work, Bruce Ames: Strong Views on Origins of Cancer,' *The New York Times*, 5 July 1994, p. C1; Philip H. Abelson, 'Testing for Carcinogens with Rodents,' *Science* (21 September 1990): 1357.

14. Gio Batta Gori, et al., *Regulatory Toxicology & Pharmacology* 6, no. 3 (1986): 261–73.

15. Samuel S. Epstein, *The Politics of Cancer* (San Francisco: Sierra Books, 1978); Herbert L. Needleman and Philip Landrigan, *Raising Children Toxic-Free* (New York: Farrar, Straus & Giroux, 1994). In 1978, the US Department of Health, Education and Welfare suggested that 20 percent of all cancers could be traced to occupational exposure to chemicals. Task Force on Environmental Cancer and Heart and Lung Disease, 'First Annual Report to Congress,' Washington, DC, 1978.

16. Bella Abzug, et al., 'Spend More on Solving Cancer Mystery,' *The New York Times*, 27 February 1995, Editorial page.

17. Mike Weilbacher, 'Toxic Shock: The Environment–Cancer Connection,' *E Magazine*, June/July 1995, pp. 28–35.

18. Umberto Veronesi, *Un Male Curabile*, 3 edition (Italy: A. Mondadori ed., 1986), p. 211.

19. Quoted in Mike Weilbacher (June/July 1995), p. 33.

20. Leslie Pardue, 'Testing for Toxins,' *E Magazine*, January/February 1994, pp. 14–16.

21. See Thomas Maugh, 'Chemical Carcinogens: The Scientific Basis for Regulation,' *Science* 201 (29 September 1978); Richard Peto, 'Distorting the Epidemiology of Cancer …,' *Nature* 284 (27 March 1980); John H. Weisburger and Gary M. Williams *Science* 214 (23 October 1981).

22. D. A. Long, *World Health Organization Monograph* 16 (1954): 45.

23. Gio Batta Gori, 'The Regulation of Carcinogenic Hazards,' *Science* 208 (18 April 1980): 256–61.

24. This proved true in 1979 when a man in Germany died from a cerebral edema after drinking 17 liters of water in a very short period of time. D. Schmahl, *CRC Critical Reviews in Toxicology* 6 (1979): 258. Aside from being dependent on dose, toxicity is related to time. For example, depending on the dose, prussic acid can kill in a matter of seconds, arsenic in a few hours or days, and cigarette smoke in a matter of years. Hence the distinction between acute (brief and severe) and chronic (long-term) toxicity.

25. T. Koppanyi and M. A. Avery, *Clinical Pharmacology & Therapeutics* 7 (1966): 250–70; Peter Wilhelm Lund, *Physiological Results of Modern Vivisection* (Germany: 1825), cited in Hans Ruesch, *Slaughter of the Innocent* (New York: Bantam Books, 1976/ Switzerland: Civitas Publications, 1983), p. 85; Joseph V. Rodricks, *Calculated Risks* (UK: Cambridge University Press, 1992), p. 40.

26. Dennis V. Parke, 'Ethical Aspects of the Safety of Medicines and Other Social Chemicals,' *Science & Engineering Ethics* 1, no. 3 (1995): 284.

27. Joseph V. Rodricks (1992), p. 41. In nutrition deprivation experiments for example, researchers would withhold certain vitamins and minerals from pregnant animals to determine what the effects would be on the mother and the offspring.

28. Joseph V. Rodricks (1992), p. 111.

29. Isaac Berenblum, 'The Modifying Influence of Dichlorethyl Sulphide on the Induction of Tumours in Mice by Tar,' *Journal of Pathology and Bacteriology*, official journal of the Pathological Society of Great Britain and Ireland, ed. A. E. Boycott, Vol. 32, Part 1 (Edinburgh: Oliver and Boyd, 1929). Berenblum also implanted metal or plastic film under the skin of animals to induce tumors. Isaac Berenblum, 'Established Principles and Unresolved Problems in Carcinogenesis,' *Journal of the National Cancer Institute* 60 (1978): 725.

30. Joseph V. Rodricks (1992), p. 111.

31. Heidi J. Welsh, *Animal Testing and Consumer Products* (Washington, DC: Investor Responsibility Research Center, 1990), p. 50.

32. Robert Sharpe, *The Cruel Deception* (Northamptonshire, UK: Thorsons, 1988), p. 95.

33. A. D. Dayan, 'Death of the LD50,' *J. Soc. Occup. Med.* 40 (1990): 85; H. M. Van Looy, 'The OECD and International Regulatory Acceptance of the Three 3Rs,' in Christoph A. Reinhardt, ed., *Alternatives to Animal Testing* (New York: VCH/ Weinheim, 1994), p. 14.

34. Dennis B. Maloney, 'Toxicity Tests in Animals: Extrapolating to Human Risks,' *Env. Health Persp.* 101, no. 5 (1993): 397.

35. In 1937, William Hueper and his colleagues at the National Cancer Institute (NCI) induced bladder tumors in dogs from administration of 2–naphthylamine. Hueper's work with 2–naphthylamine was credited with drawing public attention to the issue of chemical carcinogens in the workplace, but it was known as early as

1876 that naphtha, a petroleum by-product, caused bladder cancer in humans (though it did not cause bladder cancer in rodents).

William Hueper's experiments did not prevent 2–naphthylamine from finding its way into coal tar and cigarette smoke (International Agency for Research on Cancer, Vol. 4, 1974, Lyon, France), nor from being used in the dye and rubber industries into the early 1980s, where it caused fatal bladder cancer in hundreds of workers in the US and abroad, at which point it was finally 'removed.' OSHA, 'Industrial Exposures and Control Technologies for OSHA Regulated Hazardous Substances,' Vol. 1 of 2, Substances A–I (Washington, DC: US Department of Labor, March 1989). Prior to termination of its domestic production and use in the dye and rubber industries, the National Institute for Occupational Safety and Health (NIOSH) estimates that 15,000 workers were exposed to 2–naphthylamine during its manufacture and use in the US. NIOSH, 'Metabolic Precursors of a Known Human Carcinogen, Beta-Naphthylamine,' *Current Intelligence Bulletin* 16 (Ohio: NIOSH, 17 December 1976). The chemical is still used for research purposes.

36. Heidi J. Welsh (1990), p. 50.

37. Dennis V. Parke (1995): 287.

38. Dennis V. Parke, 'Clinical Pharmacokinetics in Drug Safety Evaluation' *ATLA* 22 (1994): 207–8.

39. William Hueper of the NCI proposed the 'linear model' in which human risk is determined based on effects observed in animals given high doses of a substance. Arnold Lehman and O. Garth Fitzhugh of the FDA devised a '100-fold safety factor' which attempted to set human toxicity thresholds using data from animal tests. This took the maximum dose at which a chemical produced no observable effect in animals, or NOEL, and divided it by a 'safety factor' of 100 to estimate humans' 'acceptable daily intake' (ADI) of chemicals from all sources in the environment. For a more complete discussion of these methods, see Chapter 2.

Here is just one example of some of the jargon used to describe statistical models: 'in this model, the shapes, arrangements, and number of sinusoids is irrelevant for substrate elimination of most substrates; only the flow through the sinusoids and the total amount of enzyme associated with each sinusoid (though not its distribution along the sinusoids) are relevant for uptake. Furthermore, in this model, all sinusoids are assumed to be functionally identical in that they have the same blood flows and enzyme content (or at least the same ratio); since all sinusoids are also assumed to have the same arterial substrate concentration, the output concentrations from all sinusoids are also identical and equal to the venous concentration.' Peter J. Robinson, discussing sinusoidal perfusion, one of three current models used to describe the metabolism of substances by the intact liver, in *Risk Analysis* 12, no. 1 (1992): 141–2.

40. Dennis V. Parke (1994): 207–9.

41. Heidi J. Welsh (1990), p. 51.

42. Personal communication with Hiromi Kamekura, Japan Anti-Vivisection Association, Tokyo, 24 August 1996.

43. Anon, 'Poland to Join OECD,' *The New York Times*, 12 July 1996, p. A6.

44. *Federal Register* (17 July 1992) Vol. 57, No. 138, p. 31721.

45. Anon, 'Lucier Named Director of ETP,' *Env. Health Persp.* 104, no. 3 (March 1996): 258.

46. Commission of the European Communities, *Development, Validation and Legal Acceptance of Alternative Methods to Animal Experiments*, Annual Report 1994 (Brussels), p. 19.

47. E. L. Harris, in A. Worden, et al., eds, *The Future of Predictive Safety Evaluation* (Boston: MTP Press), pp. 19–20, 24.

2. The numbers game: how animal-based toxicological risk assessment works

The US National Toxicology Program

'In its 16 years, the NTP has become the world's leader in designing, conducting and interpreting animal assays for toxicity.' National Toxicology Program, *Fiscal Year 1994 Annual Plan*, Draft (North Carolina: NTP, May 1994), p. 8

The array of chemical products that humans have become exposed to, and that have been tested on animals, has grown exponentially: dyes, agricultural chemicals (insecticides, fungicides, herbicides, rodenticides), soaps and detergents, synthetic fibers and rubbers, paper and textile chemicals, plastics and resins, adhesives, substances used in the processing, preservation and treatment of foods (additives), refrigerants, explosives, chemical warfare agents, cleaning and polishing materials, and cosmetics.[1] In 1993 the US Government's Office of Technology Assessment (OTA) estimated that there were approximately 62,000 man-made chemicals in commerce in the US today, with some 1,500 new chemicals being developed each year.[2] In 1995, that figure was said to be 75,000 and rising.[3]

In order to deal with this chemical threat, a chemical screening program was established by the National Cancer Institute in the 1960s and transferred to the National Toxicology Program (NTP) in Research Triangle Park, North Carolina, in 1978. The agency uses rodents, as well as short-term *in vitro* tests (carried out in glass test tubes) and epidemiological data, to predict human cancer risks from particular chemicals and their by-products. NTP, which has performed over 450 tests in the last 30 years,[4] provides data to regulatory and research agencies that are used to estimate human health risks from environmental exposures.

Although there are no statistics to demonstrate public support for federal risk assessment research, data collection for animal-based risk assessment—which has been called both a science and an art—has consumed, and continues to consume, many of the resources devoted to toxicology. In 1993, the NTP had a federally funded annual budget of \$500–\$600 million.[5] The risk assessment process is a multi-layered one which has come to involve biologists, physicists, geneticists, epidemiologists, pharmacologists, pathologists, geologists, economists, engineers, computer modelers and statisticians. The process ultimately requires risk assessors to make decisions about chemicals that have both economic value and the potential to cause cancer and other serious health effects; hence the outcome of the process necessarily acquires political and/or moral significance.

Although risk assessment research has typically focused on cancer, it has expanded its efforts to study non-cancer effects such as eye and skin irritation, respiratory ailments, reproductive and immune system disorders, phototoxicity, and neurotoxicity, among other things. According to Washington-based journalist Jan Ziegler, '[the research] is currently spread across at least twelve different federal agencies and more than 28 programs … each agency has its own set of priorities based on different constituents, legislative mandates and missions,' which often makes work fragmented and diffuse.[6] The agencies besides the Food and Drug Administration (FDA), National Institute for Occupational Safety and Health (NIOSH), National Center for Toxicological Research (NCTR) and National Institute of Environmental Health Sciences (NIEHS), participating in, and/or using data from the NTP's 'rodent bioassay' program include: The Consumer Product Safety Commission (CPSC) (similar to the UK's Consumer Policy Service), the Environmental Protection Agency (EPA), the Occupational Safety and Health Administration (OSHA), the Department of Labor (DOL), the Department of Transportation (DOT), the Department of Defense (DOD), the Department of Energy (DOE), the Department of Agriculture (USDA), the Federal Trade Commission (FTC), and the National Cancer Institute (NCI).[7] The four agencies which carry the major burden of cancer prevention are the EPA, FDA, CPSC, and OSHA.[8]

Toxicological risk assessment: a brief overview

There are many forms of risk assessment; the stated purpose of *toxicological* risk assessment, which is of interest here, is *not* to ban or regulate chemicals but to estimate the likelihood of an adverse effect on humans (and more recently wildlife and ecosystems) from exposure to chemicals.[9]

Dennis B. Maloney, a risk assessment consultant in Omaha, Nebraska, writes that, in risk assessment and toxicology in general, scientists seek to answer four basic questions: 'is a substance toxic?'; if so, what are the mechanisms of toxicity?; how much exposure makes it toxic?; and what are the best methods for estimating risk?'[10] Risk assessors use data from animal tests to answer these questions. Many turn to the NTP for that data.

How the NTP animal testing program works

The NTP's bioassay process is bureaucratic and lengthy. Maryland-based veterinarian Eric Dunayer has described it:

> Chemicals can be nominated for testing by anyone [including trade associations, consumer, and special interest groups]; participating federal agencies can nominate one priority chemical per year for a 'fast track' evaluation. After receiving nominations, the NTP's Chemical Evaluation Committee (CEC) publishes its recommendations in the *Federal Register* for public comment. Following a comment period, the CEC passes its recommendations to the NTP's Board of Scientific Counselors who pass their recommendations on to the NTP's Executive Committee which makes the final decisions as to which chemicals should be tested.[11]

Many chemicals are chosen for testing by the NTP if their molecular structure is similar to known (animal) carcinogens (a process which critics say preselects chemicals most likely to give 'positive' results). Other criteria include potential for human exposure as defined by high numbers of people exposed, production levels, and high environmental persistence.[12] In fiscal year 1996, a total of 11 chemicals were selected for testing by the NTP.[13]

Testing protocols must be approved by the Toxicology Design Review Committee (TDRC) before animal tests can begin. Most animal cancer bioassays follow standard protocols established by the NTP though, according to OSHA, the test protocols of scientific institutions are constantly being changed as new knowledge is gained, making specification of protocols impractical.[14] Moreover, different research agencies have different protocols and there is no definitive national or international standard. In 1978, EPA officials concluded that it would be impracticable to put forward standardized testing procedures since no one scheme is adequate for all the chemicals that have to be evaluated.[15]

The species and numbers of animals used in toxicity tests

'Researchers always need bodies. They just always do.' Tim Cummings, General Clinical Research Center, New England Medical Center, quoted in *The Boston Globe*, 17 November 1992, p. 67

The species of non-human animals commonly used in toxicity tests include rodents (rats, mice, guinea pigs, hamsters), dogs, cats, fish, birds (chickens, hens, pigeons), rabbits, frogs, ungulates (pigs and sheep), and primates, though other species (including wild species) are also used.[16] Monkeys are imported from Africa, Southeast Asia and South America, and bred in the United States in primate colonies. Marmosets (small primates prone to multiple births) are considered ideal for toxicology research, and chimpanzees are also used.[17]

Neither monkeys nor dogs are ideal research subjects, however, because of their long life spans, uncertain genetic makeup, and maintenance costs. According to Paul Schilling, director of Charles River Primate Corporation's primate breeding operations in Houston, Texas, monkeys have become expensive due to higher airline shipping rates and state-imposed quarantine restrictions.[18]

Rodents, primarily rats, mice and hamsters, are the 'species of choice' according to the International Agency for Research on Cancer (IARC), not because of their biochemical, physiological, or anatomical similarity to humans, but because of their small size, wide availability, low cost and short life spans.[19] Rabbits are commonly used for many of the same reasons and because they are generally docile. Certain strains of rodents are bred and specifically selected for their sensitivity to carcinogens. Countless 'inbred,' 'outbred,' 'hybrid,' 'immuno-deficient' and 'transgenic' designer rodents are available for sale or lease from breeding companies, to satisfy the desire for 'genetically pure' animals: Sprague-Dawley, Norway BDII, Lewis, Wistar, Long-Evans, Zucker, and Fischer 344 rats; Swiss, Webster, NMRI, IRC, C3H, B6C3F1 mice.[20] The use of transgenic mouse models in carcinogenesis and genetic toxicology research (the process by which foreign genes are introduced into the pronuclei of animals' cells) are being vigorously pursued by some scientists.[21] And though they have a poor reproductive rate, 'nude,' hairless rodents are specifically bred without thymus glands for cancer research because they allegedly do not reject tumor transplants.

Whether animal data, transgenic or otherwise, are relevant to humans is a contentious issue among scientists; the opportunities to obtain relevant toxicity data without the use of animals will be extensively discussed in Chapter 5.

Finally, under guidelines established by the US Public Health Service, human beings continue to be used (generally as willing subjects) in an array of experiments and clinical trials, in dozens of factories, medical centers, university hospitals and private manufacturing and bio-research firms around the country. United States law requires clinical testing of pharmaceuticals in human beings before they can be approved for general use.[22] Human volunteer studies, which eliminate the need for uncertain and costly inter-species extrapolations, are widely used by pharmaceutical, chemical, and cosmetic companies. The tests can take days or years but are appealing to research subjects because they are richly rewarded in cash. One man in Boston, who had lost his job, agreed for $1,100 to spend five four-day weeks taking escalating dosages of milk of magnesia for a pharmaceutical company.[23]

Although millions of humans are exposed to chemical threats in the environment, it is logistically impossible to use millions, or even thousands of non-humans as surrogates for humans in toxicity tests. Hence for practical reasons, most tests are performed with fifty to a hundred animals of each sex in each dose group: generally a high-dose group and a low-dose group.[24] Some six hundred animals are used in single-chemical studies which typically last two years. Commonly, two rodent (mouse and rat) and one non-rodent species (rabbit, hen, dog) are used in such studies.[25] Acute toxicity tests, such as the LD50, typically use sixty adult animals of each sex; variations of the test have used twenty animals or fewer. Developments in molecular biology and computer science, within the last two decades, have spurred the growth of technologies which eliminate the need for animals and/or reduce the numbers that are used. It is not uncommon for animals to be used more than once for different experiments, however. This is customary with rabbits in the Draize test. In an effort to decrease the total number of animals used in toxicity tests, the NTP has advocated the 'sharing of animals' between different research and testing departments. It has also advocated for the development of transgenic animals, believing that this may reduce the number of animals used in each test.[26]

But the exact *total* number of animals used in toxicity tests is difficult to determine, largely because under the US Animal Welfare Act, the Animal and Plant Health Inspection Service (APHIS) of the United States Department of Agriculture (USDA) does not require laboratories to report the numbers of rats and mice they use in research; and because those animals account for approximately 80–85 percent of the animals used, it is virtually impossible to produce an accurate figure.[27] The US Office of Technology Assessment claims that animals used in toxicity tests account for 20 percent of all the animals used in bio-medical research in the US (a figure which some say is 15 million and others 200 million),[28] placing the figure at anywhere between three and forty million.[29]

In the UK (where laboratories are required to report the number of rodents they use), government figures from 1994 revealed a decrease in the number of animals used in lethal poisoning tests, but an increase in tests for eye irritancy (despite the wide availability of non-animal methods in this area), for a total of some three million animals used—though that figure could be higher.[30] The Commission of the European Community states that it is unable to estimate how many animals were used to test cosmetic ingredients in 1994, despite the Commission's obligation to collect those statistics under Directives 86/609/EEC and 93/35/EEC.[31] Moreover, Donald W. Straughan noted in the journal *ATLA* (Vol. 23 (1995): 262–3) that, in 1991, some member states of the European Union such as Belgium and Luxembourg provided no animal use statistics; Italian data were estimated; and data from other countries were flawed. Hence, with the exception of Britain, there are still no satisfactory European data on animal use in (research and) testing.

How animal testing is performed

'the customary starting point in a toxicologic evaluation utilizes lethality as an index.' Casarett and Doull, *Principles of Toxicology*, 4th Edition (Tarrytown, NY: Pergamon Press, 1991), p. 20

It should be mentioned that there is a distinction between the *processes* used in toxicity studies that aim to measure general (non-cancer) toxicity, and those that measure cancer (as cancer is also considered to be a form of toxicity); however, because these distinctions will not be addressed in this book, and because the *methods* used to produce toxic effects are essentially the same, the reader is asked to overlook this point.

In toxicity tests, animals are generally exposed to chemicals in ways that are meant to mimic human exposure scenarios: by ingestion (or the oral route), via 'gavage,' inhalation, skin contact (or dermal irritancy), and contact with the eyes (or ocular irritancy).

The method for exposing an animal to a chemical does not always mimic the human experience, however; hair dyes were *fed* to rats for example. Toxicologists argue that hair dyes can enter the circulatory system through either the scalp or digestive tract; and since distribution of the substance throughout the animal's body is the goal of the test, feeding may be chosen as an appropriate method.

A variety of different tests are conducted; these include acute toxicity tests, chronic and sub-chronic toxicity tests, eye and skin irritation tests, carcinogenicity tests, developmental and reproductive toxicity tests, and neurotoxicity tests.[32] Such tests are required by regulatory authorities in the US, Europe and Japan. Generally, acute and sub-chronic animal tests are conducted first to screen substances for relative toxicity, and identify the dose range for toxic effects.

Short-term or acute toxicity tests last less than three months, and consist of single doses at concentrations high enough to produce toxic effects or death. It is in this category of experiments that the LD_{50} test is performed. LD or Lethal Dose 50 (and LD_{40}, LD_{30} and so on) is the dosage of a chemical in milligrams per kilogram (mg/kg) of body weight that will cause the death of 50 percent of the exposed animals in a 14–day period—generally 60 animals of one species divided equally between adult males and females.[33] The oral route is most often used because it is the cheapest and easiest way to dose an animal; inhalation and dermal studies may cost twice as much as oral studies.[34] Typically, a chemical is mixed with the animal's food and water, injected into the mouth, or delivered via gavage—down a tube that is surgically inserted into the animal's stomach. Several different dose levels of a compound are administered over a period of 14 days until half of all the animals die. The LD_{50} is then calculated from these results (for example 10 mg/kg/day).

If there is a likelihood of exposure to the material by dermal or inhalation exposure, then acute dermal and inhalation studies are performed. Acute inhalation studies (Lethal Concentration or LC_{50}) involve placing three groups of at least ten rats (or other species) in special inhalation or 'flow-through chambers' and exposing them to lethal concentrations of a vaporous substance for a period of four hours, after which they are observed for 14 days and the LC_{50} is recorded.

Sub-acute or sub-chronic tests last between one and three months and use slightly less toxic doses. Long-term, or chronic or 'repeated dose' tests, which last more than three months and generally for the lifetime of the animal, are performed to assess the cumulative toxicity of chemicals. Most animal testing is done to evaluate chronic exposure via inhalation or ingestion.[35] For the chronic or long-term test, also known as the carcinogenicity test or bioassay which lasts two years in rodents (or dogs), the animals are divided into groups of 50 to 100 adult males and females: a high-dose group, a low-dose group, and a control group that receives no treatment.

The high-dose group is tested at the maximum tolerated dose (MTD). (This testing procedure was developed in 1978 by the National Cancer Institute.) Like the LD_{50}, the MTD is chosen to be high enough to produce tumors in the animals but not so high as to kill them. A second test group is dosed at half the MTD; sometimes a third group is added; and an untreated group is monitored for rates and types of naturally occurring tumors.[36] In addition, the toxicologist must monitor food consumption rates, body weights, behavior patterns, blood and urine chemistry, and survival patterns.[37] Dunayer (1992) writes that, 'at the end of two years, all surviving animals are killed, and [their tissues] analyzed for evidence of cancer ... a two-year bioassay can produce over 40,000 pathology slides.'[38] This laborious process is described in greater detail in Chapter 3 (see 'Time and cost of testing').

Eye and skin irritation tests usually consist of a single exposure. The acute skin irritation test is typically performed in at least three groups of ten animals per sex, generally albino rabbits. Guinea pigs are commonly used for skin allergy/sensitization tests. The backs of all animals are shaved and the test substance is kept in contact with the skin for 24 hours by wrapping with an airtight plastic material. At the end of 24 hours, the plastic is removed, and the degree of skin irritation is scored according to numerous observable conditions including swelling and scarring for up to 72 hours.

In 21-day dermal studies, the substance is applied for six hours a day, five days a week, for three weeks. Toxicologist Patricia Lang writes that, 'data collected after this test include body weight, food consumption, clinical signs, blood chemistry, and [after the animal is killed], histopathology on selected organs.'[39]

In the Draize eye irritancy tests, conscious albino rabbits are immobilized in stocks, and a chemical is dropped or sprayed into one eye using the other eye as a control. Over a period of seven days, and typically without pain relief, different concentrations of chemicals are sprayed or dropped into one eye of the animal. Robert Sharpe (1988) explains that, during the experiment, 'the cornea, iris and conjunctivae are examined for signs of opacity, ulceration, haemorrhage, redness, swelling, and discharge.'[40]

Studies to determine a chemical's potential to cause a host of reproductive problems—including infertility, miscarriages, and birth defects—are also performed on a minimum of two successive generations of animals. Chemicals that damage the reproductive system and cause birth defects are called 'teratogens.' Suspected teratogens are studied by mating pairs of chemically treated animals, or chemically treated females and untreated males, and vice versa. Joseph V. Rodricks (1992) described the numerous indices of reproductive performance that are then measured: 'the "fertility index" is the percentage of matings that result in pregnancies. The "gestation index" is the percentage of pregnancies resulting in the birth of live litters. The percentage of offspring that survive four days or longer is called the "viability index."'[41]

Teratogenicity tests involve between 20 and 80 pregnant rats or rabbits and sometimes other species. The chemical to be tested is given to the animals at several dose levels during the entire period of a fetus's organ development. Because rodents will reabsorb a deformed embryo or eat a malformed fetus, fetuses are prematurely removed from the mother (either by Caesarean or by flushing them from the reproductive tract), and any physical abnormalities are observed. Rodricks explains that if a mother receives a dose that was toxic to her, it then becomes difficult to discern whether the fetus was injured by the chemical under study or due to the mother's own ill health.[42]

Hens and other animals are tested with a variety of doses at numerous exposures in acute and sub-chronic neurotoxicity tests, to determine toxic effects to the nervous system. Toxic 'endpoints' include behavioral changes, lack of coordination, motor disorders, and learning disabilities.[43] Typically, hens are injected with atropine before dosing, to prevent acute death. After the animals are killed, their nervous systems are examined under a microscope.[44]

How animal data are extrapolated to humans

'The estimated biologically effective dose could increase linearly with the de-livered dose for delivered doses exceeding the susceptibility frontier and increase exponentially (with associated low-dose linearity) for delivered doses less than the susceptibility frontier.' Robert L. Sielken Jr., 'Cancer Dose–Response Extrapolations,' *Env. Sci. Technol.* 21, no. 11 (1987): 1037

'Unfortunately, extrapolation from animal results to man remains largely problematical and no amount of mathematical sophistication can render such extrapolation more certain.' J. Higginson and C. S. Muir, International Agency for Research on Cancer, 'The Role of Epidemiology in Elucidating the Importance of Environmental Factors in Human Cancer,' *Cancer Detection and Prevention I* (Lyon: IARC, 1976), p. 81.

The process of risk assessment involves extrapolation from known conditions in a controlled laboratory experiment with non-human animals, to the uncontrollable human experience.

There is no consensus on how to extrapolate data from non-humans to humans or from one animal species to another.[45] Among the most controversial assumptions in the inter-species extrapolation process are: the relevance of high doses in animals to low-dose human exposures; the selection of the appropriate mathematical model for the extrapolation; and often the selection of the test species, as even closely related species like rats and mice can have vastly different responses from each other.

In extrapolating from one species to another, the results may depend critically on the particular statistical/mathematical model that is used.[46] These range from the simple to the increasingly complex; they may use one particular cancer theory as a foundation, and include calculations of endless biological and chemical variables.

Using the 'linearized multi-hit model' for example, and by placing 'risk' on the X axis and 'dose' on the Y axis, dose-response points are graphed to produce a curve that sweeps from the highest to the lowest recorded dose at which the animals developed tumors.[47] Scientists then consider everything else they believe about the biological effects of the tested carcinogen and introduce 'species conversion' or scaling factors for the final extrapolation to humans.[48]

The models essentially calculate the degree of probability that an exposed population of humans will get cancer from a specific chemical dose. For example, using the 'one-hit model,' and extrapolating from tobacco inhalation experiments with animals, a scientist may assume that if one hundred thousand people were each to inhale one tenth of a puff of cigarette smoke in their lifetime, one individual would get lung cancer as a consequence of that exposure, producing a human risk estimate of 1×10^{-5}.

How animal data are used within the regulatory framework*

'the level of risk that regulatory agencies have deemed acceptable in the past (10^{-4}) ... represents a working consensus on the value of human life.' C. C. Travis and H. Hattemer-Frey, 'Determining an Acceptable Level of Risk,' *Env. Sci. Technol.* 22, no. 8 (1988): 874

'the establishment of a maximum contaminant level goal (MCLG) at zero does not imply that actual harm necessarily occurs to humans at a level somewhat above zero, but rather that zero is an aspirational goal which includes a margin of safety within the context of the Safe Drinking Water Act.' Environmental Protection Agency, *Federal Register* (8 July 1987) Vol. 52, no. 130, p. 25693

Despite the inherent uncertainty in animal-to-human extrapolations,[49] the use of animal-based risk assessment data by federal regulatory agencies in the area of consumer protection is pervasive. A confusing and elaborate array of animal-based statistical data have become part

---

* Note: parts of this section include mathematical equations, formulae, and terms which will illuminate the highly technical nature of risk assessment. Readers who find this section overwhelmingly technical may choose to skip over it or return to it at a later time.

of both internal and external agency handbooks and manuals; they fill both private and public computer databases on toxicity; and they are cited in veterinary books to define 'safe doses' of anti-parasitic sprays for other animals such as cows and pigs. Different sectors work together to develop animal data for their uses; so that a company marketing a new product depends on the rules made by a regulator, who depends on the work done by a risk assessor, who may work with a statistician, who obtains his or her data from a toxicologist. All fields are inter-dependent and data derived from one discipline are used to fuel calculations and decisions made in another.

Much of the information presented below may seem mind-boggling and confusing to the layperson; some of it is extremely technical. The world of risk assessment has a language all its own which is incomprehensible at first glance, and may even seem absurd. Once one begins to speak the language of risk assessment, one is sucked into a way of reasoning that is made to seem entirely rational, despite the fact that the discipline's principles are based on the very shaky foundation of animal-to-human extrapolation. Some examples of the way animal data are used to calculate estimates of human health risks are provided below to give the reader some idea of the way it works. Descriptions follow of how this discipline has woven itself into virtually every aspect of the regulatory system.

Carcinogen classification   Rodent bioassay data are used by regulatory and research agencies to classify chemicals into categories for their carcinogenicity. The International Agency for Research on Cancer uses 'sufficient,' 'limited' or 'inadequate' evidence as the basis for its decisions, making distinctions between animal-based or human data.[50] The NTP devised letter categories to classify carcinogens: (A) for known human carcinogens, (B1 and B2) for probable human carcinogens, (C) for possible human carcinogens, (D) for known animal carcinogens, and (E) for inconclusive or no data. (Most chemicals, including lead, currently fall into the B categories; only about 30 chemicals are listed in the A category). Virtually every US federal agency, including the EPA, FDA, and OSHA, uses the NTP's classification system, though the EPA has proposed a new system to classify carcinogens as 'known/likely,' 'cannot be determined,' and 'not likely.'[51]

Toxicity profiles   Animal data (and sometimes human data if they are available) are used to generate toxicologic information used in 'toxicity profiles' for specific chemicals. The profiles are synopses which describe the range of biological effects caused by a particular chemical.

US government agencies like the EPA and the Agency for Toxic Substances and Disease Registry (ATSDR) have compiled these data into review vehicles such as the 'ATSDR Toxicity Profiles.' The ATSDR, which was mandated by Congress to develop toxicity profiles in the mid-1980s, has developed profiles for approximately 275 commonly regulated chemicals. The ATSDR hires NTP contractors to provide the data that go into its profiles. These are booklets of between fifty and several hundred pages, depending on the range of data that are available for a particular chemical. Consumers consult the profiles if they have been exposed to and/or injured by a chemical; physicians, lawyers, health advocates, and government officials also consult them, but risk assessors are the agency's principal customers.[52]

Departments of Environmental Protection (DEP) in some states publish short toxicity profiles. In Massachusetts, a state environmental law requires that toxicity profiles be done for all risk assessments performed in the state. The Comprehensive Environmental Response, Compensation and Liability Act (CERCLA), a federal EPA law, requires that toxicity profiles be provided for all risk assessments performed under CERCLA.[53]

Material Safety Data Sheets   Data from animal tests are used to create Material Safety Data Sheets (MSDS); OSHA, and EPA Toxic Substances Control Act (TSCA) and SARA Title III regulations all require MSDSs to be provided to chemical users. The MSDS defines a chemical's physical and chemical properties, lists its carcinogenicity status, describes emergency and first aid, shipping and handling, and spill procedures, defines the permissible exposure limits (PELs) for that chemical, and provides health hazard data. This latter section classifies a chemical as 'slightly toxic,' 'moderately toxic,' 'severely toxic,' 'slightly irritating,' 'mildly irritating,' and so on, based on, for example, an oral LD_{50} in mg/kg, an inhalation LC_{50} in parts per million (ppm) and/or skin/eye irritancy values from animal tests. MSDSs are published and distributed by chemical manufacturers to customers/chemical users. Manufacturers may develop MSDSs in-house or purchase them from hired consultants.[54] (Toxicologists, like Virginia C. Gordon (1993), have advocated replacing the 'outdated and subjective safety assessments' found on MSDS sheets with data from cell cultures.)[55]

Dose-response estimates, CPF and RfD/RfC/ADI   The dose-response principle is used to generate the Reference Dose (RfD) or Acceptable Daily Intake (ADI), the animal estimate of threshold which is used to determine a person's risk of experiencing a host of *non-cancer* effects, from the ingestion or inhalation of specific chemicals. Agencies like the EPA use the RfD to establish the dose of a chemical (like a pesticide residue) that is allegedly safe for an adult to consume daily for a lifetime. (The EPA now uses the RfD instead of ADI—a term which the agency says carried with it a 'non-scientific value judgement.' ADI's are still used by the FDA and the World Health Organization however; the latter developed the concept of safety factors to determine ADIs for pesticides and food additives in the early 1960s.)[56] The RfD is obtained through a formula which divides the No Observable Effect Level (NOEL)—a dose level in a test species that causes no observable effect—by a safety factor, which is usually between ten and 1,000.

$$\text{RfD} = \frac{\text{NOEL}}{1,000}$$

(Dividing the NOEL by a safety factor is supposed to produce a number that is relevant to human beings. But one must bear in mind that the NOEL itself, like the concept of threshold, is contentious since it requires the proof of a negative or a non-observable effect, which is logically and scientifically impossible.)

Since most animal testing is done to evaluate chronic or long-term exposure via inhalation and ingestion, Reference Dose values are obtained for ingestion (RfD) and inhalation (RfC) routes only, and are normally determined from chronic and sub-chronic tests in animals; some human-derived RfD values exist but they are very limited.[57]

Human exposure to a chemical is calculated using the following formula:

$$\text{Exposure} = \frac{\text{Concentration} \times \text{Intake} \times \text{Frequency} \times \text{Duration}}{\text{Body weight} \times \text{Averaging time}[58]}$$

An application of this formula would look like this:

$$\text{Exposure to mercury} = \frac{\dfrac{200\text{mg (mercury)}}{\text{kg (fish)}} \times \dfrac{0.25\text{kg}}{\text{week}} \times \dfrac{52\text{ weeks}}{\text{yr.}} \times 50\text{ years}}{70\text{kg.} \times 365\text{ days} \times 50}$$

The result of the equation is an Exposure estimate numerically represented in milligrams (or micrograms) per kilograms $\times$ day for solids, and liters per kilograms $\times$ day for liquids; for example, 0.10 mg/kg $\times$ day. That Exposure estimate is then divided by the RfD or RfC so that:

$$\text{Risk} = \frac{\text{Exposure (i.e. 0.10 mg/kg} \times \text{day)}}{\text{RfD (i.e. 0.01 mg/kg} \times \text{day)}}$$

The result of this equation produces yet another index of risk for *non-carcinogens* called the Hazard Index. The Hazard Index essentially gauges exposures that would result from doses below the Reference Dose (RfD). The Hazard Index must never be greater than one. If it is, for example, only 1.5, an exposure to a chemical in the workplace, in the environment, or at a toxic waste dump is thereby considered risky and the site must then be evacuated and/or cleaned up.

Similarly, the Carcinogen Potency Factor (CPF), which is used to calculate cancer risks only, is a measure of risk in 'units of risk' per mg/kg/day obtained from experimental data. This is expressed, for example, as

$$\frac{1 \text{ (unit of risk)}}{\text{(for every) } 2.3 \text{ mg/kg/day}}$$

Risk is then calculated by multiplying Exposure by the CPF using the formula:

$$\text{Cancer risk} = \text{Exposure} \times \text{CPF}$$

Non-linear models are applied to extrapolate cancer risks to humans.

IRIS, HEAST and other databases   Data (mostly from animals) on *non*-cancer effects for over 425 chemicals have been compiled and stored in two EPA databases: the Integrated Risk Information System (IRIS) and the Health Effects Assessment Summary Tables (HEAST) published by the EPA's Superfund Division. The IRIS database includes information on the basis for identifying a substance as a carcinogen, including the derivation of the CPR for cancer effects, the derivation of RfD for non-cancer effects, determinations of safety factors used in the RfD equation, and other information on toxicity and regulatory standards for the chemical. While the IRIS data have been subjected to extensive peer review and have been 'validated' using common extrapolation methods, the HEAST data have not been validated and the numbers are considered provisional; hence IRIS is usually searched first. Risk assessors may use these officially recognized estimates to assess quantitative measures of risk and determine whether chemical exposure levels—at a contaminated playground for example—are within an 'acceptable' range.

IRIS data are found only on-line, and IRIS access can be purchased through private vendors, via the Internet or on CD-Rom. HEAST tables are available on paper from The National Technical Information Service, a federal document repository in Springfield, Virginia.

In addition, there are databases like TOXLINE and TOXNET (and CHEMLINE and CANCERLIT), that abstract research reports from toxicology and other journals on-line. These are part of the Medical Literature Analysis and Retrieval System (MEDLARS). The MED-LARS international database system was created through a bilateral agreement to allow public institutions in foreign countries to serve as biomedical information resource centers. The National Library of Medicine in Washington, DC is a designated MEDLARS Center; participating countries include Australia, Brazil, Canada, China, Egypt, France, Germany, India, Italy, Japan, Kuwait, Mexico, South Africa, Sweden, Switzerland, Taiwan, and the UK.[59] The Toxic Substances Control Act Test Submissions, a database which includes similar information submitted by industry, is available on-line, as is the Carcinogenic Potency Database which presents an analysis of 5,000 long-term animal tests on 1,230 chemicals. The database of the International Register of Potentially Toxic Chemicals (IRPTC) in Geneva, Switzerland, sponsored by the United Nations Environment Program (UNEP), is also on-line; and anyone with access to the Internet could spend hours searching through a plethora of technical (animal-based) toxicology studies by searching the NIEHS homepage at http://www.niehs.nih.gov. The NIEHS (through the Central Data Management Office) provides copies of hundreds of NTP-conducted animal studies, as well as the Congressionally mandated *Biennial Report on Carcinogens*.

Handbooks   Animal data are exclusively used in the *Dermal Absorption Handbook*, published by the EPA, from which risk assessors obtain 'permeability constants' (for intact and abraded skin) for over 100 substances; because all of these data are derived from animals, statistical models must be used to extrapolate them to humans. The *Exposure Factors Handbook*, on the other hand, is a document compiled from extensive interviews and research with human beings, and presents data on human respiratory rates, body surface area, diet, time spent in various activities, and so on. There are no animal-derived data in this document. Using the *Handbook*, for example, the EPA has determined that the surface area of the average 150-pound male is 19,600 cm^2, and for an average female is 18,000 cm^2.

On a general level, the animal tests serve five basic functions: 1) they supply information to regulators about the range of toxic effects caused by the *accidental* and *intentional* use of chemicals, drugs and cosmetics; 2) they are used in a more formalized way by federal agencies to provide the basis for the classification and labelling of hazardous chemicals and consumer products—labels that are supposed to prevent consumers from ingesting or improperly using dangerous chemicals; 3) they are used by regulatory toxicologists to decide whether a specific chemical or drug poses a sufficiently low risk to be marketed for a stated purpose; 4) they provide the basis for regulatory standards governing human exposures to contaminants in food, air and water—whether at home, in the workplace, or in the environment; and finally 5) they are performed to avoid product liability lawsuits. Table 2.1 illustrates how various American federal agencies use animals or animal data.

Animal testing, which forms the basis of risk assessment research, directly impacts on all of our lives and the lives of animals. The tests, which are designed to mirror the ways in which humans are exposed to chemical agents, may last one day or the entire life of the animal. Data from LD50 tests, Draize tests, carcinogenicity, reproductive toxicity and neurotoxicity tests on numerous species of animals have provided the basis for virtually every federal guideline and standard in the area of environmental quality and human health. The guidelines pertain to the safe handling, transportation, storage, use and disposal of chemicals used by industries, businesses, consumers, and federal agencies. For example, the EPA has used the results of animal tests conducted at Michigan State University, in which minks were fed contaminated carp, to develop national water quality standards. The agency used the results of research on trout conducted at the University of Wyoming to formulate national sulfur dioxide emission standards.[60]

Animal test data have been used to determine the acceptable application doses for pesticides and how much residual pesticide may safely be allowed in both raw and processed foods; whether a former toxic waste dump (like Love Canal) is 'safe enough' to repopulate; whether a nuclear reactor is safe enough to operate; and whether or how the building of an incinerator will impact on the health of local residents.

Although the use of animal test data by federal regulatory agencies, research institutions and private consulting firms is pervasive, animal-to-human extrapolations continue to be laden with uncertainties, and risk assessment itself is far from foolproof. US federal regulatory agencies like the EPA have determined that, while 'zero risk' (of getting cancer or becoming sick) would be a desirable goal to strive for in this society, absolute safety is unattainable, as many contaminants such as smog, or PCBs which are stored in the fatty tissues of fish (if one eats fish), are unavoidable.[61] Consequently, 'Maximum Contaminant Levels' (MCLs—for drinking water), 'Acceptable Daily Intakes' (ADIs—for

Table 2.1 How US regulatory agencies use animal data

Federal agency	How animal data are used
Consumer Product Safety Commission	Conducts animal tests to determine the toxic potential of consumer products.
Department of Health & Human Services (ATSDR, FDA, NCI, NIEHS, NIOSH)	Conducts animal tests to determine hazards posed by drugs, cosmetics, medical devices, food and color additives, and radiological products, etc.
Environmental Protection Agency	Conducts tests to determine the toxicity of pesticides, industrial chemicals, air and water pollutants, hazardous wastes and some radiation hazards.
Department of Labor (OSHA)	Uses animal test data to identify dangerous workplace substances.
Department of Transportation	Uses animal test data to categorize different toxicity levels of hazardous materials shipped in interstate commerce.
Department of Agriculture	Conducts animal tests with agricultural drugs and preparations.
Department of Defense	Conducts experimental research in a wide variety of areas, including weapons, viruses, and chemical and biological agents.
Department of Energy	Conducts research, mostly at the privately managed Brookhaven National, Oak Ridge National, and Pacific Northwest laboratories, on the health and environmental effects of energy technologies.
Federal Trade Commission	Uses animal test data to substantiate the packing and advertising claims of companies.

Sources: National Research Council, *Use of Laboratory Animals in Biomedical and Behavioral Research* (Washington, DC: National Academy Press, 1988); Patricia Lang, 'Product Safety Assessment: A Review of Animal Testing Requirements in the US,' Reference Paper (Fall 1991), Charles River Laboratories, Wilmington, Massachusetts; Heidi J. Welsh, *Animal Testing and Consumer Products* (Washington, DC: Investor Responsibility Research Center, 1990).

exposure to chemicals in food and other environmental media), 'Permissible Exposure Levels' (PELs—for occupational exposures) or 'safe doses' have been established for humans based on what causes cancer and a range of other toxic effects (kidney damage, respiratory illness, skin rashes, blindness, reproductive effects) in animals, generally rodents, at various doses.

A 'safe dose' is one at which an individual's lifetime cancer risk does not exceed a particular level; some agencies use a numerically represented risk of one in one hundred thousand (1×10^{-5}) or lower as a standard for a safe dose, meaning that one person in one hundred thousand may develop cancer from a given chemical exposure. Clearly for some agents risks are greater.[62]

Lifetime risks of exposures to potential carcinogens have been set at one in one million for pesticides (1×10^{-6}), and between one in ten thousand and one in one million (1×10^{-4} to 10^{-6}) for airborne emissions and carcinogens in drinking water.[63] A lifetime cancer risk of one in one million (1×10^{-6}) is considered a 'societally acceptable risk' by most risk assessors, and a 'negligible risk' by the EPA,[64] although risks greater than one in ten thousand (1×10^{-4}) have been tolerated. For non-carcinogens, 'safe doses' have been set at exposures that would result in doses below the reference dose (RfD)—the animal estimate of threshold which is expressed by the Hazard Index described above. Environmentalists have criticized the EPA's standards on 'negligible risks,' however, on the grounds that they ignore cumulative risks.[65] The Maryland-based Environmental Research Foundation (ERF) charges that the EPA has set many 'tolerances' for pesticide residues on foods (some 8,500 to be more exact) at levels far higher than the agency itself has declared safe;[66] and some scientists say that, due to interspecies differences and a host of other factors related to the way animal tests are performed, safe exposure standards may be set at inappropriate levels,[67] thus unwittingly calling into question the true predictive power of the animal tests and their usefulness in safeguarding human health.

Others, like biostatistician Irwin Bross, Ellen Silbergeld, a toxicologist with the Environmental Defense Fund, and Peter Montague of ERF, have criticized risk assessment as being a ridiculously complex practice that is understandable only to the risk assessors and the statisticians themselves, which churns out data of questionable relevance to humans, and is essentially a waste of time and tax dollars.[68] Some say that effective pollution prevention measures would eliminate the need for risk assessment.[69]

Though critics of risk assessment are quick to point out the deficiencies of the discipline (which has evolved with the growth of the chemical industry), they are less likely to openly criticize the animal tests which are its backbone. In fact, as previously stated in Chapter 1, many environmental groups are in favor of animal tests. Some, including the Environmental Defense Fund (EDF), the Natural Resources Defense Council (NRDC), the World Resources Institute (WRI), and even the World Wildlife Fund (WWF), have endorsed animal tests in published reports, newspaper articles,[70] and legal documents. Some have even proposed their own testing regimes.[71] But the strongest support for animal tests has come from sectors of the federal government such as the Public Health Service, which includes the National Institutes of Health in Bethesda, Maryland and the NTP in North Carolina, and private businesses and research advocacy groups such as Charles River Breeding Laboratories in Wilmington, Massachusetts, The Society of Toxicology and the Foundation for Biomedical Research, both in Washington, DC. It is the rhetoric advanced by these groups, presented in the form of glossy promotional brochures and publications that are disseminated to schools, universities, church groups, trade organizations and the like, which may have served to legitimize these tests in the eyes of the public.

Chapter 3 will present the arguments championed by the proponents of animal testing, as well as offer a comprehensive rebuttal of those arguments on scientific grounds. Humanitarian considerations will also be addressed.

Notes

1. Joseph V. Rodricks, *Calculated Risks* (UK: Cambridge University Press, 1992), p. 10.

2. Office of Technology Assessment, *Researching Health Risks* (Washington, DC: US Government Printing Office, November 1993).

3. Victor A. Fung, et al., 'The Carcinogenesis Bioassay in Perspective: Application in Identifying Human Cancer Hazards,' *Env. Health Persp.* 103, no. 7–8 (July–August 1995): 680.

4. Joel Brinkley, 'Many Say Lab Animal Tests Fail to Measure Human Risk,' *The New York Times*, 23 March 1993, p. A1.

5. Office of Technology Assessment (November 1993).

6. Jan Ziegler, 'Health Risk Assessment Research: The OTA Report,' *Env. Health Persp.* 101, no. 5 (October 1993): 402–6.

7. Eric Dunayer, 'Testing Chemicals: Animal Testing Impedes Regulatory Action,' 1992, unpublished paper courtesy of The Physicians Committee for Responsible Medicine, Washington, DC, p. 6; personal communication with William Stokes, Environmental Toxicology Program, NIEHS, 1 November 1995.

8. It should be noted that The Agency for Toxic Substances and Disease Registry contributes resources to the NTP for the conduct of toxicology studies on chemicals

identified in priority hazardous waste sites; there are also significant toxicology research, testing and methods development activities ongoing at the EPA, the DOE and the Department of Health and Human Services (DHHS). National Toxicology Program, *Fiscal Year 1994 Annual Plan*, Draft (North Carolina: National Toxicology Program, May 1994). In addition, hundreds of private research organizations, and university and corporate laboratories, under contract by industry, conduct their own animal tests for cosmetics, household, agricultural and industrial chemicals, and pharmaceuticals. Eric Dunayer (1992), p. 7. Animals are also used by the US Air Force, for example, to test the toxicity of chemical and biological warfare agents. Harvey Clewell III, et al., *Risk Analysis* 14, no. 3 (1994): 265–76.

9. Russell Keenan, et al., 'Exposure Assessment,' *Risk Analysis* 14, no. 3 (1994): 225. Briefly, risk assessment consists of four steps; each step is complex and related to the next: (1) hazard identification: the identification of the hazard and a qualitative evaluation of its adverse health effects in the body; (2) exposure assessment: the evaluation of the routes (inhalation, ingestion) and media (soil, water, air) of exposure, as well as the dose involved, and the time and duration of exposure; (3) dose-response assessment: the process of estimating the relation between the dose of a substance and the incidence of an adverse health effect in the body (the toxic effects of all chemicals are characterized by the 'dose–response relationship,' which shows that increasing a dose will increase the severity of an effect); and (4) risk characterization: the process of estimating the probability of an adverse health effect under different conditions of exposure. Jan Ziegler (October 1993): 402–6.

10. D. Maloney, 'Toxicity Tests in Animals: Extrapolating to Human Risks,' *Env. Health Persp.* 101, no. 5 (October 1993): 396–401.

11. Eric Dunayer (1992), p. 6. National Toxicology Program (May 1994).

12. 'National Toxicology Program Final Report of the Advisory Review by the NTP Board of Scientific Counselors,' *Federal Register* (17 July 1992) Vol. 57, No. 138, p. 31724.

13. Source: Internet address, http://www.niehs.nih.gov, as of May 1996. On the NTP testing schedule for 1996 are naphthalene (dubbed a carcinogen by NIOSH in 1976), and acrylonitrile (dubbed a carcinogen by OSHA, 16 January 1978), in Edith Efron, *The Apocalyptics: Cancer and the Big Lie* (New York: Simon & Schuster, 1984), pp. 113, 153.

14. OSHA, *Federal Register* (22 January 1980) Vol. 45, No. 15, p. 5142.

15. Thomas H. Maugh, 'EPA and Toxic Substances Law: Dealing With Uncertainty,' *Science* 202 (10 November 1978): 598–602.

16. Robert Sharpe, *The Cruel Deception* (Northamptonshire, UK: Thorsons, 1988), p. 94. For example, quails, pheasants, robins and eagles were used in tests with DDT. Rachel Carson, *Silent Spring* (New York: Houghton Mifflin Company, 1994), p. 121. Rainbow trout have been used in experiments to test the carcinogenic potential of aflatoxin, a mold found in certain foods like peanuts. Joseph V. Rodricks (1992), p. xxi. North American fish are used to study the effects of aquatic pollutants. David Sarokin and Jay Schulkin, 'The Role of Pollution in Large-Scale Population Disturbances,' *Env. Sci. Technol.* 26, no. 8 (1992): 1476–84.

Fred Oehme at Kansas State University's Comparative Toxicology Lab used pigs to study the effects of agricultural chemicals on the central nervous system. Wayne Landis, director of Western Washington University's Institute of Environmental Toxicology and Chemistry, is devising methods for using the South African clawed frog to test contaminated soil at EPA's Superfund sites. A growing variety of animals are being used to study the effects of contaminants in wild species. Researchers in the Netherlands fed eleven harbor seals contaminated herring from the Baltic Sea for a two-year period to determine that environmental contaminants can impair the immune function of wild seals. Rik L. de Swart, et al., 'Impaired Immunity in Harbour Seals ...,' *Env. Health Persp.* 104, Supplement 4 (August 1996): 59.

17. Buckshire Corporation catalogue, undated, courtesy of People for the Ethical Treatment of Animals, Norfolk, Virginia. Frederick Coulston, the 79-year-old president of The Coulston Foundation in New Mexico, which manages the world's largest chimpanzee colony consisting of 540 chimps, pioneered the use of apes in tests in which chemicals are sprayed in their open eyes, a practice he still supports. Sources close to the company say his researchers tested oven cleaner on apes' eyes in 1993 despite objections from an in-house research ethics panel. Scott Allen, 'Apes on Edge,' *The Boston Globe,* 7 November 1994, pp. 1, 12.

18. Heidi Durrow, 'Primate Lab Flees NY Rules,' *Newsday,* 9 July 1991. Monkeys, which used to cost $400 to $500 in the late 1980s now cost over $2,000 each plus maintenance costs. Hazleton Research Animals, 1987 Price List. In addition, chimpanzees, widely used for AIDS research, are listed as a threatened species within the United States, and endangered for the purposes of international trade under the Convention on International Trade in Endangered Species (CITES).

19. R. Montesano, et al., *Long-Term and Short-Term Assays for Carcinogens: A Critical Appraisal* (Lyon: Oxford University Press, 1986) cited in Dunayer (1992), p. 13.

20. Pregnant animals, and animals with newborn infants are also widely sold for use in fetotoxicity and teratogenicity tests (to measure damage to both unborn and newborn infants); and most laboratories will perform surgical procedures such as castrations and removal of specific organs, upon request. Troy Soos, 'Charles River Breeding Labs,' *The Animals' Agenda,* December 1986; and Sasco 1995 Price List, Omaha, Nebraska, a division of Charles River Laboratories.

21. Raymond W. Tennant and Erroll Zeiger, 'Genetic Toxicology: Current Status of Methods of Carcinogen Identification,' *Env. Health Persp.* 100 (1992): 307–15.

22. Ann E. Weiss, *Bioethics: Dilemmas in Modern Medicine* (New Jersey: Enslow Publishers, 1985), p. 34.

23. Mark Muro, 'The New Guinea Pigs,' *The Boston Globe,* 17 November 1992, p. 63.

24. Joseph V. Rodricks (1992), p. 69. The number of human beings involved in skin irritation tests can be as small as 20 and as high as 500, depending on the substance under study (see Chapter 5, 'Human volunteer studies').

25. Beagle dogs are generally used to fulfill agency requirements for testing in a non-rodent mammal; but dogs are more expensive, more difficult to care for than rodents, and are prone to 'regurgitation' which complicates oral dosing, according to Patricia Lang, a consulting toxicologist for Charles River Laboratories (see footnote 39). Research is under way to consider the ferret as a non-rodent species to replace the use of dogs. Myron A. Mehlman, et al., *Cell Biology and Toxicology* 5, no. 3 (1989): 353. Scientists within the same organization, such as the National Cancer Institute, often disagree with each other about how many animal species should be tested before a carcinogenic finding can be applied to humans. Edith Efron, *The Apocalyptics: Cancer and the Big Lie* (New York: Simon & Schuster, 1984), p. 245.

26. *Federal Register* (17 July 1992) Vol. 57, No. 138, p. 31723.

27. National Research Council, Committee on the Use of Laboratory Animals in Biomedical and Behavioral Research, *Use of Laboratory Animals in Biomedical and Behavioral Research* (Washington, DC: National Academy Press, 1988), p. 25; see also Andrew Rowan, et al., *The Animal Research Controversy* (Massachusetts: Center for

Animals & Public Policy, Tufts University School of Veterinary Medicine, 1995), p. 156.

28. Tom Regan, ed., *Animal Sacrifices* (Philadelphia: Temple University Press, 1986), p. 18.

29. Andrew Rowan believes that the total number of animals used in research in the US is no more than 30 million annually (Anon, 'Message in a Bottle,' *The Economist*, 22 April 1995, p. 83) and that the figure for animals used in toxicity studies is 10 percent of that figure, or three million annually. Andrew Rowan, et al. (1995), p. 97.

30. Robert Sharpe, 'Rise in Vivisection ...,' *International Animal Action* 36 (Spring 1996), published by the International Association Against Painful Experiments on Animals, Hertfordshire, UK, p. 2.

31. Commission of the European Communities, *Development, Validation, and Legal Acceptance of Alternative Methods to Animal Experiments*, Annual Report 1994 (Brussels), p. 19.

32. National Research Council (1988), p. 24.

33. Personal communication with Professor Anne Marie Desmarais, Department of Civil and Environmental Engineering, Tufts University, Medford, Massachusetts, 26 July 1995.

34. The species most often used here are the mouse and rat but sometimes the rabbit and dog are used. Casarett and Doull's *Toxicology: The Basic Science of Poisons*, 4th Edition (Tarrytown, NY: Pergamon Press, 1991), p. 32.

35. Office of Technology Assessment, *Identifying and Regulating Carcinogens* (Washington, DC: US Government Printing Office, 1987).

36. See note 19.

37. Joseph V. Rodricks (1992), p. 73.

38. Eric Dunayer (1992), p. 8.

39. Patricia L. Lang, 'Product Safety Assessment ...,' Reference Paper (Fall 1991), Charles River Laboratories, Wilmington, Massachusetts, p. 6.

40. Robert Sharpe (1988), p. 101.

41. Joseph V. Rodricks (1992), p. 102.

42. Ibid., p. 105.

43. National Research Council (1988), p. 24.

44. Patricia L. Lang (Fall 1991), p. 6.

45. Three sets of extrapolations are made: 1) route-to-route extrapolations, from one route of exposure to another; 2) high- to low-dose extrapolations, of the experimental results at high-dose levels to low dose levels for the animal species; and 3) extrapolation of the low-dose results for the animal species to low-dose levels for humans. Peter J. Robinson, 'Physiologically Based Liver Modeling and Risk Assessment,' *Risk Analysis* 12, no. 1 (1992): 146. When extrapolating from high doses to low doses in animals, scientists choose the species, strain or sex that is most sensitive to the carcinogen. Jerome Cornfield, a prominent statistician, said that such conservative assumptions are required because carcinogenesis is poorly understood. Jerome Cornfield, 'Carcinogenic Risk Assessment,' *Science* 198 (1977): 695.

46. The models include the one-hit linear model, the multi-hit (K-hit) model, the multi-stage model, the extreme value model, the threshold model, the linear no-threshold model, the log-probit model, the sublinear no-threshold model, and the individualized response model. Henry C. Pitot, 'Relationships of Bioassay Data on Chemicals to their Toxic and Carcinogenic Risk for Humans,' Cancer Symposium, 'An Academic Review of the Environmental Determinants of Cancer Relevant to

Prevention,' held in cooperation with the American Cancer Society, Inc, New York, 28 February–2 March 1979, manuscript, p. 13; Joseph V. Rodricks (1992), pp. 171–9. Linear dose-response extrapolation models are used by the EPA, the Nuclear Regulatory Commission, and the DOE to regulate human exposure to mutagens, including radiation. Irwin D. Bross, 'Mathematical Models Vs. Animal Models,' in Stephen R. Kaufman and Betsy Todd, eds, *Perspectives On Animal Research* 1 (1989): 83–108, New York: Medical Research Modernization Committee.

47. The 'slope' of the curve, at the point where it departs from linearity, is known as the 'slope factor' or the 'Carcinogen Potency Factor' (CPF).

48. According to the Interagency Regulatory Liaison Group (IRLG), which represents FDA, EPA, OSHA and CPSC, among the factors that should be considered in estimating human risk from animal data are 'species conversion factors such as body surface, body weight, metabolic pathways, nutritional conditions, concurrent disease conditions, genetic variability, bacterial flora, … tissue distribution, retention and fate of the chemical.' Interagency Regulatory Liaison Group, 'Scientific Basis for Identification of Potential Carcinogens and Estimation of Risks,' *Journal of the National Cancer Institute* 63 (1979): 259.

49. D. A. Freedman and H. Zeisel, 'From Mouse-to-Man: the Quantitative Assessment of Cancer Risks,' *Statistical Science* 3 (1988): 3–56.

50. The International Agency for Research on Cancer deemed 39 chemicals and chemical processes as carcinogenic to humans based on 'sufficient evidence.' Joseph V. Rodricks (1992), p. 115. Some 100 agents or chemical processes are considered possible/probable human carcinogens based on 'sufficient evidence' in animal tests, despite the fact that in 1971 the IARC declared explicitly that no such animal-to-human extrapolations could be made. International Agency for Research on Cancer, *IARC Monographs on the Evaluation of Carcinogenic Risks to Humans; An Updating of IARC Monographs Volumes 1 to 42 Supplement 7* (Lyon: IARC, 1987); and *IARC Monographs*, untitled, Vol. 1 (1972), p. 6.

51. Anon, 'EPA's Proposed Guidelines for Carcinogen Risk Assessment,' summary, EPA Communications, Education and Public Affairs Office, Washington, DC, Document EPA/600/p92/003C, April 1996. Classification information courtesy of Professor Anne Marie Desmarais, Medford, Massachusetts.

A) = There is irrefutable epidemiologic evidence that a chemical causes cancer in humans.

B1) = There is suggestive epidemiologic evidence and irrefutable animal data of a chemical's carcinogenicity.

B2) = There is no direct human evidence, but irrefutable animal data.

C) = There are no human data; there are suggestive animal data but they are suspect.

D) = There is direct evidence that a chemical causes cancer in animals.

E) = No data.

52. Personal communication with Andrew Dorsey, technical information specialist, ATSDR, 26 July 1995.

53. Information provided by Professor Anne Marie Desmarais, Medford, Massachusetts.

54. Ibid.

55. Virginia C. Gordon, 'Applications of In Vitro Methods for the Cosmetic, Household Products, and Pharmaceutical Industries,' in Michael B. Kapis and Shayne C. Gad, *Non-Animal Techniques in Biomedical and Behavioral Research and Testing* (Florida: Lewis Publishers, 1993), p. 18.

56. Casarett and Doull (1991), p. 39.

57. RfD is measured in milligrams per kilograms per day and RfC is measured in milligrams per meter cubed.

58. For carcinogens, averaging time is represented by an individual's lifetime exposure or 365 days × 70 years; for non-carcinogens, averaging time is represented by the number of days or years a person may be exposed to a chemical.

59. Anon, 'NLM International MEDLARS Centers,' National Library of Medicine Fact Sheet, Washington, DC, August 1991.

60. Bill Breen, 'Why We Need Animal Testing,' *Garbage* (April/May 1993), p. 40. Richard Auerlich, a Michigan State University professor, fed mink contaminated carp from Lake Michigan to assess the impact contaminants, particularly PCBs and dioxins, were having on the species' reproductive ability.

61. *Critical Reviews in Toxicology* 20, no. 6 (1990): 482.

62. Joseph V. Rodricks (1992), p. 213.

63. David C. Kocher and Owen F. Hoffman, 'Regulating Environmental Carcinogens,' *Environ. Sci. Technol.* 25, no. 12 (1991): 1987.

64. Elizabeth K. Weisburger, 'Cancer-Causing Chemicals,' in *Cancer: The Outlaw Cell* (Washington, DC: American Chemical Society, 1988), p. 116. It has been postulated that about 70 percent of chemicals have a lifetime public risk greater than one in one million, and the carcinogenic effects of most chemicals may not manifest themselves until ten or twenty years after the initial exposure has taken place. Curtis C. Travis and Holly Hattemer-Frey, 'Determining an Acceptable Level of Risk,' *Environ. Sci. Technol.* 22, no. 8 (1988): 875.

65. Anon, 'EPA to Ignore Small Risks in Banning Pesticides,' *The New York Times*, 17 February 1991.

66. *Rachel's Environment & Health Weekly* No. 493 (9 May 1996), published by the Environmental Research Foundation, Annapolis, Maryland, p. 1; Mary H. Cooper, 'Regulating Pesticides: Do Americans Need More Protection from Toxic Chemicals?,' *The Congressional Quarterly Researcher* 4, no. 4 (28 January 1994), p. 82.

67. W. Howe, et al., in A. Worden, et al., eds., *The Future of Predictive Safety Evaluation* (Boston: MTP Press, 1986), p. 64.

68. See Irwin Bross, *Scientific Fraud Vs. Scientific Truth* (Eggertsville, NY: Biomedical Metatechnology Press, 1992); Ellen Silbergeld, quoted in Jan Ziegler (October 1993): 406; Andre Carothers and Peter Montague, in *Safe Food News*, published by Food and Water, Marshfield, Vermont (Spring 1993): 13.

69. In Jan Ziegler (October 1993): 406.

70. See Lawrie Mott, et al., *Handle With Care: Children and Environmental Carcinogens* (New York City, NRDC, October 1994); Robert Repetto and Sanjay S. Baliga, *Pesticides and the Immune System* (Washington, DC, WRI, April 1996); most of the studies cited in this report (which claims that pesticides are compromising human immunity), are animal studies; Dr Theo Colburn, a senior scientist at the WWF, cited animal studies to defend her belief that endocrine-disrupting chemicals like DDT were adversely impacting on human health by causing memory loss and some forms of cancer. Gina Kolata, 'Chemicals That Mimic Hormones Spark Alarm and Debate,' *The New York Times*, 19 March 1996, p. C1.

71. James T. B. Tripp and Michael E. Herz, attorneys, 'In the Matter of the Application of Signal Environmental Systems, Inc, for Permits to Construct and Operate the Brooklyn Navy Yard Resource Recovery Facility,' Post-Hearing Brief of the Environmental Defense Fund, submitted to the State of New York Department of Environmental Conservation 1 July 1988, DEC Project, No. 20–85–0306, p. 51. A

part of the text reads, 'direct acute and chronic toxicity testing is also needed to account for the potential for direct exposure to ash, given the demonstrated bio-availability and acute and chronic toxicity of substances present in ash to humans and other organisms in the environment.' In this case, Signal Environmental Systems hired a consultant, Health Risk Associates in Berkeley, California, to produce a health risk assessment which was filled with references to animal testing, but which concluded that the building of an incinerator would pose no risk to people living in the surrounding area. Allan H. Smith, et al., 'Health Risk Assessment for the Brooklyn Navy Yard Resource Recovery Facility,' (Berkeley, California: Health Risk Associates, 24 August 1987). I wrote a paper which disputed the findings of that report without recourse to animal data. E. A. Fano, 'Slash and Burn: An Analysis of Incineration in New York, and the Brooklyn Navy Yard Incinerator Controversy' (Massachusetts: Tufts University, December 1994), unpublished.

3. For the public good? Debunking the animal testing myth

The arguments in favor of animal testing

'We can't protect the environment, or people in general, without doing some animal testing. If you're pro-environment but opposed to animal testing, you're on shaky ground, because the two positions just aren't compatible with each other.' Thomas Hamm, toxicologist and veterinarian, North Carolina State University, quoted in *Garbage* (April/May 1993), p. 42

'animal studies are the only reliable alternative to human testing ... non-animal methods that are suitable and reliable ... do not exist for most needs.' Anon, 'A Look at Animal Use in the Science of Toxicology,' brochure (Washington, DC: Society of Toxicology, July 1989)

It has been established that toxicity studies are expected to demonstrate the danger/toxicity or safety of any given substance intended for humans. Advocates of toxicity tests on animals say that animal tests contribute valuable information about human hazards due to acute poisoning caused both by *accidental* and *intentional* exposures to toxic substances. On the basis of findings in animals, 'safe levels' of human exposure are determined. The safety information obtained through animal testing influences not only the decision on whether to expose humans to a substance, or to what degree, but also the manner in which human clinical trials of drugs and consumer products will be performed.[1] Animal tests, advocates say, thus protect us from the dangers of new substances at work, at home, or in the environment, and have provided data for warning labels on products which tell us what to do if a household cleaner or workplace product is accidentally spilled or swallowed.[2]

Proponents of animal tests claim that we cannot afford to wait for absolute proof of carcinogenicity in humans, and because experimenting on humans is socially and ethically unacceptable, we must heed the warnings provided by animal tests which are 'the only reliable source of information from which scientists may assess potential risks to humans.'[3] They say that risk assessment methods 'circumvent the purported deficiencies of epidemiology and allow inferences to be made that do not depend on the availability of data from human studies.'[4]

Most believe that the best predictors of human responses are often 'higher-order animals' like rats and mice.[5] Moreover, special strains of rats and mice have been developed to be particularly suitable for carcinogenicity testing. Because the natural lifetime of rodents is two to three years, they can provide information about the cancer-causing potential of test materials more quickly than longer-lived animals such as dogs or monkeys. Proponents say that most major forms of human cancer have been reproduced in mice and rats through exposure to chemical carcinogens, and that of the approximately thirty agents known to cause human cancer, almost all cause cancer in animal tests.[6]

Toxicologists say that another advantage of using genetically bred rodents is knowing the provenance of the animal from the breeder—and hence the genetic history of the animal and all its descendants—making it easier to determine whether genetics plays a role in the onset of certain effects. Because every aspect of the animal's life is controlled—its food, cage and bedding are sterilized, its water purified, the walls in the laboratory disinfected—a thorough study of the particular effects of one chemical in isolation is possible.

While researchers are aware of the differences between rodents or other animals and humans (humans are larger, live longer, frequently suffer from two or more diseases at a time, receive very different exposures than laboratory animals, and metabolize, store and excrete agents differently) they maintain that those differences are far outweighed by the similarities, and that 'a whole mammal is at least sufficiently similar to human response, to provide an index of hazard.'[7] In addition, toxicologists contend that as they acquire more knowledge about metabolism, they will come to a better understanding of the phenomenon of inter-species and inter-individual response, and will be able to compensate for those differences by devising more accurate extrapolation models.[8]

Scaling, or safety factors, are often used as a means for 'correcting' species differences in cross-species comparisons. But Daniel Menzel of the Duke Comprehensive Cancer Center in Durham, North Carolina, states that researchers need no longer resort to arbitrary judgements to calculate 'safety factors' used in animal-to-human extrapolations. Today they can use physiologically based mathematical models to estimate the exposure needed for humans to experience the same toxic effect measured experimentally in animals. First toxic effects are measured in animals, then the results are adjusted for organ size, blood flow, genetic differences, disease processes, and a host of other physiological factors common to humans, for the final extrapolation.[9] While calculating these measured parameters requires knowledge of human metabolic processes that may be highly variable and difficult to assess, some postulate that developments in computer and mathematical modeling may provide a means of improving the accuracy of the existing animal tests.[10]

Advocates say that alternative tests will never fully replace animals. Through animal testing, they believe that scientists can observe how the entire organism behaves and responds to a substance; how that substance interacts with different organs, cells and tissues; how damaged tissue grows and recovers from injury; and how a substance is absorbed, distributed, metabolized and excreted by the body.[11] At autopsy, researchers say they can observe the different routes a substance may have taken when swallowed, inhaled, injected or absorbed; they say that whole animals provide information necessary to evaluate the effects of ingestion, skin penetration, and inhalation—information that cannot be obtained in test tubes.[12]

The National Institutes of Health (NIH) (which uses public moneys to produce pro-animal testing brochures) claims that

> animals—because of their striking parallels to the human system—serve as the best, most scientifically valid surrogates for people in biomedical research and testing … Without laboratory animals, researchers would have no way of seeing how the body handles … toxins, where they are concentrating in the body, and what damage they might be causing. They would be forced to wait for a chemical accident or unanticipated toxic side effects in individuals to learn that a problem exists with exposure to certain substances. Then it would be too late.[13]

Advocates say that animal tests have laid the groundwork for understanding the harmful health effects of numerous chemicals and their by-products such as acid rain. The guinea pig is the preferred animal species for studying the respiratory effects of concentrations of polluted air similar to those experienced by people in urban areas, due to its sensitivity to these irritants.[14]

Animal tests have allegedly provided reliable indicators of what to expect for surviving victims of industrial accidents, as was the case in the Bhopal disaster in India, where poisonous gases flowed out of a manufacturing plant, killing thousands immediately and injuring thousands more.[15] In addition, advocates say that in some cases data from animal studies have prevented tragedy from occurring by serving as early warning of potential problems such as whether a chemical will cause cancer or affect reproduction; they claim that animal cancer tests prevented the commercialization of 2–acetylminofluorene, a pesticide and potent animal carcinogen; and they identified the industrial chemical bis-chloromethyl-ether as the likely cause of increased lung cancers among workers. As a result, they say, the company changed its manufacturing process and lung cancer rates declined.[16] In this vein, another advantage proponents claim is the extensive historical database of animal toxicity information that covers a wide range of substances and stretches back more than sixty years; these data provide a convenient reference to evaluate the relative dangers of different chemicals.[17]

Despite the fact that numerous toxicologists have criticized the use of the Maximum Tolerated Dose (MTD) in animal tests because of its tendency to produce erroneous results,[18] the National Research Council of the National Academy of Sciences, in a report issued February 1993, advocated continued use of the MTD as part of an overall toxicity testing strategy. James Huff of the Environmental Carcinogenesis Program at NIEHS supported the decision.[19] One toxicologist said that, 'doubts about the perfection of the MTD should not be the cause to change these dose-response studies or to alter the experimental identification and measurement of potential human risks using animal models.'[20]

Although proponents of animal testing often acknowledge the limitations of animal testing, and acknowledge inter-species and intra-species variations in animals and humans, they believe that animals and humans are more alike than they are different; and because there are allegedly no adequate substitutes for the animal model, they believe that the long-term rodent bioassay should not be abandoned.[21]

Essentially then, there are six principal reasons given to justify the use of animals in toxicity tests: (1) testing on animals removes the moral dilemma of testing on humans, or waiting for human evidence, both of which are antithetical to preventing human illness and death; (2) rodents, particularly genetically bred strains, are good biological models of human cancer and other ailments for numerous reasons; because every aspect of the animals' lives are controlled, and their genetic histories are known, experimental results are all the more accurate; (3) because it is deemed that non-human animals can be manipulated during experiments and sacrificed afterwards, scientists can observe a chemical's effect on the entire body, thereby gaining a more thorough understanding of toxicity; (4) sophisticated statistical methods can overcome inter-species differences and render animal-to-human extrapolations more reliable than ever before; (5) testing on animals provides an indication of what may happen to humans in industrial accidents, and provides data used to establish safety standards for commonly used chemicals and consumer products; and (6) human databases are simply not as comprehensive as the historical databases of animal toxicity data built up over several decades, which provide a means to evaluate chemical dangers. In the next section, as well as in Chapter 4, I shall argue that these positions are fallacious.

The reality is that all living things—animals, humans, plants—are remarkably similar and dissimilar at the same time. Pietro Croce, a pathologist in Vicenza, Italy, writes that all terrestrial beings are made up of certain fundamental chemical compounds, including the 92 elements found on earth. Yet of the five billion humans who inhabit the earth, no two are exactly alike. The same goes for animals and plants. This is evidenced by the existence of the different blood groups in humans: A, B, AB, and O; human blood, for example, contains 17 types of transferrin (the protein which transports iron in the blood), but the proportions of this protein vary among different individuals. The letter groups A, BA, B, CA, and CB are used to mark individual differences in the levels of acid phosphatase (an enzyme in red blood corpuscles) found in the human body.

All humans and animals are differentiated by the existence of numerous 'enzymatic (or proteinic) variations' of which there are millions; that is because there are millions of proteins in the body which guide, control, accelerate or slow down organic and/or biochemical reactions. British biochemist Dennis V. Parke recently said,

> almost all mammalian proteins are proteoglycans, with numerous sugar side-chains, which function as … 'bar-codes' identifying the protein's species, tissue and cell origins, and dating its biosynthesis and catabolic destruction. The very earliest events in cancer involve changes in these sugar side-chains, which result in accelerated mitosis, invasion and metastasis. These proteoglycans … are highly specific, not only to individual species, but also to specific individuals and to specific tissues, creating an intercellular communication system of unique specificity.[22]

Small differences in an individual's biochemistry can account for drastic variations in reactions among members of the same species (intra-species) and between members of different species (inter-species).[23] For example, experiments in rodents have not been able to shed light on the human toxicity of malathion, an organophosphate insecticide (and nerve agent) widely used to control various species of insects including mosquitoes. That is because rodents have a particular enzyme in their blood and liver which allows them to detoxify malathion at various doses. This enzyme is present only in humans' livers, but not in their blood stream or their blood serum. As a result, when malathion is dermally absorbed by humans and enters the bloodstream, it turns into malaoxon, a toxic metabolite which is ten thousand times more toxic than malathion.[24]

Toxicologists' attempts to use safety factors or scaling factors to 'correct' differences in cross-species comparisons are based on an admission that undeniable differences between species exist. In fact, while rats are used to predict human toxicity, companies marketing rodenticides test on rats because it is assumed that they are different enough from humans and other species to facilitate the production of highly specific poisons.[25] Ironically, though researchers complain that *in vitro* tests cannot mimic effects on the whole body, the very complexity of a living animal provides more opportunity for errors which could be avoided through the use of simpler systems. Moreover, British scientists K. Miller and S. Nicklin have said that 'mechanisms are easier to analyse in vitro than in vivo, [and] much of what is currently known about immune system responses has been discovered at the cellular level.'[26] It is an appreciation of the fundamental concept of inter and intra-species differences which lays the foundation for a discussion of the arguments against animal testing.

The arguments against

'It seems unlikely that a biological test is going to be able to make quantitative measurements of risk if that test has not been validated; has no objective or universally established criteria; is testing for the presence of a phenomenon whose mechanism is unknown; can only classify the evidence of carcinogenicity by negotiated debate; reaches different conclusions about the same substance depending on the committee, the agency, and the country; cannot identify a non-carcinogen at all; and has insufficient correlational data to predict human risk.' Edith Efron, *The Apocalyptics: Cancer and the Big Lie* (New York: Simon & Schuster, 1984), p. 332

'It is astonishing that irrational arguments continue to be used in defense of animal tests. To sustain that animal assays are the best we have for human risk assessment does not certify their adequacy or defend their misuse ...' Gio Batta Gori, 'Are Animal Tests Relevant in Cancer Risk Assessment?,' *Regul. Toxicol. Pharmacol.* 13 (1991): 226

'It is impossible to evaluate the safety of using animal studies to predict the safety of drugs and chemicals in man.' Dennis V. Parke, Emeritus Professor of Biochemistry, University of Surrey, Guildford, UK, 1 May 1996

There have always been scientists, especially within the cancer research establishment, who believed that the use of animal test data for human risk assessment was an unscientific procedure. In the 1970s, establishment scientists recognized that, without knowledge of the mechanisms of (human) cancer induction, and without epidemiological data, no one could claim to know how to predict or prevent human cancer.[27] In 1977, John Higginson of the International Agency for Research on Cancer (IARC) dismissed the predictive value of animal tests when he said, 'there is no rational biological method of extrapolating from animals to man either in terms of carcinogenic activity or dose effects.'[28]

The obstacles created by using animals as human surrogates were identified in scientific documents dating back to the 1950s.[29] Despite the fact that in the 1970s a large number of animal cancer tests conducted by the National Toxicology Program produced unreliable results, presented statistical problems, and were subject to 'subjective and controversial interpretations,'[30] the logical conclusions were not drawn. The many problems with animal tests will be discussed below.

The difficulty of inter-species extrapolation

'Extrapolation from the animal mode to humans represents something of a leap of faith.' Office of Science & Technology Policy, *Identification, Characterization, and Control of Potential Carcinogens: A Framework for Federal Decision-Making* (Washington, DC: Executive Office of the President, 1 February 1979), p. 14

'Such [animal-to-human] extrapolations would not even be attempted in most areas of science.' Chris F. Wilkinson, 'Being More Realistic About Chemical Carcinogenesis,' *Environ. Sci. Technol.* 21, no. 9 (1987): 846

Theoretical extrapolations from high to low doses and from lifetime exposures to short-term exposures in rodents have been used to estimate risks to humans. The methods used to extrapolate from animals to humans were discussed in Chapter 2. Epidemiologists Richard Doll and Richard Peto believe that extrapolations from animal studies to humans are so uncertain as to have little if any value.[31] This is due to differences in anatomy, physiology, metabolism, and biochemistry that are not considered by toxicologists.

A report entitled 'Drinking Water and Health' prepared by the Safe Drinking Water Committee (National Academy of Sciences, 1977) discusses inherent variables between animals and humans relevant in risk assessment. These include rates of chemical absorption in the body, metabolic differences in exposed animals, rates of excretion and reabsorption, and environmental and genetic differences, among other things.

The IARC has admitted that there is not one animal species the biological reactions of which are identical to humans. It has stated that although non-human primates are perceived to be similar to humans in many respects, 'there are few indications that the species of non-human primates and the breeds of dogs most commonly used in biomedical research are any closer to humans in their metabolic capacities than rodents.'[32]

Rodents for example are physiologically unable to vomit toxins whereas in humans, spastic contractions in the stomach and intestine can serve to eliminate noxious agents via vomiting; and contrary to humans who breathe from the nose and mouth, rodents are nose breathers. This allows humans to ingest toxins from two different routes at the same time, and in quantities proportional to their size. Rats and mice (as well as dogs, cats and hamsters) synthesize Vitamin C in their bodies; humans (as well as guinea pigs and primates) do not.[33] Vitamin C has long been hypothesized to have anti-tumor action. Rats have much higher activity of the 5–desaturase enzyme system, a part of the body's machinery for processing fats—the elevated presence of which is known to promote a number of degenerative diseases in humans, including cancer. In humans, however, excess fat accumulates primarily in the coronary arteries, whereas in rats it is accumulated predominately in the liver.[34] Rodents live between two and three years compared to human life spans of 65 to 75 plus years on average in the developed world. Rats have no gall bladder; in humans, the gall bladder stores bile which is released into the small intestine and aids in digestion. In addition, and in contrast to humans, rats are healthier when continually pregnant: in fact, rats are prolific and can produce up to one hundred offspring in a year; their placenta has a different structure and function than the human placenta; and they absorb iron differently.[35]

Rodents are more susceptible to cancer than humans who, because of their long life spans, have developed comparatively many more defenses against spontaneous cancers.[36] Maryland-based veterinarian Eric Dunayer writes that, 'the most commonly used mouse strain B6C3F1 has a spontaneous liver tumor rate of 15–60 percent; in contrast, mortality associated with liver tumors in the US is 0.005 percent.'[37] In bioassays, inbred strains of virtually identical animals are used; many of these have a high incidence of spontaneous tumors, making the interpretation of tumor data difficult. In 1980 Gio Batta Gori of the Division of Cancer Cause and Prevention at the National Cancer Institute (NCI) wrote that, 'the oncogenic [cancer-producing] viruses commonly infesting small rodents may be one reason for the unusually high frequency of lymphomas [lymph node tumors] in these animals.'[38] But he said that, to induce cancer in strains of animals bred to be cancer-prone deliberately introduces bias into such experiments, since the animals are bound to develop tumors one way or the other.

In *Human Epidemiology and Laboratory Correlations in Chemical Carcinogenesis* (1980), Herman Kraybill, formerly of the NCI, lists a plethora of factors which have impacted on the quality of animal experiments, including the use of rodent strains contaminated with oncogenic viruses, among other things.[39] Contrarily, in humans only the Epstein-Barr virus is considered to be an oncogenic virus as it promotes Burkitt's lymphoma which is most common in Africa.[40] It has been suggested that mice may be 3×10^4 to 10^9 (30,000 to 3,000,000,000) times more cancer prone than humans.[41] After 25 months, mice develop spontaneous tumors at a rate of 20–60 percent, depending on the strain.[42] A study of tumors in captive wild mammals, birds and reptiles found a majority of sarcomas (cancers arising in bone, connective tissue or muscle), while humans are most often afflicted by carcinomas (cancers arising in the lining membranes).[43] Many kinds of cancers that are prevalent in rodents—pituitary, liver and thyroid—are rare in humans; whereas many cancers such as prostate, colon and rectal cancers, are prevalent in humans but rare in rodents.[44] In 1995 Dennis V. Parke wrote:

> it is now realised that chemical toxicity and carcinogenicity are the consequence of the metabolic formation of 1) reactive intermediates and/or 2) reactive oxygen species (ROS) from the toxic chemical. Glutathione (GSH) protects against both, but rodents unlike man do not conserve their GSH, and use it in detoxication processes where man uses water. Moreover, rodents, having a high body surface area to body mass and therefore a much higher respiratory quotient than man, generate ROS much more extensively than occurs in man, and consequently experience GSH depletion, oxidative stress, malignancy and death at doses of chemicals that are non-toxic to humans. This has been known for at least a decade, but it is often ignored for the sake of tradition, convenience and economy.[45]

Such species variations may be extremely significant when scientists are studying cancerous tissue and attempting to determine which organs and tissues are affected by toxicity.[46] It has been argued that, for regulatory purposes, it does not matter which organ or tissue is affected by toxicity because the aim is simply to prevent cancer rates from rising. According to Gio Batta Gori, this would be true if animal tests produced simple and reproducible outcomes. But general toxicity and carcinogenicity vary from species to species and individual to individual, and with the method of administration or intake; animals are tested using methods and doses that are at odds with real-life conditions. Cancer, he says, may be induced artificially by a modulating factor like dose, or the use of a compound that is a strong carcinogen for the species or strain selected (but not for others). Consequently, he says, 'it is apparent that the current definition of carcinogens confines the validity of data to a specific experiment, restricts the opportunities for generalization, and makes it difficult to distinguish between direct carcinogens and modifying factors.'[47]

Moreover, writes veterinarian Eric Dunayer, a chemical may induce cancer in an animal, in an organ with a naturally high background cancer rate, making it 'impossible to differentiate a small rise in cancer rate from the normal background rate ... Most human carcinogens, on the other hand, have been recognized, not because they cause a large increase in cancer rates, but because they cause an increase in rare tumors—for example, asbestos and mesothelioma.'[48]

Hence the toxic effects observed in rodents may be completely irrelevant to those observed in humans because the organs that are affected, the types of cancers that are produced, the way in which they metastasize, and the rates at which they manifest themselves, are vastly different. In 1986, British scientist G. J. Turnbull stated that, 'in the rat and dog, gamma-glutamyl transpeptidase plasma levels are lower than in man and not generally useful as indicators of tissue damage, although these parameters are recommended in the OECD guidelines.'[49] This is important since toxic effects in animals are typically gauged by an examination of organs and tissues at autopsy to detect tumors/lesions, accumulation of chemical and other fluids at specific sites, and so on. Based upon these observations in animals, and an analysis of which organs are affected by a chemical, recommendations for human exposure standards are developed, and treatment modalities for injuries at specific sites in the body are made and published, in Material Safety Data Sheets for example. Ironically, the EPA's animal-to-human extrapolations do not specify which *human* tissues and organs are likely to become diseased—a fact acknowledged by the agency in a press release dated 16 April 1996 about its proposed new guidelines for carcinogen risk assessment. Moreover, toxicologist Edward Calabrese writes that, 'although human variation in response is generally greater than that observed in commonly used rodent species [as a result of human genetic heterogeneity], no reference is made in the toxicological literature as to which segment of the human population the animal model ... is thought to be related.'[50] Therefore the recommendations which emanate from the animal tests may be relevant to the animals (and even that is debatable), but one cannot determine how relevant they are to humans unless and until human data can confirm the animal findings.[51]

Joseph V. Rodricks, formerly of the FDA, raises another point in this regard. He says, 'there are hundreds of unexplained human diseases that are almost certainly non-infectious, affecting all the organs and systems of the human body, including our mental processes and behavior.' Currently, Rodricks says, we do not know what the relationship is between chemical toxicity and the actual diseases doctors are treating. The regulatory system does not ask how or whether environmental chemicals may be causing or contributing to the multitude of mysterious human diseases. It simply assumes that human health is being adequately protected by animal-derived standards for chemical exposures.[52] In this sense, the animal tests do not address the whole picture of environmental contamination; rather they focus on minutiae related to biological events caused by individual chemicals.

The use of animals often makes it difficult to determine whether mortality was influenced by a chemical or an increase in body weight. Many rodent strains have changed over time; the NTP (1994) confirmed that adult Sprague-Dawley rats have increased their weight by 300 grams over several years, while Fischer 344 rats—a strain commonly used in carcinogenicity tests—weigh 25 percent more than their predecessors. These increased body weights may have led to 'decreased lifespan and increased tumour incidences.'[53]

Serious difficulties in extrapolating from animals to humans exist due to the diversity of species' responses to substances/potential carcinogens. As early as 1938 the geneticist J. B. S. Haldane pointed out that individual humans differ in their responses to environmental agents, a fact reconfirmed by molecular epidemiologist Jack A. Taylor and molecular geneticist Douglas A. Bell in 1996;[54] and recent studies have confirmed that human susceptibility to biochemical factors affecting carcinogenesis varies widely in the population.[55] This is true between humans and non-humans, among closely related species (rats and mice), and between individuals of the same species (individual rats and/or individual humans). In a 1979 US Office of Science and Technology paper, staff scientists stated that animals did not necessarily predict for each other, let alone for humans.[56] Gori (1980, p. 257) reported that the potency of carcinogens in animal experiments can vary by a factor of 10^7. Human responses to carcinogens also vary among individuals; *in vitro* studies of human tissues have found inter-individual variations of about a hundred-fold.[57] Within a population, individual humans' risk of cancer from exposure to air pollutants have been found to vary by a factor of 10^9.[58] Berardesca and Maibach (1988) have found that different ethnic groups react differently to skin irritants; and Basketter et al. (1996) found that, in human skin patch tests, inter-individual variability was even greater than ethnic differences among Chinese, Germans and Britons.[59] These issues raise serious concerns about the reliability of both inter- and intra-species extrapolations, since one group of humans may not be representative of the entire human population. Others say that the potential problems posed by *in vitro* extrapolations from males to females, and from one human subpopulation to another, only demonstrate the need for more specific cell-based test systems.[60] However, it can be said that inter-species differences add unnecessary layers of complexity to the existing dilemma of intra-species difference. And it has been shown time and again in *in vitro* work that the use of human rather than animal tissues and fluids most closely resembles the clinical (human) situation. One recent study by Clemedson et al. (1996) concluded that, 'the finding that animal cells do not predict human toxicity perfectly will probably lead to the increased (or possibly exclusive) use of human cell lines in test batteries.'[61]

Another area in which extrapolation from animals to humans is difficult is in neurotoxicity studies in which a chemical's ability to alter behavior and damage the nervous system and the brain are measured. Though researchers have attempted to incorporate behavioral measures into animal tests, this field of research has become controversial. Signs of neurotoxicity can be detected in several ways in humans by the assessment of someone's mental state and sensory functions. But it is difficult or impossible to make such assessments in animals since rats, for example, cannot explain whether or not they are having recurring headaches, difficulty seeing, are feeling tired, depressed, nervous or nauseous. Even if they were nauseous, their inability to vomit would obscure this symptom. In this way, technicians will never know whether the symptoms that are missed in animal studies will manifest themselves in humans. Hence there are few standardized animal models for gauging behavioral changes (as well as immune system and reproductive failures) that a specific chemical may cause, nor are there any reliable ways of extrapolating the findings from such studies to humans.[62]

Yet another problem area in animal-to-human extrapolations is the statistical/mathematical model itself. According to Hoel et al. (1983), different models can yield risk estimates that vary over a wide range.[63] Estimates of lifetime risk from exposure to one part per million of vinyl chloride, for example, using different extrapolation methods, yielded risk estimates ranging from 1×10^{-2}, using the multi-hit model, to 25×10^{-4}, using the linear model (see Table in Edith Efron, *The Apocalyptics* (New York: Simon & Schuster, 1984), 369). Different scientists using the same extrapolation methods also get different results. All of these factors alone would a priori seem to invalidate animal to human extrapolations.

While noted scientists like Matthew Meselson of Harvard University have expressed their confidence in animal to human extrapolation,[64] toxicologists continually admit that the uncertainties and assumptions inherent in quantitative risk assessment are profound. At OSHA hearings in 1980 about the relevance of extrapolations from animals to humans, Richard Bates of the National Institute of Environmental Health Sciences (NIEHS) and FDA stated, with respect to all of the biological variables between species, that

> the science of toxicology will have made immense strides when it becomes able to use the results of animal experiments to precisely predict the toxic risk of a chemical to any individual or group of humans. Unfortunately, ... we do not have enough knowledge to weigh each of these factors in any particular case and come up with a reliable multiplier for converting results of animal experiments to risk for any individual human under his or her conditions of life.[65]

Scientists like biostatistician Irwin Bross and G. J. Turnbull have expressed stronger criticisms. In 1986 Turnbull stated that

> calculations of human cancer risk from chemicals by statistical models which are solely founded on arbitrary assumptions or hypotheses in biology, are a negation of science in the majority of cases. An hypothesis which cannot be tested by experimentation is not ... scientific ... although it may be fashionable dogma ... The ingenuity involved in the various models has to be admired, but the accuracy of ultra-conservative calculations is discredited.[66]

Bross believes that quantitative extrapolation from animal data to human risks is scientifically absurd because the process assumes there are exact biological parallels between humans and animals with respect to mutagenesis (the origin and development of cell mutations that can lead to cancer). Bross states, 'that these assumptions are false is apparent from numerous recent studies showing that unique human host defense systems play a key role in mutagenesis.'[67] Moreover, Bross says that while linear extrapolation may have been adequate for some of the older nineteenth-century poisons which had basic mechanisms of action, it fails completely for the newer twentieth-century mutagens which may impact on a variety of cells and organs in unknown ways and within an indeterminate timeframe.

In their comprehensive critique of statistical methods for quantitative extrapolation from animals to humans which included 150 references, statisticians Freedman and Zeisel conclude that, 'in the present state of the art, making quantitative assessments of human risk from animal experiments has little scientific merit.'[68] Toxicologists like Iain F. H. Purchase of the Zeneca Central Toxicology Laboratory in Cheshire, UK have concurred.[69]

It has never been shown scientifically that animal tests can be used to establish *qualitative* carcinogenic risk in humans either.[70] In *Statistics and Related Topics* (1981), statisticians D. Krewski and J. Van Ryzin explain that the question of how to extrapolate from animals to humans has led to the development of many statistical models; these have generated precise mathematical risk estimates that are simply not justified by the quality of the toxicology data from which they are derived.[71] Issues surrounding the qualitative validity of animal data are discussed in more detail in the section 'The animal tests have never been validated,' in this chapter.

False positives/false negatives

'Even if a chemical is found to be nontoxic in animal studies, the safety of the chemical cannot be assured.' Barbara S. Shane, 'Human Reproductive Hazards,' *Environ. Sci. Technol.* 23, no. 10 (1989): 1193

'Q: How should we interpret the appearance of tumors in one species, such as rats, and the absence of tumors in another species, such as monkeys? A: Not all tests are equally sensitive, and a negative result may mean merely that the effect was missed. Too few animals, too low a dosage, or too short a test period ... can lead to a false negative result.' National Cancer Institute pamphlet on animal testing and carcinogen identification (Washington, DC, March 1990)

No one knows for sure what the percentages of false positives and false negatives are, and whether they can be attributed to the animal tests themselves or to their statistical interpretation. There are hundreds of compounds that have been dubbed carcinogens based on at least one positive rodent bioassay. Half of all chemicals tested at the maximum tolerated dose (MTD) have produced tumors in animals.[72] With respect to non-cancer effects, Richard Kurzel of the Tufts University School of Medicine in Boston writes that any compound can be teratogenic (produce birth defects) 'if given to the right species, at the right dose, at the right time.'[73]

Although some scientists at the NTP and NIEHS say that there are 'considerable molecular and cellular similarities in carcinogenic processes among mammals, including rodents and humans,'[74] other NIEHS officials estimated that between one-third and two-thirds of substances deemed to be carcinogenic, as a result of tests in rodents, would be benign to humans at normal doses.[75] Ennever et al. found that 19 out of 20 compounds that probably were non-carcinogenic in humans were carcinogenic in rodents, indicating that the false positive rate may be as high as 95 percent.[76]

It has also been shown that tumor formations vary greatly from species to species and even between rodent strains using similar doses of a chemical. For example, N,2–fluorenylacetamide caused bladder cancer in male and female Slonaker rats, liver cancer in male and breast cancer in female Wistar rats, and intestinal cancer in male and female Piebald rats. N-nitrosodiethylamine caused liver tumors in Norway (BD II) rats, white-tailed rats, chickens, guinea pigs, NMRI mice, and Syrian golden hamsters, at doses for each species that varied by a thousandfold.[77] Ethyl carbamate caused high incidences of cancer in certain mouse strains but not in the X/Gf mouse strain.[78] Dimethyl-benzo-alpha-anthracene causes lymphomas in Swiss mice, bronchial adenomas in the Strong A mouse strain, and hepatomas (liver cancer) in male mice of other strains. Benzidine causes bladder cancer in humans, but in mice it produces tumors of the acoustic nerve, the intestine and the liver. In the mouse, carbontetrachloride (CCl_4) causes liver tumors, whereas in rats it produces cirrhosis of the liver. Chloroform ($CHCl_3$) produces liver tumors in various strains of female mice but not in male mice.

Some chemicals were found to be species-specific. For example, DDT caused liver tumors in mice but not in rats or hamsters.[79] Sodium saccharin, an artificial sweetener, caused bladder cancer only in male rats while (male and female) monkeys, hamsters and mice were unaffected, even at high doses. Epidemiological studies also failed to find any evidence of bladder cancer in humans using sodium saccharin.[80] Arsenic, though carcinogenic to humans, is not so to rodents.[81] Isoniazid (INH), used for years as a cure for human tuberculosis, causes bronchial adenocarcinomas in various mouse strains.[82] There are large differences in the responses of various species to certain classes of chemicals, like the aromatic amines (ammonia-derived compounds). Benzidine and 2–naphthylamine have caused bladder cancer in humans and dogs, but in rats they caused liver and mammary tumors; in mice and hamsters they produced mostly liver tumors.[83] N-Nitroso compounds illustrate very well the large differences in target organ metabolism between different species.[84] The examples of metabolic phenomena that are still not understood could continue *ad infinitum*.

Scientists state that there are no explicit agreed-upon criteria for conducting and interpreting tests for *non*-carcinogenicity. Epidemiologist

Robert Hoover stated that, 'it is a general principle of science that you cannot prove a negative.' Richard Peto of Oxford University added that 'animal experiments cannot demonstrate non-carcinogenicity even for animals.'[85] In addition, animals tested in the 'low dose group' often do not develop malignant tumors. But this does not mean that a 'low dose', or less, does not pose a risk to people or other animals. Rather it means that for the limited number of animals tested, or for the particular chemical under study, carcinogenic effects were not seen at that time. For example, organophosphate-based compounds such as disinfectants, marketed in Italy under the names Mipaphox, Trichlorphan, and Diptorex, caused nervous system damage in humans and other animals, yet mice were fed doses up to 1,500 mg/kg of these common compounds without any apparent negative effects, demonstrating that a negative result in an animal test is no proof that a chemical is not a carcinogen, or harmful to humans in some other way.[86] An analysis by Lave et al. (1988) demonstrated that falsely classifying chemicals as non-carcinogens could expose millions of people to a legitimate health risk, and incur social costs of hundreds of millions of dollars.[87]

For practical reasons, researchers use a few animals to represent a population of millions of humans. But the method of allowing 100 rats to represent one million humans often produces false negatives, or allows real dangers to be missed. Toxicologist F. J. Murray states that,

> what regulatory agencies are concerned about is very low risk, the theoretical one in a million. But if we try to figure what dose causes one cancer in a million individuals, you'd need more than a million rats in a test, and no one can do that. So we test on 50 or 100 rats, use much higher doses, then assume we can draw a straight line down to see what happens at low doses. But it's just not that simple.[88]

Using 600 test animals, a cancer occurring at a frequency of 5 in every 1,000 would be considered statistically insignificant and would almost certainly be regarded as a negative result. The practical implications of this are considerable since, according to rodent bioassay standards, a cancer frequency of five in one thousand translates into over one million cases of human cancer each year in the current US population of circa 280,000,000.[89] How many substances that caused no harm in rodents might be dangerous to humans? Certain well-known human carcinogens, including benzene[90] and cigarette smoke,[91] have been hard to prove in animal tests. Joseph F. Fraumeni, director of biostatistics at the National Cancer Institute, recalled how arsenic—which is not a carcinogen in animal studies—was found to cause high levels of lung cancer in smelter workers exposed to arsenic in the air.[92] Examples like these are common and could lead to the exclusion of legitimate human carcinogens from federal regulatory provisions because they did not cause tumors, or a significant number of them, in rodents. In *The Apocalyptics: Cancer and the Big Lie* (1984, p. 294), author Edith Efron writes, 'a test which is intended to discriminate between substances which do and do not cause cancer but which cannot achieve that goal is an invalid test.'

Different testing methods produce different results

'The fact that academic scientists are quarreling over such issues as mouse–man equivalence, the validity of the mouse itself as an experimental animal, the number of species and experiments required to establish the legitimacy of a carcinogen, and whether the dosing practices are falsifying the results in experiments tells us that 'regulatory' science ... is still in a precarious state.' Edith Efron, *The Apocalyptics: Cancer and the Big Lie* (New York: Simon & Schuster, 1984), p. 250

'it is easier to obtain a false negative in testing a carcinogen by inhalation than by oral administration.' William Lijinsky, 'Species Differences in Carcinogenesis,' *In Vivo* 7 (1993): 65–72

The data emanating from animal dose-response studies are influenced by many factors such as the age, nutritional status, genetic background of the individual, and the method chosen to expose the animal to the chemical (oral route, gavage, inhalation, dermal contact).[93]

In one study with methylene chloride, chronic inhalation studies produced increased lung and liver tumors in rodents whereas a drinking water study failed to produce any tumors.[94] According to veterinarian Eric Dunayer, the gavage method allows for the delivery of a precise dose, but the chemical, which is delivered in high concentrations, can damage the animal's upper gastrointestinal tract. In addition, Dunayer says, 'the absorption pattern for gavage differs from feeding studies; gavaged substances [which are typically mixed in vegetable oil that adds fat to the diet] reach high blood levels quickly then drop off rapidly, while chemicals in food and water tend to reach more steady blood levels.'[95]

Feeding studies, in which animals typically receive doses of test chemicals in their food and water, are one of the more common methods toxicologists use to study the effects of chemicals in long-term toxicity and carcinogenicity studies. British toxicologist Francis J. C. Roe believes that his peers have ignored the important role food plays in an experiment, and that 'little attempt is made to relate the pattern of diseases developed by *individual animals* to the amount of food they themselves have chosen to consume.'[96] In his book, *Calculated Risks* (1993, p. 85), Rodricks states that 'the mechanisms of absorption are many and varied, and are influenced by the type and quantity of food present at the time of chemical ingestion, the degree of acidity of various portions of the gastrointestinal tract, and even the nature and activity of the microorganisms that normally live in the intestines.'

Roe states that what and how much an animal eats during a long-term carcinogenicity test will determine how long it will live, whether and when it will develop a wide variety of benign and malignant tumors and aging-related degenerative conditions.[97] He points out that the continuous availability of food throughout a 24-hour period predisposes to obesity and diseases associated with over-nutrition. Animals who eat more will also drink more which could dilute the chemical or produce other undesired effects. Furthermore, because most commercial animal feeds have been found to be contaminated with both natural and industrial animal carcinogens such as pesticides, PCBs, estrogenic agents, fungal toxins and nitrosamines in small but variable amounts,[98] it may be impossible to determine whether tumors have been induced by over-eating contaminated foods or the chemical agent under study.[99] This applies as much to animals in test groups as to animals in control groups. J. R. Sabine of the University of Adelaide stated that every animal experiment was also a nutritional experiment in that both the quantity and types of nutrients fed the animals—fats, carbohydrates, protein, vitamins, minerals and dietary contaminants—can influence the reaction, both carcinogenic and non-carcinogenic, to a test chemical.[100]

Conversely, weight loss can be associated with several factors. Ironically, Masson (1995) writes that, 'rats readily associate food with illness, and will avoid a food if they have been ill after eating it.'[101] Hence it may be impossible to determine whether weight loss has been caused by the toxicity of the test substance, or an animal's aversion to the taste of the chemically-laced food. It has been shown that animals who eat less have a lower incidence of a wide range of diseases.

Toxicologists like Ghanta N. Rao and James Huff, who have been with the National Toxicology Program since the 1970s, admit that diet restriction would involve daily feeding of specific amounts of food to several hundred to a few thousand animals per chemical—a process that would be 'cumbersome, labor-intensive, ... expensive [and] ... subject to high rate of errors.'[102] It should also be noted that rodents are naturally nocturnal animals who actively feed at night. Because it is highly unlikely that trained technicians and laboratory staff would work during the night to feed animals according to their natural biological rhythms, it is acknowledged that rodents are forced to adapt to unnatural eating schedules.[103] Rao and Huff admit that the effects of 'modifying the inherent nocturnal circadian physiological processes [of rodents] [may be] extraordinarily complex and the mechanisms responsible for altered effects ... difficult to identify and interpret.' Rao and Huff offered no solution to this problem, concluding that 'much more research is needed in this area.'

Just as animals vary in their tastes and how they eat and drink, so do the eating patterns and intake of different foods among humans differ greatly.[104] People from different cultures or ethnic backgrounds consume different foods; portion sizes vary between individuals and indeed have been shown to vary between the sexes. Each individual's behavior and metabolism differs from those of other humans in ways that can never be fully ascertained or documented. Humans continually ingest an array of natural and synthetic chemicals in the food they eat, medications they may take, as well as from the environment. The number of chemicals believed to exist in nature is estimated to be in the millions; natural chemicals known to exist in food number in the tens of thousands. In just one cup of coffee there are some two hundred different organic chemicals—natural components of the coffee bean.[105] The compound benzo(a)pyrene (BaP) for example (which was reported by K. Bridbord at NIOSH to be an animal carcinogen in 1978), is found in vegetables and is present in cooked foods in varying amounts. Therefore, accurately to estimate a person's exposure to BaP, one would have to know what a person eats, whether that food is processed or fresh, and how it is prepared.[106]

Information on population-based food consumption patterns is available from food producers, dieticians, nutritionists, the US Department of Agriculture, and from the EPA *Exposure Factors Handbook* for example, but it is not reliable. Food consumption patterns change over time. Some people may eat in restaurants more than others where the nature of what is used in the preparation of food cannot be entirely known. Similarly, people's use or abuse of, and reactions to, prescription and over-the-counter pharmaceuticals is difficult if not impossible to monitor and/or assess. The nature and consequences of drug interactions are not addressed by animal tests.

Nutrition plays an important role in overall health. Different nutrients including vitamins, minerals, hydrocarbons, water, enzymes or proteins, amino acids and fats, are vital to keep our bodies functioning properly, combat infection and repair tissues, among other things. A lack or surplus of certain nutrients can lead to disease or a state of imbalance; for example, in humans an excess of fat and/or protein depletes calcium from the bones, leading to osteoporosis (a disease unknown to rats).[107] Nutritionists and dieticians have established that people's bodies differ in their abilities to absorb certain nutrients such as iron and calcium.[108]

Similarly, Rodricks (1992) writes that, 'individuals vary in the extent to which they can absorb the same chemical; absorption can be influenced by age, sex, health status and even dietary habits [and] ... different animal species exhibit differences in gastrointestinal absorption and dermal adsorption rates;' for example, a rat will absorb lead differently than will a human,[109] and a rabbit's skin is much more vulnerable than a human's.[110]

The nature and rate of metabolic transformations vary among individuals and different animal species. In 1982 Goldberg stated that using 'normal healthy animals' in toxicological studies disregards the special physiological needs and conditions of children, the elderly and the disabled.[111] Rodricks (1992, p. 35) states that, 'metabolism differences can be extreme, and may be the most important factor accounting for differences in response to chemical toxicity among individuals within a species.' In 1978 the British biochemist R. T. Williams stated that there were numerous variations within the metabolic patterns of various species of monkeys, carnivores and rodents.[112] Björn Ekwall, founder of the Scandinavian Society of Cell Toxicology, explained that a species difference between a human and non-human of only one toxicokinetic factor 'can completely disturb the predictability of experimental results.'[113]

Hence, an individual animal's age, genetics, and what and how much it eats, can influence the outcome of an experiment, as can the manner in which the animal is exposed to the test agent. Humans' food choices and eating patterns vary drastically from laboratory animals' in quantity, quality, substance, and method of consumption. The roles of nutrition and stress in promoting or preventing cancer in both animals and humans is a vast field of study, with many questions remaining unanswered. There is still a paucity of epidemiological data on the role that stress, and chemical carcinogens in food and the environment play in promoting human cancer. Because the mechanism of cancer is still poorly understood, and because of substantial variability in humans' and laboratory animals' living conditions, it would be irrational to draw parallels between these different species to gain insight into which factors provoke the onset of human cancers; furthermore, the vast metabolic inter- and intra-species differences among individuals, of different ages, sexes and cultures, render the results of animal tests highly questionable, at best, in terms of their relevance for humans.

The artificiality of laboratory life

'to be healthy is to be sound of mind and body. It is to be intact—not broken, damaged or injured. Health is the natural state of any creature able to take what it needs from a wholesome, supportive environment and utilize it for its well-being … comparatively few organisms are diseased beyond their natural capacity to heal themselves.' Andrée Collard, *Rape of the Wild* (Indiana: Indiana University Press, 1989) p. 81

'the human dimension clearly shows more vagaries than the controlled lab.' In Abraham H. Wandersman, 'Are People Acting Irrationally?,' *American Psychologist* 48, no. 6 (June 1993): 681–6

Ironically, toxicologists argue that because animals live in controlled, sterile environments, and their genetic history is known through their breeders, they are appropriate substitutes for humans who, toxicologists admit, do not live in controlled environments, are genetically diverse, may move widely from area to area and from job setting to job setting, making it impossible to determine which of many exposures may cause a particular illness. Although some claim that laboratory animals are 'healthier' now than they have been in the past,[114] the life of the animal who lives in a barren, sterile environment in which temperature, humidity and lighting are controlled and wall surfaces are disinfected, whose food and bedding are sterilized,[115] and who is subjected to painful and debilitating experiments, is an unhealthy and abnormal one—and one which does not parallel the average human (or animal) condition.

Issues surrounding the laboratory environment, previously raised by scientists in the 1970s, have called into serious question the validity of three decades worth of National Toxicology Program (and others') animal data. The contamination of commercial animal feeds reported in *Science* in the mid-1970s has been described above. In the same vein, spontaneous liver and breast cancer rates of 100 percent in American C3HA and C3H-AfB mouse strains, was attributed to the use of cedar chips as a bedding material. In Australia, where bedding was made of pine chips, the tumor rate was only 25 percent.[116]

Researchers have long hypothesized that both natural and man-made chemicals have the capacity to interact in the body to produce potentially carcinogenic agents. Top ranking officials, such as Norbert Page and Herman Kraybill, of the National Cancer Institute at that time concurred that contaminants in the compound being tested as well as in the air, water, diet, and bedding of the animals could introduce uncertainties or error into animal tests.[117] This issue has not been adequately addressed to date.

Under laboratory conditions, rats, who are by nature social species, are crowded together in small cages or terrariums, leading to fighting and cannibalism. Barnard and Hou write that states of stress, hunger, thirst, sleeplessness, hypersexuality, and pain, which are induced by experimental procedures, affect immunologic function.[118] Similarly, Harold Hillman, a British physiologist, asserted that the stress experienced by animals subjected to painful procedures, including the simple drawing of blood, affects every organ and/or biochemical system in the body.

David Morton, a veterinarian and head of biomedical sciences and ethics at the University of Birmingham, UK says that 'noise, restraint, isolation, crowding, regrouping, separation from mothers, surgery and anesthesia all can increase mortality, contact sensitivity, tumor susceptibility, ... metastatic spread, as well as decrease ... viral resistance [and] immune response,' among other things. It was found that the AKR mouse strain spontaneously develops a disease similar to leukemia in 90 percent of cases when kept in isolation. When housed together, the percentage of mice who fall ill drops to 25 percent.[119] In this vein, Gio Batta Gori of the NCI stated in 1980 that 'over-crowding, noise, ... and other stresses could come to be defined as carcinogens even though they may be merely modulating factors in the tests.'[120] These issues are acknowledged in EEC Directive 86/609/EEC of 24 November 1986, the regulation governing the treatment of animals used in experiments (see Annex II (2) and (3)). Item 2.5 proposes the playing of 'soft music' in laboratories since 'noises may lead to considerable change in organ functions.' The section also acknowledges that ventilation, temperature, humidity, lighting, food, housing, bedding, handling, and transport all affect an animal's biology, and hence the outcome of an experiment.

Morton has observed that rabbits isolated in single cages have abnormal bone development, exhibit neurotic behavior, and are less healthy than rabbits housed in groups. He says that, 'temperature can affect food and water intake and metabolic rate; and lighting can have an impact on reproductive performance and on the level of ... [a chemical] that will produce toxic effects.' (Albino rats are extremely sensitive to light.) In addition, Morton has seen elevated hormone levels in rabbits and rats for up to 24 hours after the animals were moved from one room to another. He said that growth hormone and immune system cells can be similarly affected while animals acclimate to change;

he concludes that, 'until we know ... the effects of the way we treat ... [animals], we are never going to be sure some of the artifacts may not be obscuring some kinds of research.'[121]

In essence, experimental conditions themselves may be causing animals to develop cancer-effects which would most likely manifest themselves in control groups as well as test groups. Hence the possibility exists that without the experimental conditions, animals may not develop tumors at all. Although, for example, EEC Directive 86/609/ EEC lists over fifty procedures that must be followed by laboratory technicians to minimize the impact of modulating environmental factors, it is highly unlikely (given human nature and lack of enforcement) that the procedures are followed at all times. Once again this raises yet unanswered questions about whether laboratory animals develop cancer from a chemical under study or from the unnatural, hostile environment in which they are forced to live.

The 'dirt' on 'germfree' animals

'The alteration, through genetic engineering, of the permanent genetic code of animals represents a unique and unprecedented assault on their dignity and biological integrity ... If we continue over the next decades to mix and match the genes of the animal kingdom to suit our desires and to gain commercial profits, it could bring about the end of nature as we have known it.' Andrew Kimbrell, *The Human Body Shop: The Engineering and Marketing of Life* (San Francisco: Harper San Francisco, 1994), 186–7.

The notion that animals can be purposely bred to be disease/pathogenfree or 'axenic' (achieved by breeding brothers with sisters and parents with children for successive generations), may work in theory, but the idea that genetically altered animals are healthy or 'normal,' and that they can function as reliable machines unaffected by external circumstances, is a Cartesian delusion.

Artificially bred animals are deprived of symbiosis with microorganisms, a phenomenon which developed with the species millions of years ago and governed its development; they are forced to live in sterile plastic or metal 'isolators' under artificial light,[122] where they are isolated from sounds, are incapable of selecting their own food in a way that is natural for them, and do not know how to accustom themselves to changes in temperature. What kinds of animals are these? What 'model' do they represent if they do not resemble even their own species? And what relationship do the results obtained from such animals have with human pathological conditions?

Italian pathologist Pietro Croce explains that genetically bred animals have numerous anatomical, biochemical, and immunologic anomalies. The anatomical anomalies include a marked enlargement of the caecum (the cul-de-sac in which the large intestine begins),[123] a thinning of the intestinal *lamina propria*,[124] hypoplasia (underdevelopment) of endothelial tissue and of the intestinal lymphatic tissue,[125] and hypoplasia of the spleen and the suprarenal glands (glands situated above the kidney).[126] Biochemical anomalies include an increase in alkaline phosphatase (an enzyme in the body that breaks up compounds made of carbohydrates and phosphates), rapid absorption of thymine, glucose, 3–methyl glucose, and d-xylose in the small intestine,[127] an increase in serum blood cholesterol,[128] the absence of phenyl sulphate, indoxyl sulphate, and urobilins in urine,[129] an increase in iron and copper in the liver, a diminished thyroid activity, and a general slowing down of the metabolism.[130]

Axenic animals' immune systems are compromised by low gamma globulin levels in their blood; gamma globulin is a protein component of blood plasma, containing antibodies effective against certain micro-organisms like infectious hepatitis.[131] In his paper, 'Alternative Test Method Development at the National Toxicology Program' (1994) William Stokes, Associate Director of Animal and Alternative Resources at the NIEHS, presents evidence that certain strains of transgenic mice—like the heterozygous P53 mouse and the TC.AC mouse—are more prone to developing both spontaneous and induced tumors, and in a much shorter time period, than their genetically unaltered counterparts. And though testing laboratories may think they are getting 'germfree' animals, undercover investigations by animal advocacy groups have prompted the USDA to bring charges against laboratory animal breeders/suppliers like the Buckshire Corporation in Perkasie, Pennsylvania. Buckshire has been charged with repeated health and animal welfare violations, including inadequate veterinary care, such as: the discovery of sick, starving, injured and freezing animals, over-crowding in cages that were too small, and the discovery of live and dead cockroaches throughout the facility.[132] Even if breeders get a clean bill of health from the USDA, however, once the animals leave the breeding facility they are exposed to numerous germs and stressful conditions while in transit to their new environments.

Caged rats are extremely susceptible to a host of bacterially induced diseases like salmonellosis, which can be caused by dirty bedding or cages; salmonellosis causes lethargy, weight loss, and partial paralysis of the hindquarters. Axenic rats, whose immune systems are already compromised, are all the more susceptible to such diseases, especially when they are housed together. Over the past five decades, various infectious agents have been recognized as causing overt disease in 'laboratory animals.' Even Charles River Laboratories, 'laboratory animal' breeders, admit that potentially pathogenic organisms like *staphylococcus aureus* or *klebsiella pneumoniae* are difficult to exclude 'without extraordinary measures.' They recommend a detailed health monitoring and diagnostic evaluation program which requires the expertise of parasitologists, microbiologists, pathologists and serologists. This involves screening for numerous viruses that are known to interfere with research, including mouse hepatitis virus, Sendai virus, sialodacryoadenitis virus, Kilham rat virus, Lymphocytic choriomeningitis virus, *Salmonella* sp., and *Citrobacter freundii* 4280, to name a few. Charles River acknowledges that labs must select which agents they wish to screen for due to the 'prevalence of agents,' and 'the cost of screening.'[133]

Because the occurrence of disease is not recorded, and because labs may not be screening for all known (and yet unknown) viruses, it is impossible to tell how many such illnesses may be affecting the results of experiments. It has been noted that injuries and diseases not expected to influence experimental results are not treated,[134] particularly when the administration of antibiotics could interfere with experimental results.

Humans make mistakes

'The variations in data from chemical analysis of samples from different animals obtained in different laboratories often led to conclusions that the wide inter-animal variations were due to insufficient numbers of animals.' Dennis V. Parke, *Science & Engineering Ethics* 1, Issue 3 (1995): 292

It is not uncommon for mistakes to be made in scientific studies, particularly in data processing and analysis. In risk assessment research, however, in which the difference between an 'acceptable' level of risk (one cancer per one million people: 1×10^{-6}) and unacceptable (one cancer per one hundred thousand: or 1×10^{-5}) is a factor of ten, the consequences of using faulty computer-generated calculations are obvious. And yet such mistakes have been made time and again.[135]

Moreover, the improper use and statistical evaluation of data, which may result in inaccurate exposure estimates, has also been a problem.[136] In reviewing animal-based studies published in prominent toxicological journals, Michael Festing, a geneticist with the Medical Research Council in Surrey, UK, found that 'nearly three out of four reports did not include correct statistical analysis.'[137] This may be aggravated by the fact that post-mortem dissections and histopathological diagnoses of animals dosed with a specific chemical are often carried out by numerous staff members in different laboratories. The analyses are subject to the skill, subjective judgement, as well as the honesty of the technicians and/or pathologists. Historically there have been problems with false, missing and/or misrepresented data, or scientific misconduct.[138]

The animal tests have never been validated

'It is generally recognized that the traditional in vivo procedures were accepted without validation.' H. M. Van Looy, 'OECD and Acceptance of the Three Rs,' in *Alternatives to Animal Testing*, C. A. Reinhardt, ed. (New York: VCH/ Weinheim, 1994), p. 18

'Historically, the greatest failing of risk assessments for both human health and the environment has been the lack of follow-up studies to determine the efficacy of actions taken and, incidentally, to validate the assessment methodology.' G. W. Suter and J. M. Loar, 'Weighing the Ecological Risk of Hazardous Waste Sites,' *Environ. Sci. Technol.* 26, no. 3 (1992)

A plethora of reports have been produced solely to *define* validation. According to the British Fund for the Replacement of Animals in Medical Experiments (FRAME), 'validation is the process whereby relevance and reliability [of a test method] are established for a particular purpose;'[139] in this case, animal tests were designed to determine whether a chemical causes cancer and other toxic effects (in the animal) under given conditions. Validation programs must prove that such a test method produces data that are reproducible, reliable and relevant to *humans*; and it must be possible to extrapolate the data from such tests to the human situation.[140] It should be pointed out that, traditionally, the infallibility of a scientific method is dependent on two conditions: first, the existence of a thesis or an idea, and second, a means of testing that idea.

While several studies have been conducted to validate non-animal toxicity testing methods such as *in vitro* tests, against classical animal tests, the latter have never been formally validated—a fact to which numerous prominent scientists like Curtis Harris, Umberto Saffiotti and Arthur Upton of the NCI have conceded; in other words it has never been scientifically shown that animal tests could be used to establish qualitative or quantitative carcinogenic risk for humans. The situation today is no different than it was over twenty years ago, as William Stokes of the NIEHS recently confirmed.[141] David Salsburg of Pfizer Central Research reviewed the scientific literature and determined that the rodent bioassay had never been validated. Salsburg tried to validate the animal test himself by analyzing the results of past experiments and concluded that the current animal-based testing system could not be validated.[142]

Because there is no standard of proof for the animal tests—of their capacity to shed light on the human mechanisms of cancer or of their usefulness in safeguarding human health—it is unknown how well animal tests compare with the human situation.[143] According to H. R. Hertzfeld and T. D. Myers, contributors to a 1986 US Office of Technology Assessment report, *Alternatives to Animal Use in Research Testing and Education*, 'it is concluded that the lifetime feeding study has never been subjected to proper validation as an assay for human carcinogens. When an attempt is made to validate it on the basis of these reported studies and those in literature, it appears to lack acceptable specificity and sensitivity.'[144] Rodricks (1992, p. 200) states that the results of most risk assessments, which rely on the data generated by animal tests, have also 'not been subjected to empirical study and verification. ... Indeed, the results of most risk assessments ... are scientific hypotheses that are not generally testable with any practicable epidemiological method.' Rodricks suggests that such assessments, when they are made, should not pretend to represent 'normal science.'[145] Author Edith Efron concurs and adds that toxicologists are barely capable of testing the thesis that a substance causes cancer in a given animal strain. Without human data, they cannot test their thesis that the animal data can predict for humans.[146] (Ironically, human data can only be acquired either by waiting until humans have contracted cancer or by studying humans in the process of being exposed to carcinogens.) Despite this fact, animal testing was a priori accepted as the gold standard by which all other testing methods were forced to compare in order to prove safety or harm.[147]

As alluded to above, attempts have been made to assess how accurately animal tests predict human responses to the same chemical. It is often claimed that the standard rodent cancer tests are accurate in predicting human carcinogenicity about 90 percent of the time.[148] Given that the animal data can only be compared to a handful of known human carcinogens, such a high confidence level is suspect. In one study published in 1983, David Salsburg reported that animals predicted cancer in man less than 50 percent of the time.[149] Although the testing of pharmaceuticals has not been explored in this book *per se*, an indication of the unreliability of animal tests for human responses can be obtained by looking at data from drug trials. One survey found only a 5–25 percent correlation between the harmful side effects of drugs in people and the results of animal experiments.[150] Another comparison between human and animal test data found that, at most, only one out of four side effects predicted by animal experiments actually occurred in people.[151]

Based on extrapolations between rats and mice, Gold et al. estimated that rodent-to-human extrapolation would be right about 75 percent of the time. Maryland-based veterinarian Eric Dunayer suggests, however, that the high concordance was influenced by a positive test rate of over 50 percent, possibly a result of dosing animals at the maximum tolerated dose (MTD).[152] Another analysis by toxicologist F. J. Di Carlo (1984) found marked patterns of discordance in the reactions of mice and rats to different chemicals.[153] Current US federal guidelines for carcinogen testing ignore such sources of variability which cannot be controlled.

Only the regulatory scientist, writes Edith Efron, acts in advance of knowledge and justifies it as science; in fact the rationalization to defend action without knowledge is moral because, 'the process of animal–man extrapolation is a hypothesis that can never be tested by the science that produces it.'[154] Efron writes that because the 'validity' of the animal tests has *not* been assessed (and because the criteria for the technical adequacy of the tests are over a decade old), the use of animal cancer tests to predict human cancer is *not* objective.[155] To condone unethical standards which would be unacceptable in other branches of science, and to base regulatory decisions upon such uncertain scientific knowledge, is bad public policy.

In contrast, the criteria for the validation of non-animal testing methods to predict toxicity are being subjected to the most scrupulous validation procedures. In 1981, Michael Balls, then with the Fund for the Replacement of Animals in Medical Experiments (FRAME) said that an alternative method will never replace an established animal procedure and/or be accepted by regulatory authorities 'until it has been rigorously and independently validated by a number of reputable research groups.'[156] Regulating bodies like the OECD say that validation must also be adequate to gain international recognition.[157] Furthermore, alternative methods must be 'no less relevant, no less reproducible, and no less useful for identifying the toxic potential of chemicals, their toxic potencies, and the hazards they might represent under certain conditions of exposure—as a basis for risk assessment.'[158]

It is important to scrutinize the rigorous standards which have been established for *in vitro* tests, given that they are expected to predict human toxicity just as well as, or better than, the animal tests which have never been validated. In 1987, four different stages of the validation process were defined by Balls et al. of FRAME. By 1990, John Frazier of the Johns Hopkins Center for Alternatives to Animal Testing

(CAAT) in Baltimore, Maryland published criteria for the selection of tests and chemicals for validation; in addition he proposed six factors that he felt should be taken into consideration in the selection of test chemicals.[159] In January 1990, the (12) Amden principles for validation were agreed upon behind closed doors by a group of scientists (including Balls) in Amden, Switzerland.[160] Both Ekwall (1992) and Flint (1992) criticized the report as being too inflexible and complex. The OECD also published a 62-page report in 1990 entitled, *Scientific Criteria for Validation of In Vitro Toxicity Tests*. In 1991, a new FRAME report was published detailing 16 recommendations for the validation and acceptance of alternative methods. It said,

> [validation] consists of four main steps, namely intra-laboratory assessment,[161] inter-laboratory assessment,[162] [including a blind trial], test database development, and evaluation,[163] and is preceded by test development and acceptance. The purpose of a validation study should be fully defined, particularly in relation to the level of assessment, and in relation to the type of test required, the type of toxicity to be evaluated, and the chemical spectrum of interest. Tests should only be considered for inclusion in validation studies if the specific purposes for which they have been developed are well defined and consistent with the overall objectives of the validation study. In addition, they must have been adequately developed, standardized and documented, and a need for them in relation to the availability of other tests must have been demonstrated. The incorporation of new methods into practice will be facilitated … if the results of validation studies are subjected to independent assessment … Relevant national and international agencies, industry associations, and data banks should be kept informed of all validation programmes, from early planning through to completion. The results of validation programmes, together with full test protocols and details of statistical methods, should be published in the peer-review literature, and data sets should be made available to all interested parties.[164]

If this seems daunting, it is. Yet similar criteria were put forward again in January 1996 at an OECD workshop in Sweden on the 'Harmonization of Validation and Acceptance Criteria for Alternative Toxicological Test Methods.'[165] Such schemes, however, appear to recreate the complexity inherent in the animal testing regimes. In 1981 Weisburger and Williams noted that, 'when the NCI began carcinogen screening programs in 1962, a test of a given chemical performed in one animal species took … eight months and cost about $10–15,000.' Twenty years later, they write, tests of a chemical for multiple observational endpoints began to be required, testing took up to 64 months, and cost as much as $500,000.[166] The validation process for *in vitro* tests has become so scrupulous and costly (and the difficulties that have been established so formidable) that it currently takes ten to fifteen years to validate a new method.[167]

Pam Logemann, Director of Worldwide In Vitro Lab Technology Sales, at Advanced Tissue Sciences (ATS) in La Jolla, California says that validation programs need not be so lengthy or complicated. In fact, ATS conducted six simple validation trials with its artificial skin technology, Skin^2 between 1990 and 1996. Logemann reported that some 400 chemicals tested with Skin^2 have been 'validated' against classic animal data—the regulatory 'gold standard'—by large companies like Procter & Gamble, but they have not done anything with the results. Companies are apparently reluctant to submit the data to regulators for fear of legal repercussions from regulators and consumers; and regulatory bodies have been reluctant to phase out animal tests, however meaningless, even when presented with data from completed *in vitro* validation trials.[168]

Ironically, scientists are still not in agreement on the principles for the validation of 'alternative' test methods. A draft report by the *ad hoc* Interagency Coordinating Committee on the Validation of Alternative Methods (ICCVAM), a group of 15 federal agencies assembled by the NIEHS in 1994, attempts to address that (see Chapter 5); but the language of the report itself, and the influence and input of special interests, may hinder the adoption of clear-cut criteria.[169] There is also debate about whether it is counterproductive to validate *in vitro* data against animal test results, and to use animal tissues and cells for *in vitro* tests. Some scientists believe that the use of human tissue avoids the problem of species variation.[170] These and other issues related to validation will be explored further in Chapter 5.

It is paradoxical that *in vitro* tests should be charged with being insufficiently validated when the principle of validation itself is still being defined, and particularly as the animal tests themselves (against which *in vitro* tests are being compared), have never been validated. Indeed, the question of whether the animal tests are even *valid*, given all the issues discussed in this chapter, has not been explored. Given the enormous time and cost required for animal tests (see below), and the number of chemicals awaiting testing, this question becomes more significant as federal resources shrink. In an age when human fertilization and embryo culture can be successfully performed *in vitro*,[171] when it has been shown that it is possible to perform neurobiological and developmental research at the cellular level;[172] screen for irritants,[173] mutagens,[174] and carcinogens *in vitro*, quickly and cheaply;[175] and predict drug effects without using animals,[176] this double standard for the validation of *in vitro* tests should enrage animal testing opponents. If the same rigorous validation standards were demanded for the animal tests, their fallaciousness would soon be revealed.

A criticism of specific tests and methods

'That different countries use different LD50 values for similar hazard categories only proves the regulatory convenience and lack of real scientific merit [of the method]' Gerhard Zbinden quoted in Heidi J. Welsh, *Animal Testing and Consumer Products* (Washington, DC: Investor Responsibility Research Center, 1990), p. 51

Stephen R. Kaufman, of the Medical Research Modernization Committee in New York City, writes that most animal tests are supposedly intended to identify subtle toxic effects, but they perform poorly in this regard.[177] The chronic human exposure scenario is a reality which simply cannot be recreated in all its complexity in the laboratory. Since many chemical agents that are potential carcinogens undergo chemical transformation before humans encounter them, there is no a priori basis for predicting whether the carcinogenic potency of these agents will be lost, retained, or enhanced in this process. Both the Lethal Dose or LD50 and Maximum Tolerated Dose (MTD) tests have been criticized for their inability to shed light on the synergistic health effects of the chronic, low doses of thousands of chemicals humans are exposed to—in combination—over a lifetime,[178] particularly when extrapolating from the high doses of one chemical typically administered to animals over a 90-day period. In 1983, David P. Rall, then Director of the NTP said, 'I do not think the LD50 test provides much useful information about the health hazards to humans.'[179]

LD50 values vary greatly from laboratory to laboratory, and the values are highly influenced by the sex, species, and diet of the animal, among other things. LD50 values for one substance and one animal species have varied as much as tenfold, a situation which has caused researchers to press for repeated tests with as many animal species as possible in an effort to obtain meaningful results. However, increasing the number of species has merely served to increase the variability of the results. For example, it was found that for methyl-fluoracetin, monkeys were 73 percent, and mice 44 percent more resistant to the compound than dogs. (The LD50 values for each of these species were 11.0 mg/kg, 6.7 mg/kg and 0.15 mg/kg respectively.) Cats, rats, guinea pigs and rabbits had equally varying values.[180]

In addition, lethality and weight loss (and reduced food and water consumption)—conditions that the LD50 and MTD are designed to produce—are hardly realistic parameters by which to measure adverse health effects in humans. Because the LD50 focuses on *when* animals die and not *why* they die, information derived from cases of accidental poisonings in humans is much more useful.

It is common for animals in LD50 tests to be dosed with enormous quantities of a substance. In one experiment involving the sweetener cyclamate, test animals were given the human equivalent of 552 bottles of soft drinks a day; in two experiments with trichloroethylene (TCE)— a chemical once used as a flavor enhancer in foods, an extraction agent in decaffeinating coffee, and as a dry-cleaning and degreasing agent— rats were given the human equivalent of 5×10^7 (or 50,000,000) cups of coffee a day. The doses used in the rodent bioassays of TCE typically exceeded those consumed by humans by a factor of more than one million.[181] In another experiment involving a potent pesticide, Herman Kraybill of the NCI reported that the amount in pounds used for the lifetime rodent bioassay (two years) exceeded the amount available from a manufacturer in his total annual production.[182] In one notorious Alar study released in 1989, mice were fed 35,000 times the amount of Alar normally consumed by children.[183]

While, in most studies, the dose of a chemical administered to animals is half of the Maximum Tolerated Dose, that dose is still hundreds or thousands of times the expected human exposure level.[184] In an article in *Science* (249 (31 August 1990): 970), Ames and Gold stated that dosing at the MTD could be thought of as 'chronic wounding.' Such high levels of a chemical, which drench the metabolic process with poison, not only overwhelm the body's natural defenses, but violate the basic threshold principle of toxicology. The threshold principle states that all mammals have thresholds for chemicals and that the body possesses a self-healing mechanism which allows it to detoxify itself if it has been poisoned. Some toxicologists argue that for most toxic processes a threshold exists, though this is a topic of ongoing debate as definitive evidence of this phenomenon has not been presented. Researchers argue that for carcinogenicity on the other hand (in keeping with the 'one-hit' hypothesis discussed in Chapter 1), no threshold is assumed to exist, despite the fact that many animal carcinogens are effectively detoxified at low levels.[185] Disturbing questions on this issue have been raised by many reports and studies, and remain unresolved.[186]

Herman Kraybill of the NCI stated that high dosing can falsify an experiment in two ways: it can either poison the cells and tissues so severely as to prevent a carcinogenic response that might otherwise have occurred, or it can so overload and change metabolic processes as to cause a carcinogenic response that might not have occurred.[187] An

NIEHS study of oxazepam—a direct chemical relative of Valium and one of the US's most-often prescribed drugs—completed in 1992, caused a 100 percent incidence of aggressive tumors in rodents. A costly and time-consuming examination of frozen DNA sections from the diseased animals found that this was a result of dosing at the Maximum Tolerated Dose.[188] Indeed, a National Toxicology Program policy statement from 1992 says that 'approximately two-thirds of the NTP carcinogens would not be considered carcinogens if the MTD was not used.'[189]

Similar arguments have been made in criticism of the Draize test, the sole purpose of which is essentially to measure damage caused to the eye by a test substance. A popular criticism is that the test has been more effective in detecting severe irritants rather than moderate ones; in addition, the test does not provide information on subtle or chronic effects, nor information relevant to the effective *treatment* of accidental injury.[190] Like the LD50, test results vary widely from laboratory to laboratory because of minor changes in test protocols, and different laboratory workers' interpretations of injury which are translated into scoring assessments.[191] In a survey of intra- and inter-laboratory variability of Draize test results, Weil and Scala concluded that the Draize test should not be recommended by federal agencies as standard procedure in toxicology testing.[192] The rabbit's eye is structurally and physiologically different from the human eye, which complicates the interpretation of test results.[193] The rabbit's cornea makes up 25 percent of the rabbit's eye, while in humans it makes up only 7 percent. Rabbits blink a few times every hour compared to humans who blink circa twelve times per minute; they have a third eyelid, and a less effective tearing mechanism due to a milky secretion from a species-specific gland which makes them unable to wash away or dilute an irritant.[194] Furthermore, rabbits have a higher threshold of pain, making it difficult to determine whether a product would be painful for humans. Many of these basic facts are acknowledged in the international OECD guidelines for the testing of chemicals. In a section entitled, 'Interpretation of test results' they state that, 'extrapolation of the results of eye irritation studies in animals to man is valid only to a limited degree.'[195]

According to biostatistician Irwin Bross, toxicologists who are used to studying signs of acute toxicity are not experts in mutagenesis, a phenomenon which he believes is the most important factor in cancer induction.[196] Bross explained that there is an erroneous tendency to equate tumor formation with cancer. The hallmark of a cancer is that it will spread to other sites in the body. Because animals are often poisoned by dosing at the MTD, cells are killed and cannot clone themselves so that tumors cannot metastasize; hence the mutagenesis phenomenon cannot be observed or considered. In addition, there are many kinds of tumors and not all of them are malignant; this applies to both humans and animals. Whether a tumor will *become* malignant (after multiple, or chronic exposures to a mutagen) is a critical issue; but little if anything is known of the ultimate molecular events that determine the transformation of normal cells into cancer cells. Pathologists who study animal tissues after animals are sacrificed may observe a cellular abnormality, but they cannot detect what caused a malignancy, how it was caused, or when. Moreover, says Bross, because toxicologists are used to studying acute toxic effects in animals, most would not know how to recognize chronic effects. And even then, chronic effects observed in specially bred, genetically homogeneous animals may not be relevant to humans who are so genetically diverse. In fact, one of the problems with detecting toxicity in humans is that the majority of humans do not die from acute poisoning; rare toxicities are what kill a lot of people. Tightly monitored and well-conducted human studies could provide early measures of toxicity in humans and detect these rare forms of toxicity. Epidemiological threats could be readily identified and exposure stopped immediately.[197] Bross believes that the current use of animal models has served to cover up serious human health hazards rather than detect them since the *mutagenic* effects of chemicals occur at doses that, at present, are likely to be called 'safe' by government agencies focused on acute toxicity tests like the Draize, MTD and LD50.

In conclusion, the reasoning behind dosing animals with quantities of chemicals that are irrelevant to natural human (or animal) conditions is that these methods will more reliably produce acute toxic effects, including tumors, in statistically significant numbers. In most cases, the pathology of these tumors is poorly understood. The testing methods are not only crude and lacking in their ability to gauge subtle effects or mutagenicity, but they are inherently biased, as critics like Gio Batta Gori point out, since they often cause a metabolic overload which inevitably produces disease. In this way, the body is not allowed to recover, and both the threshold principle of toxicity and the mutation theory of cancer—deemed important by many toxicologists and scientists—are ignored. Given the classic tradition of looking for and recording acute toxic effects in animals, there is no system in place which allows pathologists to measure subtle and/or chronic toxic effects—those most commonly experienced by humans.

Humanitarian considerations

'The performance of an animal during an experiment depends very much on its confidence in man, something which has to be developed.' EEC Directive 86/609/EEC of 24 November 1986, Item 3.10.2

'All humane methods of killing animals require expertise which can only be attained by appropriate training.' EEC Directive 86/609/EEC, Item 3.12.1

'Ultimately, the desecrator of animal life ends up desecrating all life including his own, for he ... denies the complex interactions of all life systems ... In the end he has amassed crushing amounts of information but has grown not at all in knowledge or understanding.' Andrée Collard, *Rape of the Wild* (Indiana: Indiana University Press, 1989), p. 70

Although this work specifically addresses the scientific issues sur-rounding animal testing, the manner in which the tests are performed necessarily raises ethical and social issues which cannot be ignored— particularly since the performance of these crude and often redundant tests is considered routine in toxicology laboratories in the United States and elsewhere; and also because the justification for using animals as human surrogates is a moral one. A majority of scientists claim that while it is unethical to experiment on humans, it is acceptable to experiment upon non-humans. Society itself teaches us that we are separated from animals by differences in our degrees of sentience and intelligence, a principle rarely explored in the scientific literature, perhaps for fear that it would quickly be debunked.[198] Acknowledging similarities between humans and animals would create emotional obligations between a scientist and his or her subject that would make carrying out animal experiments inconceivable. Hence, the depersonal-ization of animals in research enables them to be viewed as separate and different from humans, and facilitates their exploitation. Animals are clinically referred to as 'bioassays,' 'biologic or surrogate test systems,' 'subjects,' and 'models;'[199] in the laboratory, rather than being given names, they are assigned numbers: A1, B1, C1, which depersonal-izes them further; strains of genetically bred animals are identified by letter codes such as the B6C3F1 mouse strain, the SHR/NCrlBR rat strain, and so on.

Despite these attempts to alienate us from animals, many non-invasive scientific investigations have narrowed the gap between our-selves and the rest of the animal kingdom. Jeffrey M. Masson's critically acclaimed book, *When Elephants Weep: The Emotional Lives of Animals* (1995), offers undeniable proof that non-human animals (including rodents) feel, think, reason, communicate, have sophisticated social systems, act self-consciously, and behave altruistically towards each other. Some scientists believe that rats, for example, are smarter than horses, cows and other animals. Small rodents' (and monkeys') brains make up a larger percentage of their body weight than ours do; relative brain size is typically correlated to the possession of higher central nervous system functions. Because dolphins have a higher brain-to-body-mass ratio than we do, and we know that they are supremely intelligent mammals, possessing sensory and auditory capabilities unknown to us (such as the ability to 'see' through solid objects), it would follow that rodents and monkeys also have a well-adapted higher central nervous system that can be linked to a developed intelligence, by human standards.[200]

Pet rats are reputed to become as attached to their owners as dogs.[201] In a series of experiments on parental love, female rats have been observed to be fiercely maternal towards their own pups and those of other species.[202] Marmosets are frequently used in toxicity tests, yet marmoset fathers have been observed washing newborns, caring for them, and mashing fruit in their fingers for newly weaned babies.[203] Birds, such as geese who mate for life, and mammals including dogs and chimpanzees, have been observed grieving for the death of a mate, and may die of heartbreak over the loss of a companion. Primates (and marine mammals) have been known to die of grief after being taken from the wild and imprisoned in laboratories.[204]

Jeffrey Masson writes that, 'fear can set animals running, diving, hiding, screaming for help, … bristling their quills, or baring their teeth.' Similarly to humans, frightened animals experience trembling, chattering of the teeth, and a rapid heartbeat among other things; they may cower or freeze in place, and very great fear can produce shock. In the August 1995 issue of *National Geographic* magazine, an article about African voodoo rituals described a chicken who died of fright as five men pointed knives at its throat during a ceremonial dance in which the animal was to be sacrificed.[205] Chickens are commonly used in neurotoxicity tests.

While the knowledge we have about non-human animals should make it more difficult to rationalize inhumane experimentation on them, it has not. The LD50, which is still performed to satisfy regulatory requirements, has been described by Swiss toxicologist Gerhard Zbinden as little more than a 'ritual mass execution of animals.'[206] In toxicity tests, animals are forced to eat and drink chemicals using such crude methods as gavage—a process whereby a tube is surgically inserted directly into the stomach; they are placed in inhalation/gas chambers and forced to breathe vapor, given intravenous and subcutaneous injections, and have chemicals painted on their skin and dropped or sprayed in their eyes. In LD50 tests, which are frequently funded by the Environmental Protection Agency and are still required in Japan, animals have been made to suffer convulsions, severe abdominal pain, seizures, tremors and diarrhoea; they have been made to bleed from their genitals, eyes and mouth, vomit uncontrollably, self-mutilate, become paralyzed, lose kidney function, and fall into comas.[207] Guinea pigs, routinely used in inhalation experiments, commonly die of asphyxiation due to a constriction of their bronchial airways. In reproductive studies, pregnant animals are fed chemicals and induced to abort their young; rats and rabbits typically have their entire uteruses removed before expected delivery dates so that fetuses may be examined and dissected. Rabbits, who are often used multiple times in Draize irritancy tests, become severely stressed and dehydrated, and have been known to break their backs trying to escape from the stocks in which they are immobilized;[208] while some federal laboratories no longer use stocks and allow the rabbits access to food and water,[209] the test itself is still performed. The British Animals (Scientific Procedures) Act of 1986 (Schedule 1, p. 21) describes 'Standard Methods of Humane Killing' (of animals used in research and testing). These include dislocation of the neck, concussion by striking the back of the head, and decapitation.

Masson states that an animal experimenter will almost inevitably deny that animals suffer the way humans do, even though scientists who have heard rats and other animals moan, cry, whimper and scream in laboratories know that is nonsense. Such denial is necessary to assuage the guilt associated with the knowledge that one is being cruel.

Yet studies have revealed that mammals and birds can experience pain because they have a central nervous system.[210] In an attempt to collect data about the nature of pain involved in animal experiments, the US Department of Agriculture established a 'pain scale,' which allows researchers (who are rarely trained to detect or assess pain) to rate experiments in terms of painfulness—A being painless, and E being severe pain not relieved by drugs. Toxicity experiments are commonly placed into the C category (momentary pain or distress),[211] even though in The Netherlands, performance of the LD50 is considered to cause *severe* animal suffering.[212]

The US Animal Welfare Act of 1966, designed to improve conditions for 'warm-blooded laboratory animals' in the United States does not cover rodents, birds or farm animals; moreover, the definition of pain is left up to the individual researcher, and certain loopholes in the Act allow experimenters to claim that (1) pain is a necessary component of an experiment, and (2) that the use of pain-alleviating drugs and/or anesthesia would alter the results of an experiment. The latter is also the case in the UK Act (Sections 1, 2, 5, 14) and the EEC Directive 86/609/EEC of 24 November 1986 (Article 8). Hence, there is no system in place which truly protects animals from pain in experimentation.[213]

In light of this, animal welfare groups have attempted to reduce the number of animals used in experiments. This has resulted in animals being used multiple times in different experiments; and despite claims to the contrary,[214] redundancy is still rampant in toxicology laboratories. It is not uncommon for one substance to be tested by dozens of different laboratories, as a perusal of the toxicology literature will confirm. And in his review of animal studies published in leading toxicology journals, British geneticist Michael Festing found that 'many [researchers] waste animals by using far more than necessary.'[215] The NIEHS used 85,000 mice in one saccharin study in an attempt to obtain a 'meaningful' result.[216]

Often, when the human hazards are already known, animal experiments are performed to reproduce the results obtained in humans. For example, in 1968, 1,057 Japanese were poisoned with PCBs as a result of a leak in a heat exchanger which contaminated rice oil. Though the human victims of this tragedy, whose health problems were studied for over a decade, had provided reams of epidemiological information on PCB poisoning in humans, rhesus monkeys were fed purified PCBs decades later in an attempt to reproduce symptoms of PCB poisoning found in humans.[217] Researchers at New York University exposed young leghorn chickens to second-hand cigarette smoke six hours a day for 16 weeks, at concentrations 300 times greater than human real-life exposures. The chickens developed arterial plaques, leading the researchers to conclude that the studies confirmed what was already known from human epidemiological studies—environmental tobacco smoke can lead to heart disease.[218] The money used to fund such experiments would have been better spent on public health education campaigns.

The causal link between benzene and human leukemia was established as early as 1928.[219] Fourteen separate animal trials, starting in 1932, failed to show that benzene caused cancer.[220] Only during the late 1980s were researchers finally able to induce cancer in animals by overdosing them with benzene. But this has not stopped researchers from using public funds to continue to subject thousands of animals to lethal tests with the chemical, its derivatives, and its byproducts. Mice and rats have been forced to inhale unleaded gasoline in chronic tests. Robert Snyder at Rutgers University has been exposing rats to benzene and toluene, in an attempt to 'reduce benzene toxicity by modifying its metabolism in rats.'[221] The money used to fund such futile animal experiments would be better spent on alternative fuel, electric, natural gas and/or solar-powered vehicle development, pollution prevention programs, and in-depth analyses of decades worth of epidemiological data on benzene toxicity.[222] Since 1970 there has been a 40 percent increase in the number of US cities that are below EPA air quality standards; and 90 million Americans currently live in areas that violate the national health safety standards for smog.[223] It is highly doubtful that experiments on rats will contribute towards a solution to such political and economic problems.

The very manner in which animals are bred to be 'germfree' conjures up images of mad scientists in a world completely out of touch with humanity. In order to obtain 'germfree' or microbiologically sterile animals, Charles River Laboratories developed the Caesarean-Originated-Barrier Sustained (COBS) system, now used by other breeding laboratories. This was modeled after methods developed by Reyniers in 1946 and Foster (founder of Charles River Laboratories) in 1959.[224]

First, to avoid all-night vigils, and delay normal delivery of a newborn animal until a day Caesarean surgery can be undertaken, progesterone injections are typically administered to rodents daily from the 17th day of pregnancy. In 1986 Troy Soos reported that, when it is time to perform the Caesarean,

> the healthy mother [rat or rabbit or cat] is killed by having her neck broken shortly before she would have given birth. Her entire uterus is surgically removed and placed in a sterile isolator. [A gloved surgeon has 10 to 15 minutes after the death of the mother to perform a hysterectomy from within a sterile chamber]; the uterus is cut open, allowing the germfree pups to be 'born' in a germfree environment. The young [orphaned] animals are [placed with a lactating female from another germfree colony], [and] later housed in a barrier building equipped with air filters, temperature and humidity controls, and pasteurized feed. The only germs to which the animals are exposed are administered in a carefully prepared mixture intended to aid digestion and stimulate immunity ... To minimize the risk of contagion from human handling, rodents are sent to the shipping room via mechanical chutes.[225]

It should shock us that such a violation of life has become an integral component of a vast commercial enterprise. Thousands of people perform these violent acts without questioning them; we have turned living beings into disposable commodities. In 1978, medical historian Hans Ruesch wrote:

> the progressive blunting of human feelings, which occurs inescapably in all those who engage in systematic torture, is an extremely serious matter. As vivisection is being practiced on an increasing scale … there is a constant, world-wide increase in the number of individuals who get conditioned to disregard the sufferings of other sentient beings … The international health authorities … who provide the guidelines for all other countries—are not merely blind to this danger, but are part of it.[226]

And the general public has unwittingly been drawn into supporting this life-destroying paradigm since, under the present economic structure, the majority of consumer products found in stores and supermarkets have been tested on animals unless a label claims otherwise. In *Rape of the Wild* (1989, p. 77), eco-feminist scholar Andrée Collard wrote that consumerism thrives on the apathy and thoughtlessness of the consumer who, though often well enough informed, continues to buy commodities, foods and products which support life-destroying industries like animal research. Similarly, author Carol Adams writes, 'it is because we are consumers [of cosmetics, cleaners, etc.] that many [animal] experiments continue.'[227]

Although controlled clinical trials have been enormously useful in advancing our understanding of human reactions to drugs and consumer products (and human diseases and their treatments),[228] Italian pathologist Pietro Croce believes that the most heinous forms of *human* experimentation witnessed in this century are an inevitable consequence of the culture of animal experimentation, in which living beings are viewed as tools for research.[229] Human experimentation is currently performed in all scientifically advanced countries, particularly in the area of pharmaceutical development, but also to test the toxicity of commercial products. The term 'human guinea pig' is commonly used to describe people willingly and unwillingly involved in such experiments.[230] Croce says that, in the end, human beings are the only reliable experimental subjects, and so researchers, though they deny it, continually strive to come as close to human experimentation as possible. Often they succeed, as in the case of 'volunteer studies' (or experiments with terminally ill patients).[231]

In one of the earliest attempts to communicate these ideas to the general public, George Bernard Shaw (1856–1950) adapted a play from his book, *The Doctor's Dilemma,* in which he wrote:

> once grant the ethics of the vivisectionists and you not only sanction the experiment on the human subject, but make it the first duty of the vivisector. If a guinea pig may be sacrificed for the sake of the very little that can be learnt from it, shall not a [hu]man be sacrificed for the sake of the great deal that can be learnt from him?[232]

Time and cost of testing

'Long-term animal cancer bioassays … are expensive, time-consuming and often inconclusive … Given the large numbers of potential carcinogens in the environment, it is imperative that methods be developed for predicting the carcinogenic potency of a compound based on results from short-term assays.' Curtis C. Travis, et al., 'Prediction of Carcinogenic Potency … ,' *Mutation Research* 241 (1990): 21–36

As was previously stated, the federal risk assessment research done in the United States by the National Toxicology Program is funded by taxpayers at a cost of $500–$600 million annually.[233] The cost of running a typical rodent test or 'bioassay' is between $2 million and $4 million.[234] The Chemical Manufacturers Association states that test rules may require a number of tests to be conducted on an individual chemical and the total cost per chemical can be as high as $5 million.[235] With some 75,000 chemicals awaiting evaluation, to test all of those chemicals for carcinogenicity could cost over $375 billion.

From the chemical nomination process to the initiation of animal testing takes three years; the animal testing process takes another three to five years. Six to ten years may elapse between the time a chemical is nominated for testing and the publication of the final report.[236] After the bioassays are run, pathological specimens must be evaluated, and statistical analyses on the data performed. Edith Efron writes that,

> according to the NCI, the scientist who is trying to discover whether a chemical has produced tumors in excess of those which occur spontaneously in control groups, must examine every tissue and every organ in the body of every animal in both test and control groups. He must do this for preliminary sets of studies in toxicity and dose-setting as well as for the final study. The analysis includes gross necropsies of 'gross lesions; tissue masses or suspect tumors and regional lymph nodes; skin; mandibular lymph node; mammary gland; salivary gland; larynx; trachea; lungs and bronchi; heart; thyroids; parathyroids; esophagus; stomach; duodenum; jejunum; ileum; cecum; colon; rectum; mesenteric lymph node; liver; thigh muscle; sciatic nerve; sternebrae, vertebrae or femur [plus marrow]; costochondral junction, rib; thymus; gallbladder; pancreas; spleen; kidneys; adrenals; bladder; seminal vesicles; prostate; testes; ovaries; uterus; nasal cavity; brain; pituitary; eyes; spinal cord.' He must dissect all these tissues and organs, prepare blood smears, fix slices of them in formalin, prepare cross sections and slides. Then he must do detailed histopathologic [tissue] analyses of most of these same organs. Then he must write out reports of his discoveries.[237]

Dennis V. Parke writes that such diagnoses are fraught with potential error due to human carelessness, and lack of adequate training of pathologists and technicians.[238] If a pathologist performs all of the aforementioned examinations for each animal in the course of *one* animal test, he or she may end up with as many as 50,000 or more slides that no one can ever fully review. Because the bioassays are tediously slow, no more than 10 to 15 chemicals are selected for testing each year.[239] At that pace, to carry out tests for all of the chemicals currently in use would take over 1,000 years.[240] In 1978, Umberto Saffiotti of the NCI stated that even if all the new substances that were invented each year (in excess of 1,000) were to be tested, there would be no way to test those that had already been introduced into the environment.[241]

To date, despite concerns over the carcinogenic potential of the more than 75,000 chemicals that pervade every aspect of our lives, 'adequate toxicological data' are available for just 10–20 percent of those chemicals,[242] and most are animal data. In 1995, journalist Leslie Lang reported that 'of the 50 top-production chemicals in the United States (which total nearly 700 billion pounds per year) more than two thirds have yet to be evaluated for carcinogenicity in animals.'[243] But Lave at al. (1988) concluded that, 'the [rodent] bioassay often does not provide information commensurate with its cost,' implying that current regulatory policies are flawed. Short-term tests and computer-based structure activity analysis, the authors say, give a preliminary indication of the likelihood that a chemical is a carcinogen. They conclude that resources should be devoted to improving the sensitivity, specificity, and cost-effectiveness of alternative methods such as *in vitro* test schemes.[244]

It has been pointed out by the US Office of Technology Assessment that the costs of environmental illness run into the billions of dollars. These include 'pollution-related acute respiratory conditions, occupational diseases and certain cancers.'[245] Because the current animal-based testing system has not been able to stem the tide of industrial pollution, a case could be made that it has in part been responsible for driving up national health care costs. There is also the question of the environmental (and additional economic) costs of animal testing, since as per EEC regulations (86/609/EEC) for example, toxicology laboratories must annually 'dispose' of and/or incinerate millions of animal carcasses whose biological tissues are laden with toxic and hazardous chemicals. Many cages and pens are also 'disposable.' This issue has not been explored to date.

The many problems with animal tests have been discussed. Clearly the animal test is an inefficient screening tool and a grossly imperfect predictor of human toxicity and disease. Rodents—'germfree,' transgenic, or otherwise—are *not* good biological models of humans, or other animals for that matter. Because of innumerable physiological and metabolic differences between and among species (many of which have yet to be discovered), animal-derived toxicity data may have little if any relevance to human beings. Controversial dosing practices and stressful laboratory conditions call into question the value of animal-to-human extrapolations and the vast databases of animal toxicity data. Regulators are currently forging environmental safety standards based on data from these highly erratic, inhumane, time-consuming and expensive testing methods which have never been scientifically validated. The general public has been swayed by proponents' claims that animal tests protect them from harmful substances when in fact their efficacy is impossible to establish due to the lack of corresponding human data.

In addition, the public is unaware that the government often ignores the results of its own animal tests, so that even when data demonstrate a substance's cancer-causing potential, that chemical is not banned but allowed to remain on the market (sometimes but not always) accompanied by appropriate warning labels. In other cases, agencies like FDA or EPA may classify substances found in foods or water as 'unavoidable contaminants', and hence set legal tolerance levels for them. Ironically, virtually every food product on the market today contains some constituent (including essential and naturally occurring vitamins and minerals) that has been shown to be carcinogenic in at least one animal species.[246]

Several examples of specific products which the EPA and other agencies have failed to regulate, despite evidence of harm from animal tests, will be discussed in Chapter 4. As it stands, current consumer product labelling is 'grossly inadequate,' according to the Cancer Prevention Coalition (CPC), a Chicago-based non-profit organization. Ingredients and contaminants are not listed for foods and household products. CPC states that, 'while cosmetics are labeled for major ingredients, they are not for hidden carcinogens such as contaminants and precursors. Furthermore, no information is provided on the labels about the chronic risks of cancer and other toxic effects, despite the fact that such information has been available in government and industry files for decades.'[247] If government agencies do in fact believe the results of their own animal tests which show a product to be toxic and/or carcinogenic, why haven't they banned these allegedly harmful animal carcinogens rather than allow their continued use? Why aren't hazardous products labelled to inform consumers of their cancer-causing potential? And why haven't safer alternatives been developed and marketed?

The database of the American Association of Poison Control Centers (AAPCC) in Washington, DC, now contains 16 million human poison exposure cases with the majority of those being acute exposures to household products; it is unknown how many cases of poisoning go unreported each year.[248] In addition, most physicians do not know how to recognize or diagnose chemically induced illnesses, particularly when symptoms are chronic rather than acute.[249]

Many environmentalists and health advocates believe that the answer lies in banning the production of toxic chemicals from the outset, or reducing our chemical dependency. So far, this has not happened; in fact production rates for (potentially carcinogenic) synthetic industrial chemicals in the US increased fifteenfold from 6.7 million metric tonnes in 1945 to 102 million metric tonnes annually in 1985.[250] In California alone, pesticide use climbed by 31 percent between 1991 and 1993.[251] Animal testing has neither slowed this growth, nor shed light on the cumulative hazards of nations' chemical buildup.

The ambiguity inherent in animal test results has been used to the advantage of chemical manufacturers and federal regulatory agencies seeking to achieve desired policy objectives—objectives which often place profits before public health and safety. When seeking registration for a new product, chemical manufacturers may test a chemical in an 'appropriate' animal species, or at certain doses, to 'prove' that a new product does not cause cancer or produce toxicity according to current regulatory standards. In some cases, chemical companies may 'explain away' positive evidence in animal studies. The French company Rhône-Poulenc attributed the bladder cancer in male rats caused by its pesticide Aliette, to the rats' 'unusual urine chemistry.' Aliette remains on the market.[252]

Biostatistician Irwin Bross, former Director for 24 years of the Roswell Park Memorial Institute for Cancer Research in Buffalo, New York, asserts that government agencies frequently deny positive human evidence by citing negative results with laboratory animals when it is convenient to do so. He says that, 'whenever government agencies or polluting corporations want to cover up an environmental hazard, they can always find an animal study to 'prove' their claim. They can even do a new animal study which will come out the way that they want by choosing the "right" animal model system.'[253] Johannes Clemmensen of Denmark, a renowned epidemiologist in environmental cancer, said that to ignore relevant human experience and accept animal data is ludicrous and scientifically 'unsound.'[254]

Conversely, governments may ignore animal data when it is convenient to do so. Soldiers who served in the Persian Gulf War from

1990 to 1991 had insecticides sprayed on their clothing, insect repellents rubbed on their skin, and took an experimental drug, pyridostigmine, as a precaution against chemical warfare agents. They are now plagued by skin, stomach, joint, and neurological disorders dubbed the Gulf War Syndrome. A US government panel studying the veterans' ailments dismissed the incriminating results of chicken experiments as hypothetical. Because the government could face lawsuits from thousands of ailing veterans (9000 out of 500,000 have already filed disability claims), it is highly unlikely that it would heed the results of the chicken studies.[255] (Ironically, the for-profit Coulston International Corporation—related to the Coulston Foundation which conducts toxicity tests on primates—made millions of dollars providing the US Department of Defense with permethrin, an animal-tested insecticide implicated as a possible cause of Gulf War Syndrome.)[256]

Companies sometimes use animal data to imply superiority over a competitor's product.[257] Debates over the validity of animal test results have resulted in costly litigation between manufacturers and the federal government. As scientists, industry representatives and federal regulators argue over the significance of these results, dangerous products are allowed to remain on the market where the public continues to be exposed to them. Ultimately, animal tests do not mitigate the dangers to public safety posed by industrial chemicals as their proponents would have us believe. Rather they are part of a regulatory bureaucracy which has lost sight of its mandate to protect human health.

Revolutions in chemical testing and screening technologies have produced methods that are faster, cheaper and often superior to animal tests in terms of their accuracy when compared with human toxicity data. Although the many problems with animal testing discussed in this chapter have been acknowledged by mainstream scientists for decades, political, economic and scientific obstacles are impeding change. The following chapters will address these issues.

Notes

1. Anon, 'Animal Research and Human Health: The Use of Animals in Product Safety Testing,' brochure (Washington, DC: Foundation for Biomedical Research, Undated).

2. Anon, 'Animals: The Vital Link to Health and Safety,' brochure (Bethesda: Partners in Discovery, 1992). (Partners in Discovery includes representatives of government agencies, medical institutions, and research-based pharmaceutical companies; the group was formed as part of the NIH centennial observance of 1987 and addresses 'issues important to the health and vitality of biomedical research in the US').

3. See note 1.

4. Michael Gough, 'Estimating Cancer Mortality,' *Environ. Sci. Technol.* 23, no. 8 (1989): 929.

5. Partners in Discovery (1992), p. 5. This brochure refers to rodents as 'higher-order animals,' and refers to worms and salamanders as 'lower-order animals.' But the characteristics which qualify rodents as 'higher-order animals' are not explained. The only point made in this regard is that rats and mice account for about 90 percent of the animals used in research, perhaps (falsely) implying that they are used to this extent because they accurately parallel human anatomy and physiology. Evolutionary biologists might contend that primates are higher-order animals because they most closely resemble humans, and that rodents are in fact 'lower-order animals.'

6. Dennis M. Maloney, 'Toxicity Tests in Animals … ,' *Env. Health Persp.* 101, no. 5 (October 1993): 400; Victor A. Fung, et al., 'The Carcinogenesis Bioassay in Perspective: Application in Identifying Human Cancer,' *Env. Health Persp.* 103, no. 7–8 (July–August 1995): 680–2.

7. Partners in Discovery (1992); Alan Goldberg and Frederick Wehr in *Non-Animal Techniques in Biomedical and Behavioral Research and Testing*, M. B. Kapis and S. C. Gad, eds (Florida: Lewis Publishers, 1993), p. 7. They claim, for example, that mammals have similar respiratory tract anatomies. Daniel B. Menzel, 'Physiological Pharmacokinetic Modeling,' *Environ. Sci. Technol.* 21, no. 10 (1987): 946.

8. Joseph V. Rodricks, *Calculated Risks* (UK: Cambridge University Press, 1992), p. 35.

9. Daniel B. Menzel (1987): 944–58; Editorial, 'Developing Confidence in Risk Assessments Based on Physiological Toxicokinetic Models,' *Env. Health Persp.* 104, no. 3 (March 1996): 242.

10. Virginia C. Gordon, in M. B. Kapis and S. C. Gad, eds (1993), p. 11.

11. Joseph V. Rodricks (1992), p. 37.

12. See note 10.

13. Anon, 'With Respect to Life: Protecting Human Health and the Environment through Laboratory Animal Research,' brochure (Bethesda: National Institutes of Health, August 1990).

14. Ibid.

15. Ibid.

16. Ibid.

17. Heidi J. Welsh, *Animal Testing and Consumer Products* (Washington, DC: Investor Responsibility Research Center, 1990), p. 57.

18. Joel Brinkley, 'Many Say Lab Animal Tests Fail to Measure Human Risk,' *The New York Times*, 23 March 1993, p. A1.

19. Dennis M. Maloney (October 1993): 397.

20. Ibid.

21. Ibid.: 400; US Food and Drug Administration, Statement to the Maryland Governor's Task Force to Study Animal Testing, 17 April 1989.

22. Personal communication between Dennis V. Parke and André Menache, President, Doctors and Lawyers for Responsible Medicine, UK, 1 May 1996, courtesy of Dennis V. Parke, Surrey, UK.

23. Pietro Croce, *Vivisection or Science: A Choice to Make*, 5th edition (Firenze, Italy: Movimento Nazionale Ecologico, 1992), p. 30.

24. R. Talcott, et al., 'Malathion Carboxyl Esterase Titer and its Relation to Malathion Toxicity,' *Tox. & Appl. Pharm.* 50 (1979): 501–4. A. R. Main and P. E. Braid, 'Hydrolysis of Malathion by Ali-Esterases In Vitro and In Vivo,' *Biochemical Journal* 84 (1962): 255–63.

25. Robert Sharpe, *Science on Trial: The Human Cost of Animal Experiments* (Sheffield, UK: Awareness Publishing Ltd, 1994), p. 141.

26. K. Miller and S. Nicklin, in *The Future of Predictive Safety Evaluation*, A. Worden, et al., eds (Boston: MTP Press, 1986), p. 185.

27. See Edith Efron, *The Apocalyptics: Cancer and the Big Lie* (New York: Simon & Schuster, 1984), Chapter 11.

28. John Higginson quoted in Edith Efron (1984), p. 373.

39. See Gio Batta Gori, 'The Regulation of Carcinogenic Hazards,' *Science* 208 (18 April 1980): 256–61, for a list of references.

30. John H. Weisburger and Gary M. Williams, 'Carcinogen Testing: Current Problems and New Approaches,' *Science* 214 (23 October 1981): 401–7.

31. Michael Gough (1989): 926.

32. R. Montesano, et al., *Long-Term and Short-Term Assays for Carcinogens: A Critical Appraisal* (Lyon: Oxford University Press, 1986).

33. Pietro Croce (1992), p. 20.

34. Ibid., p. 46.

35. M. B. Reddy and J. D. Cook, 'Assessment of Dietary Determinants of Nonheme-Iron Absorption in Humans and Rats,' *American Journal of Clinical Nutrition* 54 (1991): 723–8; *Casarett and Doull's Toxicology* (New York: Macmillan, 1980), p. 162.

36. Richard Doll and Richard Peto, 'The Causes of Cancer ... ,' *Journal of the National Cancer Institute* 66 (1981): 1191–308.

37. D. B. Clayson, et al., 'The Power and Interpretation of the Carcinogenicity Bioassay,' *Reg. Tox. Pharm.* 3 (1983): 329–48; Philip H. Abelson, 'Diet and Cancer in Humans and Rodents,' *Science* 255 (1992): 141, cited in Eric Dunayer, 'Testing Chemicals: Animal Testing Impedes Regulatory Action,' 1992, unpublished paper courtesy of the Physicians Committee for Responsible Medicine, Washington, DC, p. 19.

38. Gio Batta Gori (18 April 1980): 257. Historically, federal agencies have revealed an automatic bias for positive findings in animal tests regardless of their validity. Often when animal data contradict each other, positive (carcinogenic) findings are given priority over the non-carcinogenic findings. See Edith Efron (1984) for a discussion of this issue.

39. Herman Kraybill, *Human Epidemiology and Laboratory Correlations in Chemical Carcinogenesis* (Norwood, New Jersey: Ablex, 1980). In 1976 Umberto Saffiotti of the NCI, which had the largest carcinogen screening program in the world, observed that of the 6,000 chemicals that had been tested for carcinogenicity, many were conducted on very small numbers of animals, without adequate controls and by protocols now considered inadequate. Edith Efron (1984), p. 381. In 1978 Thomas Maugh of *Science* reported that tests were conducted with impure substances and rare concoctions of chemicals to which humans would probably never be exposed; moreover pathology work was inadequate in many cases. Edith Efron (1984), pp. 298–300.

40. Pietro Croce (1992), p. 69.

41. Gio Batta Gori (18 April 1980): 258.

42. Pietro Croce (1992), p. 56.

43. M. Effron, et al., 'Nature and Rate of Neoplasia Found in Captive Wild Mammals, Birds and Reptiles at Necropsy,' *J. Natl. Cancer Inst.* 59 (1977): 185–98.

44. A. Monro, *Reg. Tox. Pharm.* 18 (1993): 115–35.

45. Dennis V. Parke, 'Ethical Aspects of the Safety of Medicines and Other Social Chemicals,' *Science & Engineering Ethics* 1, Issue 3 (1995): 291.

46. Jeff Diner, 'A Compendium of Alternatives to the Use of Live Animals in Research and Testing,' brochure, publication sponsored by The American Anti-

Vivisection Society (Jenkintown, Pennsylvania: December 1989), p. 33. Some suggest that it is important to study tissue from the species which naturally develops the disease, and more useful to study cancerous tissue in cell and tissue culture, where the mechanisms of cell growth can be more easily determined and where the effects of potentially useful substances on the cells can be explored.

47. Gio Batta Gori (18 April 1980): 258–61.

48. Dunayer (1992), p. 15; E. McConnell, 'The Maximum Tolerated Dose: The Debate,' *J. Amer. Cell. Toxic.* 8 (1989): 1115–120.

49. G. J. Turnbull, in A. Worden, et al., eds (1986), p. 125.

50. Edward J. Calabrese, 'Animal Extrapolation: a Look Inside the Toxicologist's Black Box,' *Environ. Sci. Technol.* 21, no. 7 (1987): 622.

51. Michael Gough (1989): 925–30.

52. Joseph V. Rodricks (1992), p. 228.

53. *National Toxicology Program: Fiscal Year 1994,* Annual Plan, Draft (North Carolina: National Toxicology Program, May 1994): 147; Eric Dunayer (1992), p. 20.

54. John Manuel, 'Environment, Genes, and Cancer,' *Env. Health Persp.* 104, no. 3 (March 1996): 257

55. E. J. Calabrese, *Principles of Animal Extrapolation* (New York: John Wiley & Sons, 1983).

56. Office of Science and Technology Policy, *Identification, Characterization, and Control of Potential Human Carcinogens: A Framework for Federal Decision-Making* (Washington, DC: Executive Office of the President, February 1979), p. 9.

57. Interagency Regulatory Liaison Group, 'Scientific Basis for Identification of Potential Carcinogens and Estimation of Risks,' *Journal of the National Cancer Institute* 63 (1979): 259.

58. Gio Batta Gori, *Air Pollution and Cancer in Man,* Lorenzo Tomatis, et al., eds (Lyon: IARC, 1977), pp. 99–111.

59. E. Berardesca and I. H. Maibach, 'Racial Differences in Sodium Lauryl Sulphate Induced Cutaneous Irritation: Black and White,' *Contact Dermatitis* 18 (1988): 65–70; D. A. Basketter, et al., 'Individual Ethnic and Seasonal Variability in Irritant Susceptibility of Skin: the Implications for a Predictive Human Patch Test,' *Contact Dermatitis* 35 (1996): 208–13.

60. Vicki Glaser, 'In Vitro Test Systems Getting a Close Look by Industry and the FDA,' *Genetic Engineering News,* 15 April 1995, p. 6.

61. C. Clemedsen, et al., 'MEIC Evaluation Part II … ,' *ATLA* 24, Supplement (1996): 308; J. T. Emerman, et al., *In Vitro Cellular & Developmental Biology* 23 (1987): 134; P. Roberts et al., *Drug Metabolism & Disposition* 19 (1991): 841–3; G. M. Hawksworth, *Human & Experimental Toxicology* 13 (1994): 568–73; R. Jober, et al., *Toxicol. In Vitro* 6 (1992): 47–52.

62. Gordon Graff, 'The Chlorine Controversy,' *Technology Review,* January 1995, p. 59.

63. D. G. Hoel, et al., 'Implications of Nonlinear Kinetics on Risk Estimation in Carcinogenesis,' *Science* 219 (1983): 1032–6.

64. Matthew Meselson et al., 'The Meselson Report,' Harvard University (1975) cited in Edith Efron (1984), p. 363; see Chapter 13, footnote 40 for full references.

65. OSHA, *Federal Register* (22 January 1980) Vol. 45, No. 15, p. 5122.

66. G. J. Turnbull in A. Worden, et al., eds (1986), p. 127.

67. Irwin Bross, 'Mathematical Models Vs. Animal Models,' *Perspectives in Medical Research* 1 (1989): 83–108, Medical Research Modernization Committee, New York.

68. D. A. Freedman and H. Zeisel, 'From Mouse-to-Man: the Quantitative Assessment of Cancer Risks,' *Statistical Science* 3 (1988): 3–56.

69. Iain F. H. Purchase, 'In Vitro Toxicology Methods in Risk Assessment,' *ATLA* 24 (1996): 327.

70. Edith Efron (1984), p. 374.

71. D. Krewski and J. Van Ryzin, in *Statistics and Related Topics*, M. Csorgo, et al., eds (Amsterdam: Elsevier/North Holland, 1981), pp. 201–31.

72. Lois S. Gold, et al., 'Interspecies Extrapolation in Carcinogenesis: Prediction Between Rats and Mice,' *Env. Health Persp.* 81 (1989): 211–19, cited in Eric Dunayer (1992), p. 18.

73. Richard B. Kurzel, 'The Effect of Environmental Pollutants on Human Reproduction,' *Environ. Sci. Technol.* 15, no. 6 (June 1981): 638.

74. Victor A. Fung, et al., 'The Carcinogenesis Bioassay in Perspective ... ,' *Env. Health Persp.* 103, no. 7–8 (July–August 1995): 682.

75. Leslie Pardue, 'Testing for Toxins,' *E Magazine*, January/February 1994; see also, Joel Brinkley (23 March 1993), p. A1.

76. Lester B. Lave, et al., 'Information Value of the Rodent Bioassay,' *Nature* 336 (15 December 1988): 631–3.

77. D. B. Clayson, et al., 'The Power and Interpretation of the Carcinogenicity Bioassay,' *Reg. Tox. Pharm.* 3 (1983): 329–48, cited in Eric Dunayer (1992), p. 17.

78. Elizabeth Weisburger, 'Cancer-Causing Chemicals,' in *Cancer: The Outlaw Cell* (Washington, DC: American Chemical Society, 1988).

79. C. F. Wurster, 'DDT Proved Neither Essential Nor Safe,' *BioScience* 23 (1973): 106.

80. S. M. Cohen, et al., 'Cell Proliferation in Carcinogenesis,' *Science* 249 (1990): 1007–11, cited in Eric Dunayer (1992), p. 19.

81. Joel Brinkley (23 March 1993), p. A16. Animal experiments with arsenic began in 1911, but it wasn't until 1981 (70 years later) that experimenters were able to induce cancer in animals by dosing them with arsenic. Robert Sharpe, 'Occupational Hazards,' *The AV Magazine*, published by the American Anti-Vivisection Society, Jenkintown, Pennsylvania (January/February 1995), p. 7.

82. C. Biancifiori and L. Severi, 'The Relation of Isoniazid (INH) and Allied Compounds to Carcinogenesis in Some Species of Small Laboratory Animals,' *Brit. J. Cancer* 20 (1966): 528–38.

83. *IARC Monograph* 29 (Lyon: 1982).

84. See William Lijinsky, 'Species Differences in Carcinogenesis,' *In Vivo* 7 (1993): 65–72, and 'Chemical Structure of Nitrosamines Related to Carcinogenesis,' in *Nitrosamines and Related N-Nitroso Compounds*, Richard N. Loeppky, et al., eds, ACS Symposium Series 553, August 1992 (Washington, DC: American Chemical Society, 1994), Chapter 20.

85. OSHA (22 January 1980) pp. 5028, 5051.

86. Pietro Croce (1992), p. 24.

87. Lester B. Lave, et al. (15 December 1988): 631–3.

88. Frederick J. Murray, quoted in Mike Weilbacher, *E Magazine*, June/July 1995, p. 32.

89. C. F. Wilkinson, 'Being More Realistic About Chemical Carcinogenesis,' *Environ. Sci. Technol.* 21 (1987): 843–7.

90. See note 87.

91. E. McConnell (1989): 1115–20.

92. Joel Brinkley (23 March 1993), p. A16.

93. It should be noted here that while test animals are given direct, concentrated doses of a chemical, many chemical agents that are potential carcinogens undergo

chemical transformation before humans encounter them in varying concentrations; many carcinogens encountered in air and water come from sources far from the point of exposure. For example, smokestack particulates may travel many miles through wind and rain, where they will mix with other chemicals before precipitating onto a surface. This sheds light on the controversial nature of most dose-response studies.

94. Daniel B. Menzel (1987): 948. Inhalation exposure also has inherent problems. To begin with, writes veterinarian Eric Dunayer, 'rodents are obligate nose breathers, have smaller airways, abundant nasal 'turbinates' [scroll-like, spongy bones of the nasal passages] and different lung anatomy. Aerosols may precipitate on the animal's fur and then be ingested during grooming, adding an uncontrolled oral dose. Animals can hide their noses in their fur to filter out noxious vapors ... ,' thus controlling the dose they receive. Montesano et al. (1986), cited in Eric Dunayer (1992), 14.

95. Eric Dunayer (1992), pp. 13–14.

96. Francis J. C. Roe, Letters to the Editor, *Fund. & Appl. Tox.* 16 (1991): 616–18.

97. Excessive food intake in rodents has been linked to increasing incidences of mammary and pituitary tumors and kidney disease in male rats. G. N. Rao and J. Huff, Letters to the Editor, *Fund. & Appl. Tox.* 16 (1991): 617–18.

98. Jeffrey R. Smith, *Science* 202 (1978): 192; Burchfield et al., in *Advances in Modern Toxicology*, Myron A. Mehlman, ed. (Washington, DC: Hemisphere, 1977).

99. Edith Efron (1984), p. 253.

100. J. R. Sabine, 'Susceptibility to Cancer and the Influence of Nutrition,' *Nutr. Cancer* 1, no. 3 (1979): 52–7.

101. Jeffrey M. Masson, *When Elephants Weep: The Emotional Lives of Animals* (New York: Delacorte Press, 1995), p. 54.

102. G. N. Rao and J. Huff (1991).

103. Ibid.

104. Joseph V. Rodricks (1992), p. 18.

105. Ibid., p. 5.

106. Paul J. Lioy, 'Assessing Total Human Exposure to Contaminants,' *Environ. Sci. Technol.* 24, no. 7 (1990): 944.

107. James F. Balch and Phyllis A. Balch, *Prescriptions for Nutritional Healing* (New York: Avery Publishing Group, Inc., 1990), p. 18.

108. Joseph V. Rodricks (1992), p. 26.

109. M. B. Reddy and J. D. Cook (1991).

110. Joseph V. Rodricks (1992), p. 31.

111. L. Goldberg, *The Next 25 Years in Toxicology Safety Evaluation and Regulation of Chemicals* (Basel: Karger, 1982), pp. 193–99.

112. R. T. Williams, 'Species Variations in the Pathways of Drug Metabolism,' *Env. Health Persp.* 133, no. 22 (1978).

113. Björn Ekwall, 'Toxicology Beyond the LD50,' in Conference proceedings, Doctors in Britain Against Animal Experiments, now Doctors and Lawyers for Responsible Medicine (London: April 1991).

114. Neil S. Lipman and Steven L. Seps, 'Alternatives: A Perspective on Progress,' *The AV Magazine* (September/October 1995), p. 16.

115. See note 13.

116. J. R. Sabine, et al., 'Spontaneous Tumors in CH-Avy and CH-Avy B Mice ... ,' *J. Nat. Cancer Inst.* 50 (1973): 1237–42.

117. Anon, 'General Criteria for Assessing the Carcinogenicity of Chemical Substances,' *Journal of the National Cancer Institute* 58 (1977): 462.

118. Neal Barnard and S. Hou, 'Inherent Stress—the Tough Life in Lab Routine,' *Lab Animal* 17 (1988): 21–7.

119. G. Mathé, *Inchiesta Sul Cancro* (Milan, Italy: Rizzoli, ed., 1979), cited in Pietro Croce (1992), p. 407.

120. Gio Batta Gori (18 April 1980): 256–61.

121. Paul Cotton, 'Animals and Science Benefit From "Replace, Reduce, Refine" Effort,' *Journal of the American Medical Association* 270 (22–29 December 1993): 2906.

122. It is well-known that although rodents, who are nocturnal animals, are subjected to artificially bright lights in the laboratory, they prefer dim lighting or darkness much of the time, and cannot tolerate more than 15 minutes of direct sunlight in the wild. See J. L. Kavanau, 'Behavior of Captive White-Footed Mice,' *Science* 155 (31 March 1967): 1623–39.

123. H. A. Gordon and B. S. Wostmann, 'Morphological Studies on the Germfree Albino Rat,' *Anat. Rec.* 137, no. 1 (1960): 65, in Pietro Croce (1992), p. 63.

124. The *lamina propria* is a thin, elastic layer of protein found under the epithelium, or lining, of the intestine.

125. Hypoplasia is a condition in which cells are abnormal or deficient and organs remain immature or subnormal in size; endothelial tissue is a type of tissue composed of a single layer of smooth, thin cells which line the heart, blood vessels, lymphatic and serous cavities; lymphatic pertains to the lymph—a yellowish, coagulable fluid containing white blood cells in a plasma-like liquid which is derived from body tissues and conveyed to the blood stream by lymphatic vessels.

126. H. A. Gordon and B. S. Wostmann (1960): 65.

127. H. A. Gordon, 'The Germfree Animal … ,' *Amer. J. Digest. Dis.* 5 (1960): 841, in Pietro Croce (1992), p. 63.

128. Bruce N. Ames, 'Principles and Methods for Their Detection,' in A. Hollander, ed., *Chemical Mutagens*, Vol. 1 (New York: Plenum Press, 1971), 261–82, in Pietro Croce (1992), p. 63.

129. Urobilins are urinary secretions which give urine its yellow color. B. E. Gustaffson and L. S. Lanke, 'Bilirubin and Urobilins in Germfree, Ex-Germfree and Conventional Rats,' *J. Exp. Med.* 112 (1960): 975, in Pietro Croce (1992), p. 63.

130. A. Desplaces, et al., 'Etude de la Fonction Thyroidienne du Rat Privé de Bacteries (Germfree),' *C.R. Acad. Sci.* 257 (1963): 756–8, in Pietro Croce (1992), p. 63.

131. S. Sell, 'Gamma Globulin Metabolism in Germ-free Guinea Pigs,' *J. Immunol.* 92, no. 4 (1964): 559, in Pietro Croce (1992), p. 63.

132. Christine Bahls, 'Lab Animal Supplier Faulted on Conditions,' *The Philadelphia Inquirer*, February 1995, p. BC1; Mary Beth Sweetland, 'Dirty Dealer,' *The Animals' Agenda* 14, no. 6 (1994): 18–19.

133. Charles River Laboratories, 'A Laboratory Animal Health Monitoring Program: Rationale and Development' (Winter 1990) source: Internet address, http://www.criver.com/techdocs/hmradev.h. as of July 1996.

134. Troy Soos, 'Charles River Breeding Labs,' *The Animals' Agenda* (December 1986): 10.

135. Margaret A. Hellmann, 'Data Validation,' *Environ. Sci. Technol.* 23, no. 6 (1989): 640.

136. Russell E. Keenan, 'Exposure Assessment: Then, Now, and … in the Future,' *Risk Analysis* 14, no. 3 (1994): 227.

137. Paul Cotton (22–29 December 1993): 2905–7.

138. Dennis V. Parke (1995): 293–4; Philip J. Hilts, 'Misconduct in Science is Not Rare, a Survey Finds,' *The New York Times*, 12 November 1993.

139. 'Animals and Alternatives in Toxicology: Present Status and Future Prospects,' The Second Report of the FRAME Toxicity Committee, *ATLA* 19 (1991): 124.

140. Erik Walum, et al., 'Principles for the Validation of In Vitro Toxicology Test Methods,' *Toxic. In Vitro* 8, no. 4 (1994): 807–12.

141. Personal communication with William Stokes, National Institute for Environmental Health Sciences, Research Triangle Park, North Carolina, June 1994.

142. D. Salsburg, 'The Lifetime Feeding Study in Mice and Rats—an Examination of its Validity as a Bioassay for Human Carcinogens,' *Fund. & Appl. Tox.* 3 (1983): 63–7, cited in Eric Dunayer (1992), p. 20.

143. Edith Efron (1984), pp. 328–29.

144. In testimony of former US Senator Paul E. Tsongas before the House Appropriations Subcommittee on Labor, Health and Human Services, Education, and Related Agencies, Washington, DC (19 April 1990), p. 335.

145. Joseph V. Rodricks (1992), pp. 200–1.

146. Edith Efron (1984), p. 383.

147. Personal communication with Franklin Loew, Dean, Cornell University School of Veterinary Medicine, Ithaca, New York, 25 September 1995.

148. Myra Sklarew, 'Toxicity Tests in Animals: Alternative Models,' *Env. Health Persp.* 101, no. 4 (September 1993): 288.

149. D. Salsburg (1983): 63–7.

150. R. Heywood, 'Clinical Toxicity—Could it Have Been Predicted? Postmarket Experience,' in *Animal Toxicity Studies: Their Relevance for Man*, C. E. Lumley, S. R. Walker, eds (London: Lancaster Quay Publishing, 1989). See also J. T. Litchfield Jr., *Clinical Pharmacology & Therapeutics* 3 (1962): 665–72; F. I. McMahon, *Medical World News* 6 (1965): 168.

151. A. P. Fletcher, *Journal of the Royal Society of Medicine* 71 (1978): 693–8.

152. Lois S. Gold, et al. (1989): 211–19, cited in Eric Dunayer (1992), p. 16.

153. F. J. Di Carlo, 'Carcinogenesis Bioassay Data: Correlation by Species and Sex,' *Drug Metab. Rev.* 15 (1984): 409–13.

154. Edith Efron (1984), p. 381.

155. Ibid., p. 329. For a complete discussion of this topic, see Chapter 11 of Efron's book, 'The Case of the Missing Predictions.'

156. E. Walum, et al. (1994): 807–12.

157. R. J. Fielder, 'Acceptance of In Vitro Studies by Regulatory Authorities,' *Toxicology In Vitro* 8, No. 4 (1993): 911–16.

158. See note 139: pp. 116–38.

159. J. M. Frazier, 'Scientific Criteria for Validation of In Vitro Toxicity Tests,' *OECD Environment Monographs*, no. 36 (1990): 1–66.

160. Personal communication with Ethel Thurston, AFAAR, New York City, 8 July 1996.

161. In 1987, Michael Balls and Richard Clothier defined intra-laboratory validation as the period during which the method is developed, its mechanistic basis established, and its strengths and limitations are determined. M. Balls and R. Clothier, 'Validation of Alternative Toxicity Test Systems: Lessons Learned and to be Learned,' *Molecular Toxicology* 1 (1987): 547–59.

162. In 1987, Balls, et al. defined this as the period when the scientific quality of the new test protocol is determined.

163. In 1987, Balls, et al. said that extra-laboratory validation was fulfilled when the new test competes with other methods for usefulness in providing data relevant to real-world problems.

164. FRAME Toxicity Committee (1991): 116–38. In 1987, Balls, et al. discussed the need for regulatory validation, the process by which an alternative test becomes accepted by regulatory agencies. In 1993, Goldberg et al. of the Johns Hopkins Center for Alternatives to Animal Testing (CAAT), Sub-committee on Validation and Technology Transfer, presented yet another framework for validation. A. M. Goldberg, et al., 'Framework for Validation ... ,' *Journal of the American College of Toxicology* 12 (1993): 23–30.

165. K. Lovekari, 'In Vitro Toxicology and the Test Guidelines,' *ATLA* 24 (1996): 435–8

166. John H. Weisburger and Gary M. Williams, 'Carcinogen Testing: Current Problems and New Approaches,' *Science* 214 (23 October 1981): 401.

167. Lavinia Pioda, 'The Position of the Authorities,' in *Alternatives to Animal Testing*, Christoph A. Reinhardt, ed. (New York: VCH/Weinheim, 1994), p. 176.

168. Personal communication with Pam Logemann, ATS, La Jolla, California, 14 August 1996; B. Ekwall, *AATEX* 1 (1992): 127–41.

169. 'Validation and Regulatory Acceptance of Toxicological Test Methods,' a report of the *ad hoc* Interagency Coordinating Committee on the Validation of Alternative Methods (Draft) (North Carolina: NIEHS, 16 October 1995).

170. J. C. Petricciani, I. Levenbrook and R. Locke, *Investigational New Drugs* 1 (1983): 297–302; R. Jover, et al., *Toxicology In Vitro* 6 (1992): 47–52; G. M. Hawksworth, *Human & Experimental Toxicology* 13 (1994): 568–73.

171. Horst Spielmann, et al., 'ZEBET: Three Years of the National German Center for Documentation and Evaluation of Alternatives to Animal Experiments at the Federal Health Office (BGA) in Berlin,' in Christoph A. Reinhardt, ed. (1994), p. 84.

172. Christoph A. Reinhardt, 'The SIAT Research, Testing and Consulting Program in the Area of In Vitro Toxicology ... ,' in Christoph A. Reinhardt, ed. (1994), p. 92.

173. See Chapter 5.

174. H. F. Stich and R. H. C. San, eds, *Short-Term Tests for Chemical Carcinogens* (New York: Springer-Verlag, 1981).

175. See *Mutagenesis* 4 (1989) for several examples.

176. N. R. Farnsworth and J. M. Pezzuto, paper presented at University of Panama workshop sponsored by the International Foundation for Science, 1982. Reproduced in the British *Lord Dowding Fund Bulletin* 21 (1984): 26–34.

177. Stephen R. Kaufman, 'Scientific Problems With Animal Models,' *Perspectives in Medical Research* 4 (1993), Medical Research Modernization Committee, New York City.

178. See J. Morrison, et al., 'The Purpose and Value of LD50 Determinations,' in *Modern Trends in Toxicology, Volume 1*, E. Boyland and R. Goulding, eds (UK: Butterworth, 1968), pp. 1–17. See G. Zbinden and M. Flury-Roversi (1981).

179. David P. Rall quoted in S. R. Kaufman and M. J. Cohen, 'The Clinical Relevance of the LD50,' *Veterinary and Human Toxicology* 29, no. 1 (February 1987): 39–41.

180. Pietro Croce (1992), pp. 109–10.

181. Edward J. Calabrese (1987): 622.

182. Edith Efron (1984), p. 248.

183. John F. Ross, 'Risk: Where Do Real Dangers Lie?,' *The Smithsonian*, November 1995, pp. 42–53.

184. D. B. Clayson, et al. (1983): 329–48, cited in Eric Dunayer (1992), p. 22.

185. J. K. Haseman, 'Issues in Carcinogenicity Testing: Dose Selection,' *Fund. &*
Appl. Tox. 5 (1985): 66–78.

186. See Gio Batta Gori, *Science* 209 (18 April 1980): 256–61, for a list of references.

187. Edith Efron (1984), p. 248.

188. Joel Brinkley (23 March 1993), p. A1.

189. *Federal Register* (17 July 1992) Vol. 57, No. 138, p. 31723.

190. F. E. Freeberg, et al., *Fund. & Appl. Tox.* 7 (1986): 626–34. See Internet address,
http://www.envirolink.arrs/avar/testing, Ned Buyukmihci, 'Safety Testing of Products for Human Use ... ' (as of June 1996) for references of numerous scientific
papers which challenge the value of animal testing.

191. Heidi J. Welsh (1990), p. 71.

192. C. S. Weil and R. A. Scala, *Toxicology and Applied Pharmacology* 19 (1971): 276–
360.

193. R. B. Kemp, et al., *Cytobios* 36 (1983): 153–9.

194. D. W. Swanston, 'Assessment of the Validity of Animal Techniques in Eye
Irritation Testing,' *Food Chem. Toxicol.* 23 (1985): 169–73. In *The Cruel Deception*
(Northamptonshire, UK: Thorsons, 1988), pp. 101–4, Robert Sharpe documents several cases in which data from rabbits have proved misleading for humans. Primates
are considered to be more relevant but expense, availability and temperament have
precluded their use in eye irritation tests. Rats have also been excluded because they
are not sufficiently docile. Edward J. Calabrese, *Principles of Animal Extrapolation* (New
York: John Wiley & Sons, 1983).

195. *OECD Guidelines for Testing of Chemicals*, Vol. 2 (1987), Guideline 405 (Paris:
Organization for Economic Cooperation and Development, 1981), p. 8.

196. The theory that cancer is caused by low doses of mutagens has been supported
by John C. Bailar, formerly of the NCI, Bruce Ames, and F. W. Sunderman of the
IARC among others. C. Waldren (1986), A. Seifert (1987), and K. Messing (1989)
have all performed epidemiological studies and *in vitro* studies with human chromosomes which confirm this theory.

197. Personal communication with Irwin Bross, Eggertsville, New York, 24 October
1995.

198. Masson notes that the deep fears experienced by animals in laboratories have
never been the object of study, possibly because 'the ethical dilemma created by
causing such fear is too transparent to be acknowledged by the scientific community.'
Jeffrey M. Masson, *When Elephants Weep: The Emotional Lives of Animals* (New York:
Delacorte, 1995), p. 57.

199. See Curtis D. Klaassen and David L. Eaton, 'Principles of Toxicology,' in
Casarett and Doull's *Toxicology: The Basic Science of Poisons*, 4th Edition (Tarrytown,
NY: Pergamon Press, 1991), pp. 12–49.

200. Jeffrey M. Masson (1995), p. 28; personal communication with Murry Cohen,
a practicing psychiatrist in Annandale, Virginia, 14 December 1995. Cohen stressed
that because human beings are the species by which all other living creatures are
measured, the subject of animal intelligence has never been deemed worthy of
exploration by neuroscientists and cognitive psychologists. Masson's book may help
to change that.

201. Susan Fox, *Rats* (New Jersey: TFH Publications, 1988).

202. Jeffrey M. Masson (1995), pp. 69, 75. Rats are also an important part of the
ecosystem, forming links in the food webs of many communities, and eating a variety
of insects, thereby keeping insect populations under control. Moreover, rats deposit
seeds in the ground when they forage and defecate, providing plant cover for the
earth. Susan Fox (1988).

203. Jeffrey M. Masson (1995), p. 71.

204. Ibid., pp. 86–96.

205. Carol Beckwith and Angela Fisher, 'The African Roots of Voodoo,' *National Geographic* (August 1995), p. 109.

206. Leonard Rack and Henry Spira, 'Animal Rights and Modern Toxicology,' *Tox. Ind. Health* 5, no. 1 (1989): 133–43.

207. M. Van den Heuvel, *Human and Experimental Toxicology* 9 (1990): 369–70; Heidi J. Welsh (1990), p. 67. In Japan, some 2,900 animals (dogs, rabbits, rodents) are killed to test a new chemical. *The AV Magazine* (Winter 1997), p. 5.

208. Tom Regan, *Animal Sacrifices* (Philadelphia: Temple University Press, 1986), p. 22.

209. Consumer Product Safety Commission, Animal Testing Policy, *Federal Register* (30 May 1984) Vol. 49, No. 105, p. 22523.

210. Andrew Rowan, et al., *The Animal Research Controversy* (Massachusetts: Center for Animals & Public Policy, Tufts University School of Veterinary Medicine, 1995), p. 76.

211. Ibid., p. 21.

212. L. F. M. Von Zutphen, 'Animal Use and Alternatives: Developments in The Netherlands,' in Christoph A. Reinhardt, ed. (1994), p. 58.

213. Michael D. Metzler, 'Viewpoint: Animals in Research,' *Journal of the American Medical Association* 261 (1989): 785.

214. See notes 13–16.

215. Paul Cotton (22–29 December 1993): 2905–7. This point of view was echoed by Alan Goldberg and John Frazier in an August 1989 article in *Scientific American*.

216. Joel Brinkley (23 March 1993), p. A1.

217. Richard B. Kurzel (June 1981): 632.

218. Richard Stone, 'Study Implicates Second-Hand Smoke,' *Science* 264 (1 April 1994): 30.

219. P. DeLore and C. Borgomono, 'Acute Leukemia Following Benzene Poisoning,' *Journal de Médecin de Lyon* 9 (1928): 227–36.

220. D. M. De Marini, et al., in *Benchmarks: Alternative Methods in Toxicology*, Myron A. Mehlman, ed. (Princeton, NJ: Princeton Scientific Publishing 1989).

221. Leslie Lang, 'Strange Brew,' *Env. Health Persp.* 103, no. 2 (February 1995): 144.

222. David Riggle, 'Amory Lovins: From Megawatts to Hypercars,' *In Business*, March/April 1995: 18–23. See pages 8 and 16 for articles about benzene-free vehicles. In the summer of 1993, Cincinnati started to run part of its bus fleet on soydiesel, a fuel made from soybeans. The 1990 Clean Air Act Amendments, and the 1992 Comprehensive Energy Policy Act—which mandates that government fleets purchase alternative fuels—will hopefully spark more developments like these. Dianne Molvig, 'Taking the Soybean Bus,' *E Magazine*, September/October 1995, p. 16.

223. Mike Weilbacher, 'Toxic Shock: The Environment–Cancer Connection,' *E Magazine*, June/July 1995, p. 30; Cable News Network, 7 November 1995.

224. Andrée Collard, *Rape of the Wild* (Indiana: Indiana University Press, 1989), p. 73. See pp. 71–5 for Collard's feminist theory about the social and cultural significance of such unethical practices.

225. Troy Soos (December 1986), pp. 8–9.

226. Hans Ruesch, *Slaughter of the Innocent* (New York: Bantam Books, 1976 and Switzerland: Civitas Publications, 1986), p. 295. Added to this concern is the discovery that cruelty to animals is indicative of an incipient antisocial character disorder. Because cruelty to animals typically precedes cruelty to people, it has been elevated

in clinical significance to equality with the latter in the *Psychiatric Diagnostic and Statistical Manual* of 1994. Sigmund Freud initially corroborated these associations in 1905, which are cited in an extensive study on the subject by Ascione (1993). Alan R. Felthous, MD and Stephen R. Kellert, PhD, 'Violence Against Animals and People: Is Aggression Against Living Creatures Generalized?,' *Bull. Amer. Acad. Psych. & Law* 14, no. 1 (1986); Frank R. Ascione, 'Children Who are Cruel to Animals: A Review of Research and Implications for Developmental Psychopathology,' *Anthrozoos* 6, no. 4 (1993) and references therein; see also the work of Randall Lockwood, of the Humane Society of the United States, Washington, DC.

227. Carol Adams, *Neither Man Nor Beast* (New York: Continuum, 1994), pp. 52–3.

228. Robert Sharpe, *Consenting Guinea Pigs: The Human Participants Who Advance Medicine*, published by the American Anti-Vivisection Society, Jenkintown, Pennsylvania (1993).

229. See: Associated Press, 'Parents Fear Babies Killed for Organs,' *Vancouver Sun*, 12 June 1995. Andrew Kimbrell, director of the International Center for Technology Assessment in Washington, DC, lends credence to these ideas in his book *The Human Body Shop: The Engineering and Marketing of Life* (San Francisco: Harper San Francisco, 1994). In it, he uncovers information about the marketing of the *human* body, including the sale of blood, organs, and fetal tissue; the merchandising of human fertility; and the engineering and manipulation of genes, viruses, and microbes.

230. Public Citizen Health Research Group, 'Medical Research Guinea Pig or True Volunteer,' *Health Letter* (Washington, DC), Vol. 6, no. 11 (November 1990): 1.

231. See Philip J. Hilts, 'Mixed-Species Organ is Set for Transplant,' *The New York Times*, 28 July 1995, p. A10; 'FDA Panel Backs New Breast Cancer Drug,' *The New York Times*, 19 October 1995, p. A19. Taxotere was approved to treat dying breast cancer patients 'despite its high incidence of dangerous side effects.'

232. George Bernard Shaw, *The Doctor's Dilemma* (New York: Viking Penguin, 1950 and Garland, 1981).

233. Office of Technology Assessment, *Researching Health Risks* (Washington, DC: US Government Printing Office, November 1993).

234. Leslie Lang, 'Mouse or Molecule?,' *Env. Health Persp.* 103, no. 4 (April 1995): 334–6.

235. *US Chemical Industry Statistical Handbook* (Washington, DC: Chemical Manufacturers Association, 1994), p. 113.

236. Eric Dunayer (1992), 6; Joel Brinkley (23 March 1993), p. A16.

237. Edith Efron (1984), pp. 255–6.

238. Dennis V. Parke (1995), p. 293.

239. Leslie Lang (April 1995): 334.

240. Eric Dunayer (1992), p. 8.

241. Thomas H. Maugh, 'Chemical Carcinogens: The Scientific Basis for Regulation,' *Science* 201 (1978): 1202.

242. The National Research Council only has toxicity data for 2 percent of the chemicals used in commerce, according to Mike Weilbacher, *E Magazine* (June/July 1995), p. 30; according to Richard Griesemer of the NIEHS, about 1,000–1,200 chemicals have been 'adequately tested on animals for carcinogenicity.' Bill Breen, 'Why We Need Animal Testing,' *Garbage* (April/May 1993), p. 42.

243. Leslie Lang (April 1995): 334.

244. Lester B. Lave, et al. (15 December 1988): 631–3.

245. Jan Ziegler, 'Health Risk Assessment Research: The OTA Report,' *Env. Health Persp.* 101, no. 5 (October 1993): 404.

246. Peter Barton Hutt, 'Public Policy Issues in Regulating Carcinogens,' *Food Drug Cosmetic Law Journal* 33, no. 10 (1978): 548–9. According to a Cable News Network (CNN) report on 28 August 1995, almost every apple tested by the US Department of Agriculture in 1993 had traces of pesticides; celery and peaches followed. Chlorine, which is used as a water purification agent, is an animal carcinogen; yet the risks associated with drinking untreated water were deemed to outweigh the risks of suspending chlorination, and so, in 1979, the FDA relinquished any claim to jurisdiction over the materials used to treat drinking water. FDA and EPA, 'Drinking Water Technical Assistance: Implementation Plan for Control of Direct and Indirect Additives to Drinking Water ... ,' *Federal Register* (1979), Vol. 44, p. 42775.

247. Cancer Prevention Coalition, 'Hidden Hazards: Cancer Risks in the Home,' press release, 22 September 1995, Chicago, Illinois, courtesy of Keith Ashdown, Director of Communications.

248. Toby L. Litovitz, et al., *1994 Annual Report of the American Association of Poison Control Centers Toxic Exposure Surveillance System* (Washington, DC: AAPCC, 1994), pp. 551–3. It is probable that, when combined with OSHA and EPA statistics on occupational exposures, and proprietary information from hospital, insurance company, and industry databases, national poisoning figures could be much higher. In 1994, 2.3 million human poison exposures are estimated to have been reported to all US poison centers, an increase of 10 percent compared with 1993 reports. AAPCC adjusted that figure to 4.5 million to account for under-reporting.

249. Eric Chivian, et al., eds, *Critical Condition: Human Health and the Environment* (Cambridge, MA: The MIT Press, 1993), pp. 9–10.

250. Sandra Postel, 'Controlling Toxic Substances,' in Lester R. Brown, et al., *State of the World 1988: A Worldwatch Report ...* (New York: W. W. Norton & Co., 1988), p. 119.

251. Anon, 'Pestifornia Here I Come,' *Earth Island Journal* Winter (Southern Hemisphere) 1996, published by Earth Island Institute, San Francisco, p. 13.

252. John H. Cushman Jr., 'EPA Plans Radical Change in Calculation of Cancer Risk,' *The New York Times*, 16 April 1996, p. A1.

253. Irwin Bross, 'How Animal Research Can Kill You,' *The AV Magazine*, published by The American Anti-Vivisection Society (November 1983), pp. 5–7.

254. *Federal Register* (22 January 1980) Vol. 45, No. 15, p. 5037.

255. Philip J. Hilts, 'Researchers Say Chemicals May Have Led to War Illness,' *The New York Times*, 17 April 1996, p. A17; Philip Shenon, 'Gulf War Illness May be Linked to Gas Exposure, Pentagon Says,' *The New York Times*, 22 June 1996, p. A1; 'Update—Gulf War Mystery,' *The Newshour* with Jim Lehrer, Public Broadcasting Service (PBS), 24 May 1996, transcript. Because human nervous system syndromes develop slowly and their detection is dependent on the clinical examinations used, and because the veterans were exposed to chemicals similar to ones used in civilian life, like the pesticide malathion, government officials may be hoping that causal links will become murkier with time.

256. Anon, 'Coulston Product Implicated in Gulf War Syndrome,' *The IDA Magazine*, published by In Defense of Animals, Mill Valley, California, p. 11.

257. L. Ekman, et al., *Lancet* (17 February 1990): 419–20.

4. Human health at risk

'it is more profitable to continue cancer research and violate more lives—animals, plants, and humans—than to eliminate the major carcinogenic materials that pour out from the vast industrial complex considered *vital* to a *healthy* economy.' Andrée Collard, *Rape of the Wild* (Indiana: Indiana University Press, 1989), p. 82

'I have to say we don't serve the American people very well right now. But that's where we are.' Kenneth Olden, Director, National Institute of Environmental Health Sciences, quoted in *The New York Times*, 23 March 1993, p. A16.

'it is probably true that this major [carcinogen bioassay] program by NCI and now NTP has done very little to account for the majority of human cancers.' John H. Weisburger, *Fundamental & Applied Toxicology* 22, no. 4 (May 1994): 485

Despite the admitted inadequacies of animal test data, and evidence of poor correlations between animals and humans, federal regulators and scientific advisory committees defend the animal tests and the policies that emanate from them. The claims for their necessity persist primarily because, the toxicologists argue, it would be unethical to experiment on humans and because, they say, there are no other acceptable options.

But even after decades of animal tests, humans and wildlife continue to be exposed to an ever-expanding arsenal of synthetic chemicals in their air, water and food, with unknown consequences. As early as 1933, Arthur Kallet (then of Consumers Union) and F. J. Schlink (of the US Bureau of Standards) wrote a book entitled *One Hundred Thousand Guinea Pigs: Dangers in Everyday Foods, Drugs and Cosmetics* (Vanguard, 1933), in which they expressed deep concern about the potential cancer-causing substances consumed by humans in foods, medicines, cosmetics, insecticides and so on. In his book, *A Nation of Guinea Pigs* (1979), the lawyer Marshall Shapo wrote that 'commercialization can be viewed as a form of experiment—one that entails more varied and often prolonged exposures than can be replicated in any laboratory setting.' Indeed, according to David Sarokin, Director of Special Projects in the Environmental Assistance Division of the US EPA, of the circa 75,000 chemicals now on the market, *o percent* of them have been banned.[1] A much larger number are regulated, though Jim Bradshaw of the EPA's Information Management Division conceded that fragmented regulatory programs make it virtually impossible to determine an exact figure.[2]

Although many scientists and regulators would claim that animal tests have been useful in establishing safety standards for environmental pollutants, I will show that the standards are not protective and enforcement is severely deficient; moreover, the complex and political nature of federal regulations makes the *prevention* of chemical releases virtually impossible. Both state and federal environmental agencies allow polluters to release toxic chemicals into the environment. Current federal guidelines for the testing of chemicals do not sanction non-animal testing regimes which could speed up testing and remove offending chemicals from the market much more quickly. Comprehensive legislative revisions could do much to improve this state of affairs; but efforts to reform the system have been hindered, as I will explain below and in subsequent chapters.

Only in very rare cases have results from animal tests been heeded and offending chemicals removed from the US market, as in the cases of the artificial Red Dye 2 and the pesticide DDT. However, decisions to ban such products have been based more on conjecture than fact, due to the array of conflicting studies and lack of confirmatory human data.[3] Debates over the significance of animal test results have often delayed regulatory action for years.

Countless drugs and consumer products deemed to be toxic and/or carcinogenic in animal tests remain in common use (both in the US and abroad). These include DDT (sprayed on bananas in Ecuador and exported back to the US) and the artificial sweetener saccharin (both of which experts now say are not as harmful as once believed),[4] the preservative nitrite, and the teratogen thalidomide,[5] to name just a few. One study found that countries continue to accept—and the US continues to produce and export—pesticides that were banned or severely restricted (or never registered) in the US and the country of destination. Current law allows American manufacturers to do this. Once shipments arrive, the chemicals can be purchased openly and easily.[6] This indicates that even when governments take the decisive step of banning a hazardous product, it cannot be assumed that the product will no longer be used or imported. Whether this is due to inadequate surveillance or outright disregard of local environmental policies means nothing to the people, animals and ecosystems that suffer the consequences of exposure.

Chemicals are frequently left on the market even when there is direct evidence that they are harmful to *humans*. Captan, a fungicide with a molecular structure akin to thalidomide, is still sprayed on cherries, apples, cantaloupes, pears, eggplants, lettuce, corn, wheat and potatoes, despite the fact that it has caused birth defects in humans.[7] (In 1990, more than 70 percent of fungicide applications in America were aerially applied.)[8] Chlordane, a chlorinated hydrocarbon insecticide, was introduced in 1948; it was eventually tested in animals and dubbed a probable human carcinogen in 1977, almost 30 years after it had been introduced. In 1982, the National Research Council characterized chlordane as a hazard at any dose. In 1986 the EPA reported that chlordane was the most frequently misused or misapplied termiticide. Although Velsicol, the manufacturer, stopped selling chlordane for consumer use in the United States in 1987 (after it had been used in and around over 30 million homes), the company was still licensed to export it. Then, in 1988, EPA shockingly allowed chlordane to be applied at 150 residences across the US (at unknown concentrations in many cases), and decided that air monitoring would be done for two years to detect whether there were levels in the air. A 1994 study of people exposed to the chemical in Houston, Texas in 1987 and 1988 revealed prolonged impairment of neurophysiological and psychological functions. The authors of the study advocated prohibiting human exposure to chlordane.[9]

In an attempt to deal with these problems, environmental and animal advocacy groups have campaigned to replace industrial carcinogens with non-toxic alternatives, and replace animal tests with more credible technologies. Once the failings of the current animal-based testing system are exposed, the implementation of such goals will be seen as socially desirable. In this chapter, I shall focus on specific cases which illustrate those failings.

Criticism of the risk assessment process

'In general, whether the regulatory procedures have protected the public health cannot be proved because none of the studies commonly employed can with certainty predict the nature of the human response or the degree of human sensitivity, and no attempts have been made to assess the efficacy of regulatory control on human disease patterns.' D. M. Conning and K. R. Butterworth, in *The Future of Predictive Safety Evaluation*, A. Worden, et al., eds (Boston, MA: MTP Press, 1986), p. 102

'The system for measuring risks and benefits is itself subject to enormous political manipulation. And devising precise human "tolerances" to chemicals is, at

best, an inexact science.' Editorial, 'Truth, Justice, and the Delaney Clause,'
The Amicus Journal, published by the Natural Resources Defense Council, New
York City (Fall 1992): 6

'[Risk assessment is] basically a fraud ... the goal of which is to obtain per-
mission to kill people and destroy the environment.' Peter Montague quoted in
Safe Food News, published by Food and Water, Marshfield, Vermont (Spring 1993),
p. 12

George Lucier (director of the Environmental Toxicology Program at
the NIEHS) says that, due to the lack of good human data, regulatory
agencies are often forced to make decisions on the safety of chemicals
based on inadequate information. Federal agencies routinely draft air
and water quality standards for the entire population using data from
risk assessments that are fraught with unverified assumptions, including
the notion that humans and non-humans react similarly to chemicals;
that age, sex, or genetics do not influence individuals' biological sensitivities; and that the effects of one chemical are independent of the
effects of others.[10]

In spite of the fact that we are exposed to a cacophony of chemical
mixtures, risk assessment research has typically focused on the effects
of specific chemicals (tested on animals in the artificial laboratory
environment). In fact, the vast majority of established exposure standards are for single compounds and, currently, more than 95 percent of
the resources in toxicology are devoted to single-chemical studies. Such
a fragmented analysis weakens our ability to grasp the true nature of
the problem of chemical overload and to act upon it intelligently. In
the same vein Frederick Kutz, a toxicologist at the US EPA, says that
'the traditional narrow focus on specific pollutants and acute environmental effects has resulted in neglect of growing systemic problems
[which inevitably impact our health], such as stratospheric ozone depletion, ... wetlands loss,' and air pollution.[11] A US Commission on Risk
Assessment and Risk Management now says that risk assessments should
consider the larger spectrum of preexisting chemical pollution and its
impact on human health.[12] Yet some toxicologists believe that the
addition of 'mixtures research' to the risk assessment process would
add a layer of complexity to an already uncertain enterprise;[13] the
nature of most chemical interactions in humans and animals remains a
mystery. Al Meyerhoff, a lawyer with the Natural Resources Defense
Council, stated that 'we still do not know whether humans are more or
less sensitive than laboratory animals to carcinogens and whether one
carcinogen may increase the cancer-causing effects of another.'[14]

With the excuse that the addition of safety factors in animal-to-human extrapolations has led to the establishment of very conservative exposure standards for carcinogens, humans have been allowed to ingest and bioaccumulate 'safe doses' of countless animal carcinogens. As early as 1960, conservation biologist Rachel Carson charged that the establishment of 'safe doses' of chemicals in our food, air and water would guarantee the slow poisoning of humans and all life on earth, since the piling up of 'safe doses' of chemicals from many different sources creates a total exposure that cannot be measured.

Toxicologists claim that if, for every chemical, we knew the point at which toxicity begins to appear, we could then act to prevent exposures from ever reaching toxic doses. But most environmental agents cause a range of symptoms and, as author Edith Efron writes, 'there is no way on earth, now or ever, of identifying, in advance, a safe dose of a carcinogen that will hold for the entire population, or for a random slice of a population, or in fact, for anybody at all.'[15] Even The National Cancer Institute (NCI) concurs on this point. In a pamphlet about the role of animal testing in carcinogen identification published in March 1990, the NCI states that, 'there is no adequate evidence that there is a safe level of exposure for any carcinogen ... In addition, a low exposure that might be safe for one person might cause cancer in another.'

According to Anthony Cortese, an environmental consultant and former Commissioner of the Massachusetts Department of Environmental Protection, many risk assessors have not been adequately grounded in human disease biology and toxicology,[16] and hence may not understand the consequences of the recommendations they make. And because chemically induced cancers may have a latency period of up to forty years, we may realize in the next century that Rachel Carson was right: that current environmental standards are indeed inadequate, and that more drastic measures are, and were, needed to protect human health.

Currently, enforcement of anti-pollution measures by the EPA is weak; since 1980, the US General Accounting Office has published 22 reports examining the weakness of federal pesticide control programs.[17] EPA statistics, cited in *E Magazine* (June/July 1995), reveal that 13 pesticides identified as contaminants in 1972 are still in use; the number of cases of non-compliance with pesticide regulations in 1993 was 633, and only 42 fines were assessed for those cases. Furthermore, whether and how regulators (and corporations) act upon the data generated by risk assessments today is unclear. After identifying more than a hundred dangerous chemicals in the New Orleans municipal water supply under the Safe Drinking Water Act of 1974, regulators had set acceptable exposure standards for only nine of those chemicals fifteen years later.

Experiences with the Toxic Substances Control Act and the Clean Air Act have been similar.[18]

Tests of drinking water sampled in people's homes by the Environmental Working Group (EWG)—a non-profit organization in Washington, DC—between 15 May and 2 July 1995, found as many as nine different herbicides or herbicide by-products in the *treated* tap water of major midwestern cities. The weed killers found most often were atrazine (used on corn and sorghum) and cyanazine (used on field corn, sweet corn and cotton). According to studies conducted by the makers of the weed killers and submitted to the EPA, animal tests with the chemicals produced cancer as well as disruption of the endocrine system, reproductive failure, sexual dysfunction and birth defects.[19] EWG estimated that 18,000 human infants 'drank infant formula reconstituted with tap water contaminated with at least one weed killer at an average concentration that exceeded federal standards for the entire six week study period.'[20]

The means to enforce compliance with federal exposure standards (ADIs, PELs, MCLs, etc.) are lacking. In 1995, as a result of Republican-led budget cuts, the EPA was forced to cancel hundreds of pollution inspections at factories, water treatment plants and other sites nationwide—evidence that efforts to enforce environmental laws can often be subject to political phenomena;[21] and there have never been any follow-up/validation studies to determine the efficacy of federal risk assessment/management programs, in terms of whether they actually serve to protect human health.[22] In addition, these programs are being carried out as state and federal environmental agencies are giving polluters the license to release toxic contaminants into our air and waterways.[23] How, then, can the success or failure of federal risk assessment/management programs ever be gauged?

On occasions when regulatory agencies have had the opportunity to protect humans from carcinogens in advance, through legislation which prevented their use or release, the goals of the legislation have been relaxed—based on considerations of cost and technical feasibility.

Getting away with murder

Richard Peto writes that even when use of a chemical has proven dangerous to humans, 'industrial consortia may actively lobby for controls so weak that they leave no reasonable safety margin.'[24] In the case of benzene—a known human carcinogen, and primary component of gasoline and kerosene—the economic consequences of doing without gasoline, or finding viable non-polluting alternatives to it, are weighed against the risk of getting cancer from exposure to it which are as high as one in one thousand (1×10^{-3}) according to EPA figures.[25] Some 11.67 billion pounds of benzene entered commerce in 1989, enough to give every US citizen leukemia given long enough exposure.[26] As noted in Chapter 3, ongoing animal experiments with benzene and its by-products have not prevented the release of this human carcinogen into the environment. Marc Lappé (1991) writes that '[although the EPA] has identified twelve major industry groups or activities that are responsible for most benzene emissions,' it has been slow in regulating those industries.[27] In a 1989 report, the EPA admitted that motor vehicle particulates account for more than 76 percent of benzene emissions; yet in New York City for example, which has been in violation of federal Clean Air Act standards for over a decade, air quality is declining and federal officials projected an 11 percent increase in urban area diesel pollution between 1985 and 1995.[28] William Pease, professor in the School of Public Health at the University of California, Berkeley stated:

> if you look at the regulation of hazardous air pollutants under the Clean Air Act, we're talking about known human carcinogens like benzene taking as long as ten years to develop control rules for major sources ... In the meantime, people are being exposed. This isn't even treating them like guinea pigs; this is exposing them to a known human leukemogen.[29]

Another striking example is that of the Delaney Clause, which was enacted in 1958 to bar carcinogenic additives from entering the food supply, and was recently repealed by the US Congress. Experts claimed that the Clause was 'scientifically unsupportable.' The FDA, which enforced the Delaney Clause, took the position that while the clause applied to processed foods (where a pesticide is added to a crop after harvesting), it did not apply to fresh produce—a paradox; however, in a 1994 pesticide exposé, Mary H. Cooper wrote that because it is impossible to determine which fruits and vegetables end up in a can and which in the fresh produce section, regulators permitted pesticide residues on both types of food as long as the residues posed a 'negligible' cancer risk.[30] In addition, certain classes of food ingredients not covered by the Clause were permitted; regulations legally allowed for 40 pesticides in carrots, 67 in strawberries, and 82 in grapes.[31]

Similarly, the new law which replaces the Delaney Clause will allow pesticides and additives on both fresh and processed food if there is a 'reasonable certainty of no harm' from exposure to the chemicals. The legislation's standards could be relaxed further, if necessary, 'to maintain a steady food supply.' Ironically, though stripped of its original rigorous standards of 'zero risk' for carcinogens, the law *adds* a new regulatory burden which requires the EPA to screen for chemicals that could cause reproductive harm (presumably in animals).[32] But currently, although the FDA is supposed to test samples of food to ensure that pesticide residues are not detected which are above EPA's established 'safe tolerance levels,' FDA chemists allegedly fail to report 43 percent of all the violations they find.[33] It is unclear how the new law will resolve existing shortcomings related to enforcement.

In May 1989, the Natural Resources Defense Council joined several others in filing a lawsuit in the US District Court in Sacramento, California, requiring the EPA to strictly enforce the provisions of the Delaney Clause. In 1992 the Supreme Court ruled that the EPA had been violating the law by allowing trace amounts of pesticides in food it believed were safe (based on animal tests). Ironically, in February 1993, the EPA released a list of 35 pesticides that it said would be banned or restricted because tests on animals produced cancers at the Maximum Tolerated Dose.[34] This demonstrates that animal tests, which provide such varied results depending on the dose given and species used, can be used to justify politically convenient regulatory decisions that may have little or no scientific basis; and the EPA's repentant gestures are too little, too late.

Statistics show that the United States' pollution prevention goals are not being met. From 1983 to 1993, the US chemical industry expanded its output by 35 percent.[35] Today, pesticides are produced at a feverish pace compared to that of 40 years ago, and EPA has done little to curtail their overall use;[36] seven hundred and fifty million (750,000,000) pounds of some twenty thousand (20,000) different pesticides are poured over the American landscape annually. EPA itself estimates that 84 percent of US households use pesticides. Bizarrely, while some pesticides like diazinon are banned for use on golf courses and certain crops, their use in households is unregulated.[37] (Though still high, European figures pale in comparison: about 600 different pesticides, herbicides and fungicides are used in agricultural, forestry and horticultural sectors in Europe.)[38] One hundred and seventy five million (175,000,000) pounds of toxic insecticides, and seventy five million (75,000,000) pounds of fungicides, were applied to US food crops in 1991.[39] The EPA, which routinely monitors drinking, surface and ground water, recently detected 78 different pesticides in the water wells of 38 states; in the mid-West, 44 streams were found to contain contaminants in excess of the EPA's proposed drinking water standards.[40] Yet, as of July 1996, of the USDA's 111,414 employees,[41] only three have been assigned to the development of organic agriculture—an area of development which could eliminate or greatly reduce the need for synthetic pesticides and herbicides.[42]

Even though polychlorinated biphenyls (PCBs), deemed carcinogens in animal tests,[43] were banned in the early 1980s, every man's semen currently co-mingles with 35 different kinds of PCBs, ethers and phenols, and every woman's breast milk contains a brew of pesticides like chlordane, dieldrin, lindane and mirex, mixed with some 65 isomers of PCBs and dioxins—all proven animal carcinogens.[44] According to Greenpeace, 177 synthetic chlorine-based chemicals have been identified in the tissues and fluids of the American public.[45] Many of these toxins may be stored in fatty tissues for decades. Contrary to animal testing proponents' claims, animal tests cannot predict which of these components may cause toxicity to humans, particularly at low levels, and especially if exposures occurred during childhood or *in utero*. There is evidence that children who were exposed to dioxins and PCBs in the womb now have impaired memory and attention deficits.[46]

The environment has already given us clear signs of toxic overload.[47] Animal tests have not prevented the release of toxic chemicals into the environment and they cannot prevent or predict the consequences of those releases.

Why animal tests do not protect humans from toxins

'[Federal] agencies often draw their toxicologists from industry, and after their tour of duty in government is over, it is to industry that they return. Manufacturers are large contributors to political campaigns. As a result, there is tremendous pressure to do as little as possible to restrict industry profits.' Neal Barnard, Director, Physicians Committee for Responsible Medicine, Washington, DC, 1990

Several cases illustrate the dangers of relying on animal test data to protect human health. First, much of the time, concerns are raised about a chemical that has already been on the market for decades, meaning that humans and wildlife have already been exposed to health risks. Such was the case with trichloroethylene or TCE (see p. 114), and DES, which was used as a growth promotant in cattle and poultry, and prescribed as a drug to prevent miscarriages between 1940 and 1970. DES caused birth defects and vaginal cancers in daughters whose mothers took the drug. An estimated fifty million (50,000,000) people were exposed to DES before its use was discontinued.[48] It is only ever because of an industrial accident or the grim documentation of human illness caused by chemicals like DES that federal agencies are forced to take action against a product.

Second, federal scientists and industry representatives' discrepant opinions about the significance of results from animal tests, generally in rodents, has led to repeated testing of the same chemical in different species of animals; and government agencies frequently ignore the results of their own and other scientists' animal tests. For example, in December 1995, scientists announced that phenolphthalein, a substance used for almost a century in over-the-counter laxatives, caused cancer in rodents. The drug remains on the market because both the NTP and NIEHS acknowledge the 'difficulty in extrapolating human risk from animal studies.' Additional studies are being conducted.[49]

Recently, experiments in which glass fibers were injected into rats produced enough tumors for the NTP to declare that fiberglass was a possible human carcinogen. (Fiberglass had already been reported to be an animal carcinogen in 1974 by Pott, et al., and Wagner, et al.)[50] Industry vigorously fought the NTP finding, contending that it was based on faulty science. Using data from its own study in which rats inhaled higher levels of fibers than the average person breathes, Richard Versen of Schuller International, a fiberglass manufacturer, said that the animals in the company's study did not develop lung cancer. Indeed, 60 years worth of fiberglass inhalation experiments on animals have yielded negative results.[51] The government dismissed Schuller International's study on the grounds that rats are nose-breathers and humans breathe through the nose *and* mouth (a fact highlighted in Chapter 3). But Versen retorted that people are not injected with fiberglass as the rats in the NTP study were.[52]

In another case, 23 carcinogenicity (including 16 dermal) studies in rodents with benzoyl peroxide (a popular over-the-counter acne medication on the market for thirty years) yielded negative results. Positive results (skin tumors) were obtained in one particularly sensitive, SENCAR mouse strain. Procter & Gamble makes a popular anti-acne ointment containing benzoyl peroxide. A. L. Kraus, et al., P & G toxicologists, dismissed the mouse studies claiming that they were poorly done, that human epidemiological evidence contradicted them, that the mouse skin tumors only occurred under specific experimental conditions and only with specific mouse strains, and that mouse and human skin are significantly different physiologically. They concluded that 'available scientific evidence does not allow the results of [the rodent studies] to be meaningfully applied to human safety assessment.'[53] It is this sort of (politically and financially motivated) disagreement over the significance of animal test results which leads to a call for more animal tests to prove or disprove a desired theory. Because the ambiguity of test results increases with the number and variety of species used, each new generation of testing prompts further controversy between scientists within government and industry, which in turn further delays regulation.

The lack of coordination between US regulatory agencies and the diverse priorities of the departments within each agency, ensure that animal test results often end up being sidelined. Toxicologists and epidemiologists, for example, pursue different goals in their research; although the former frequently write up reports for the latter, most epidemiologists don't take animal-based toxicology studies seriously. In 1991 the results came in from rat and mouse studies that 1,2,3-trichloropropane, an industrial solvent used as a paint and varnish remover and degreasing agent, caused animals to become riddled with tumors in several organs. Workers regularly wash themselves with the solvent which penetrates their skin. Richard Irwin, an NCI toxicologist who wrote the 1,2,3-trichloropropane report for the NTP, said it would be helpful to collect human data for the solvent because people were being exposed to it. But Allen Wilcox, an NTP epidemiologist, said that NTP was not looking at the solvent. The NCI epidemiologists, who get the animal study reports regularly, were also not looking at it and said they never initiated an epidemiological study based on animal data. Joseph Fraumeni, head of epidemiology at the NCI, said he hadn't even heard of 1,2,3-trichloropropane. Edward Stein, a health scientist for OSHA, said the agency had done no surveys on the chemical and had not changed its standards for it since 1989. Stein claimed that manufacturers were responsible for alerting users as to the chemical's dangers, but he did not know whether worker training programs informed employees about how to use the chemical properly.[54] Clearly, animal tests with 1,2,3-trichloropropane were aimless and wasteful, and contributed nothing to preventing workers' exposure to this potentially toxic/carcinogenic substance.

In some cases, animal studies have actually harmed workers. Experiments in the 1930s, for example, revealed that rabbits who inhaled metallic aluminum did not get silicosis (a debilitating lung disease) after exposure to silica dust. And so, in the 1940s and 1950s, workers exposed to silica dust on the job were made to pass through special chambers to inhale aluminum powder. Epidemiological studies later revealed that Canadian workers who breathed the powder showed signs of Alzheimer's disease; and workers in the aluminum industry have reportedly high risks of lung disease and cancer.[55] Similarly, hundreds of people died in the 1970s after being exposed to paraquat. The herbicide, which was thought to have a low toxicity based on experiments with rats, turned out to be highly toxic to humans in minute doses. More than 14 tons of paraquat were exported out of the United States every day between 1991 and 1994.[56]

On numerous occasions, bans against certain substances deemed to be carcinogenic in animals have been lifted because the animal-to-human extrapolations were found to be unreliable, and because human experience defied the animal findings.[57] Such was the case with the sweetener saccharin (tested in mice, rats, hamsters and monkeys),[58] the food flavoring agent cinnamyl anthranilate, and the solvent methylene chloride, used widely in decaffeination, food and computer chip manufacturing processes.[59]

More often than not, chemicals are left on the market despite positive evidence of cancer in animals, and over a decade may pass before a chemical is suspended or withdrawn. Industry has lobbied vigorously and mounted elaborate public relations campaigns to oppose the withdrawal of chemicals until the lengthy review process is finished.[60] Such was the case with Alar or daminozide, used widely on apples since 1968 to control ripening time on the tree. As the EPA ignored 25 years of incriminating animal studies, public pressure forced Uniroyal, Alar's maker, to voluntarily withdraw the chemical in 1989. By then the company had earned $20 million a year since 1964 selling the chemical to apple growers and others.[61] As Andrée Collard wrote in *Rape of the Wild* (1988, p. 149),

> many more animals will be sacrificed while the EPA waits for the results of 'further studies' and many more people will be exposed to the danger … before the EPA makes a ruling … In the absence of strong human data, the EPA's decision to restrict the use of [a chemical] is heavily based on a cost–benefit analysis.

Indeed, under the EPA's interpretation of the Federal Fungicide, Rodenticide and Insecticide Act (FIFRA), the agency is allowed to weigh the risks of exposing the public to a potentially dangerous pesticide against the financial losses that would be incurred if that chemical were banned or severely restricted. In addition, Rodricks (1992) reports that, 'the EPA tolerates higher risks for exposures to pesticides incurred by workers who manufacture, distribute, or apply pesticides, than they do for the general population.'[62] Nothing illustrates this point better than the case of the deadly pesticide parathion.

Particular chemicals as examples

Parathion   Like malathion, parathion (or Alkron, Alleron, Corothion, Genthion, Geofos, Lethalaire, Niran, Orthopos, Paradusto, and Stathion, as it is also called) is an organophosphate and member of the nerve gas family; it has been tested on numerous animal species in whom it caused cancer, birth defects, neurotoxicity, and retinal de-generation.[63] Though it is listed as a suspected animal carcinogen, mutagen and teratogen,[64] parathion has been in use in the United States since 1948—and despite overwhelming evidence of its debilitating effects on *humans* which have included paralysis, blindness, violent vomiting, poisoning and death from amounts as minute as 0.00424 ounce.[65]

In her book *Silent Spring* (1994 edition, p. 126), Rachel Carson called parathion a 'universal killer' because of its ability to kill a variety of wildlife and poison workers handling foliage sprayed with the chemical. Millions of pounds of parathion are now applied to fields and orchards in the US by hand sprayers, motorized blowers and dusters, and by airplane. According to the EPA and the California Department of Food and Agriculture, parathion has poisoned more than 650 field workers and killed 100 since 1966. The pesticide is estimated to have caused 80 percent of all pesticide poisonings in Central America in the 1970s, and ranked second as the cause of reported systemic and respiratory pesticide-related illness in California between 1984 and 1990; it continues to cause extensive poisonings throughout the world, even among workers taking all possible precautions.[66] But the chemical's manufacturer, the Danish company Cheminova A/S, complained that it would lose $10 million a year if a ban became effective; the cost of an allegedly safer substitute, diazinon, was deemed too great for far-mers, and would presumably result in higher prices for consumers. And so in 1991, scientists at EPA stated that the economic benefits of continuing to apply parathion to roughly four million acres of fruits, vegetables, nuts, and grains in the US (including peaches, nectarines, plums, apples, lettuce, broccoli, onions and wheat) outweighed the hazards to wildlife and people.[67]

Summary Despite having caused cancer, neurotoxicity and other effects in laboratory animals and poisoned and killed hundreds of workers and non-target species, cost–benefit decisions have allowed parathion—a toxic pesticide—to remain on the market and be sprayed on fields and orchards in the United States. Chemical manufacturers have profited handsomely from such regulatory decisions. Organic farmers and alternative farming associations such as the Rodale Institute in Kutztown, Pennsylvania are encouraging a move away from the use of toxic agricultural chemicals. They advocate using crop rotation, mech-anical cultivation, integrated pest management,[68] and natural biological pesticides such as the larvicide *bacillus thuringiensis israelensis* (BTI)[69] instead.

Trichloroethylene (TCE) Trichloroethylene (TCE) has been in use since the 1940s in the production of spices, as a general anesthetic in medicine and dentistry, an extraction solvent in decaffeinated coffee, and a flavor enhancer in beer.[70]

Over a dozen TCE animal tests/cancer bioassays have been performed by the National Cancer Institute (NCI), the National Toxicology Program (NTP), the Manufacturing Chemists Association (MCA), and several independent scientists, in at least four strains of mice, four strains of rats, and one strain of hamster, at doses ranging up to 2,400 parts per million—with wildly varying results.[71] Numerous reproductive and developmental toxicity studies have been conducted at various concentrations in different strains of mice and rabbits with negative results. Some experiments found TCE to be toxic and teratogenic in rats.[72]

TCE's uses were curtailed and it was dubbed a 'suspected carcinogen' in 1976, and later a 'probable human carcinogen' (after it had already been on the market for thirty years) when a study by the NCI stated that in very high experimental dosages of up to 2,339 mg/kg/day, TCE caused liver tumors in B6C3F1 mice.[73] In spite of these results, TCE was approved for extensive use in food production by the FDA into the late 1970s, and continued to be used as an anesthetic by the health profession. It was not until the early 1980s that specific laws, regulations and exposure limits for TCE were promulgated.[74]

Today, while TCE is no longer used in food production or dry cleaning, it is still used as a degreasing solvent, in chemical processing, and in adhesives. There are no official restrictions on the chemical's use; in fact, TCE is so ubiquitous, it was listed among the EPA's 17 high-priority chemicals under the agency's 33–50 program—a voluntary initiative seeking commitments from companies to halve their reported releases of high-volume industrial chemicals by 1995.[75] In 1988, 49,071,464 pounds of TCE were released into the air;[76] it has been released into nations' waterways (both in the US and other countries like Czechoslovakia) by industry and consumers; it has been found in more than half of the US's hazardous waste sites. Frank Schaumburg, professor of environmental engineering at the University of Oregon, said: 'it is highly likely that our ability to detect and measure contaminants far exceeds our ability to properly and responsibly evaluate the impacts of those concentrations on human health, on other biological life, and on overall environmental quality.'[77]

Summary Even though TCE was used for decades before its carcinogenicity was questioned, and though it caused cancer and birth defects in numerous species of animals, the chemical was not banned but merely regulated. Ambiguous animal test data delayed regulatory action. Existing regulations do not prevent this toxic chemical from being released in large quantities into the environment.

Lindane Despite having caused cancer and damaged the nervous systems of animals and people, lindane, a chlorinated hydrocarbon pesticide, has been in use since the 1970s. In the early 1970s, Nagasaki, et al. fed 660 mg/kg technical grade BHC (the primary ingredient in lindane) to mice, who developed benign liver tumors. These test results were ignored by regulatory agencies. Thorpe and Walker (1973) fed mice even higher doses of lindane which induced both benign and malignant tumors in 93 percent of male and 69 percent of female mice, some of which metastasized to the lung.[78] Veterinarian Eric Dunayer wrote that,

> other studies have yielded both positive and negative results, but most have been criticized for using too low a dose of lindane in the high treatment group. In all, lindane has been tested in six oral bioassays using mice. Two experiments showed increased liver tumors as well as other malignant and benign tumors; four studies were considered inadequate even though two of the four showed increased evidence of liver tumors. Three studies in rats yielded two assays considered inadequate and a third showed increase in thyroid tumors in female rats. Based on these findings, the IARC finally concluded that lindane is carcinogenic in mice and possibly carcinogenic in humans.[79]

In 1977, the NCI performed its own rodent carcinogen bioassays in rats and mice which yielded negative results.[80] Ten years later, in 1987, Dunayer reports that the EPA canceled lindane's use in vaporizers and for 'direct application to aquatic environments,' citing its carcinogenic potential, teratogenic and reproductive effects, and acute toxicity to aquatic wildlife. To avert a complete ban on lindane, registrants agreed to label the chemical, warning applicators to use greater protection when using it.[81] In April 1990, over a hundred people died after attending a wedding feast in Northern India when lindane powder was mistakenly added to the flour for the wedding meal.[82]

Despite all this, lindane remains on the market today. It is applied to various food crops including avocados and pecans, ornamental trees, and forestry products; it is also used in a diluted solution in lotions, creams and shampoos to treat parasites, lice and scabies in livestock, dogs and humans.[83] Several generic brands of lindane-based pesticide and delousing agents are readily available in markets, and hardware and garden supply stores. The Purina company sells an antiparasitic dog dip with a 5 percent lindane solution, though such dips have been found to be toxic to dogs and cats.[84] Ortho sells a pesticide through lawn care stores with a 20 percent lindane solution.[85]

Recent publicity by the National Pediculosis Foundation (NPF) in Boston, Massachusetts revealed that Kwell, a brand of delousing shampoo with a 1 percent lindane solution (deemed safe based on animal tests), has caused chronic, incurable body rashes, seizures and blindness in hundreds of humans who have used the product *as directed* over the last two decades[86]—a product which was considered safe by the Food and Drug Administration 'when used as directed.'[87] It has also been linked to childhood brain cancer.[88] Although current regulations require that animal tests be used to set dose levels for drugs and consumer products before human trials begin, the lindane case serves to illustrate the failure of animal tests to establish 'safe' dose levels for human beings.

Researchers at the Multicenter for Evaluation of In Vitro Cytotoxicity (MEIC) project in Sweden have modeled human toxic doses and concentrations with the use of *in vitro* toxicity and toxicokinetic data.[89] Robert Sharpe, a scientist and author in Sheffield, UK, confirmed that *in vitro* systems are capable of successfully estimating human lethal doses; results have correlated well with reported human lethal doses, hence such tests could be used to set safe dose levels for chemicals in products intended for human use.[90] Phil Casterton, senior scientist in the Product Safety Department at Amway (a Michigan-based multibillion dollar personal and home care products company), asserts that mild dose-response studies could be done *in vitro*, particularly for substances that cannot be identified as mild irritants in animals.[91] Moreover, it is ultimately through (legally mandated) human trials of drugs and consumer products (in which patients and volunteers receive tiny incremental doses of a substance until the appropriate dose is found), and years of human use, that the safety of a chemical can ever truly be determined.

Although diluted solutions of citronella oil (an insect repellant), melaleuca (tea tree) oil (a disinfectant and antiviral agent), or thyme oil (an antiseptic) have been suggested as natural alternatives to toxic delousing agents,[92] conventional doctors are not familiar with herbal remedies and consequently do not endorse them. According to the National Pediculosis Foundation, research into safer alternatives has never been pursued. In the meantime, the Foundation is advocating prevention, and sending consumer complaints to the FDA. One staff member suggested that it would be safer to live with lice than risk the side effects of lindane-based delousing agents.[93] Public Citizen, a Washington-based health advocacy group, filed a petition with the FDA in June 1995 to have lindane taken off the market.

Summary Decades' worth of ambiguous animal tests (in which some animals developed tumors, birth defects, or no effects) eventually led to the weak regulation of a product which is clearly toxic to humans, pets and wildlife. Despite its toxicity, lindane is readily available in home and garden stores, is used on food crops, and in personal care and pet products. Clearly, research into safer alternatives (for humans and pets) is needed as the use of less toxic substances would prevent future tragedies. Those already in existence should be promoted more forcefully. A shift to organic farming would further reduce health risks for all life forms.

Dioxin Dioxins are a family of chemical compounds that are by-products of industrial processes. More than 95 percent of all dioxin emissions come from combustion and incineration activities. Epidemiological studies of humans (mostly males) exposed to large doses of dioxin in industrial accidents, including studies of Vietnam veterans exposed to Agent Orange, provide positive evidence of severe skin reactions, neurological damage, alterations in reproductive hormones, birth defects, and some forms of cancer related to the exposures.[94] As a result of this information, the US government has allegedly spent billions of dollars to clean up dioxin in the environment.[95]

Despite evidence from epidemiological studies which would appear conclusive enough to convict dioxin as a known human carcinogen, the EPA has dubbed dioxin a 'probable carcinogen.' According to the agency, this means that direct evidence of carcinogenicity to humans is characterized as inconclusive. Ironically, health and environmental advocates who wish to indict dioxin frequently cite animal data rather than human data, to show that dioxin is toxic in the most minute doses. Yet the EPA's own animal data are riddled with contradictions. Male and female rabbits, hamsters, mice, rats, monkeys, chickens, minks and guinea pigs of different ages, used in acute tests with dioxin, responded in vastly different ways, both between and among species. Between species in the LD_{50} there was a 5,000–8,000-fold difference in response; and different strains of the same species (rodents) showed more than a 300-fold variation, leading the EPA to describe the range of responses as 'extensive,' 'dramatic,' and 'enormous.'[96] Interestingly, it is unclear how much weight the animal or human data carry for governments establishing safety standards. Government-regulated safety exposures for dioxin vary greatly from country to country because different countries use diverse statistical methods to establish exposure limits. Dennis B. Maloney, a risk assessment consultant in Omaha, Nebraska writes that, 'some countries allow more than 1,000 times the acceptable US levels to be released into the environment, even though the same data (liver tumors in female rats) were used worldwide to establish [standards of acceptable] risks' for dioxin.[97] In *Dying for Dioxin* (1995), author Lois Gibbs states that most Americans have already been exposed to their lifetime maximum 'safe' dosage of dioxin.

To date, despite decades' worth of epidemiological evidence that shows dioxin to be harmful to humans, and admissions by the EPA that the animal data may be questionable and biased, no official, definitive conclusions about the health risks to *humans* from dioxin have been reached by regulatory agencies.

Summary The dioxin case demonstrates that animal testing has not aided regulatory agencies and toxicologists in determining *human* health risks. Decades of animal tests have again produced confusing data, clouded scientific judgement and delayed regulation. In 1994 the American Public Health Association, a professional society, called on industry to reduce or eliminate chlorinated organic compounds in its products and processes, as did the environmental group Greenpeace.[98] While the EPA continues to review the dioxin data, it finally instituted rulings, effective as of September 1995, forcing incinerator operators to reduce their dioxin emissions by 99 percent.[99] This is heartening, but because dioxins are extremely persistent, accumulating both in the environment and in biological tissues, current efforts to curb release of dioxins may be too little too late. Dioxins continue to be released into the environment.

DDT (Dichloro-Diphenyl-Trichloro-Ethane) The chlorinated hydrocarbon pesticide DDT was first developed for use as an insecticide in 1939. Because of its molecular structure DDT, and compounds like it, take decades and sometimes centuries to degrade in the environment; traces of it have been found in soils twenty years after its application, in the bodies of penguins and seals in Antarctica, and in frogs living at very high altitudes in remote regions of the Sierra Nevada mountains.[100]

DDT was tested for decades on mice, rats, hamsters, and other species. In 1969 Innes, et al. dosed mice with 853 times the average amount of DDT found in the human diet, doses that Herman Kraybill of the NCI said rendered toxicological evaluations and comparisons with the human experience 'difficult.'[101]

DDT appeared to produce liver tumors only in mice (at abnormally high doses)[102] but it did not cause any malignancies in female rats, hamsters, Osborne-Mendel rats and B6C3F1 mice. The NCI, along with several research laboratories, performed animal tests with DDT into the 1970s, with its metabolites p,p'- DDE, DDE, DDD, DDA, with a major contaminant of DDT: TDE, and in combination with other carcinogens like dimethylnitrosamine (DMNA) which appeared to intensify carcinogenic responses.[103]

Fifteen years after Rachel Carson elucidated the dangers to humans of DDT in her book *Silent Spring*, however, and even after DDT was banned for use in the United States in 1972, scientists continued to debate the relevance of the mouse studies for humans. At OSHA hearings in 1978, officials stated that the question of whether DDT caused cancer in humans, and whether it could definitively be classified as a human carcinogen, was 'unanswerable.' But cancer was not the only ailment by which the harmful effects of the chemical could have been gauged. Knowledge of the symptoms of acute poisoning from DDT was provided by several British scientists who deliberately exposed themselves to DDT by applying it on their skin in the 1940s. Symptoms included aching limbs, muscular weakness, and spasms of extreme nervous tension.[104] And the FDA had warnings as early as 1950 about DDT's persistence in the human body. Various occupational studies had revealed that workers in insecticide plants were storing 648 parts per million of DDT in their bodies, and the average person was storing 5.3–7.4 parts per million.[105] DDT was also reported to cause chromosome abnormalities in human lymph cells *in vitro*.[106]

Despite these findings some still demurred, like John A. Moore, a former assistant EPA administrator and now head of the private Institute for Evaluating Health Risks, who said new data show that DDT poses 'a relatively modest cancer risk.'[107] Perhaps that is why DDT analogues like dicofol, kelthane, and methoxychlor are still in use in the US[108] and why nearly fifty million (50,000,000) pounds of the allegedly cancer-causing pesticide have continued to be manufactured each year and exported to developing countries—a practice sanctioned by the United States under the Federal Insecticide, Fungicide and Rodenticide Act (FIFRA) and by branches of the World Health Organization.[109] Ironically, the principal use of 70 percent of the pesticides in developing countries is for crops grown for export to industrialized countries.

Summary Human and *in vitro* evidence of DDT's toxicity and persistence in biological tissues was known as early as the 1940s–50s.

Rachel Carson elucidated the harm DDT caused to wildlife and the environment in her book *Silent Spring*, first published in 1962. This did not prevent DDT from being used for another decade, nor from it being tested in numerous animal species at unrealistic dose levels even after the chemical had been banned. The ambiguous data generated by these tests continue to spark scientific debates. Despite the US ban on DDT in 1972, both US and international regulations allow for humans' continued ingestion of this presumed animal carcinogen and human poison.

Several points which illustrate the failure of animal tests to protect human health have been made thus far:

1. Because animal tests are so ambiguous, studies are often repeated; debates over test results are so drawn out that regulation is delayed. Products typically remain on the market until decisions are reached. Chemicals may stay on the market for decades *before* they are chosen for testing, leaving humans and wildlife exposed to unknown dangers. Cost–benefit analyses play a large role in these decisions and industry has benefited from them.

2. Regulatory agencies frequently ignore the results of their own animal tests and risk assessments. Rarely, if ever, are toxic substances banned as a result of animal tests (in numerous strains and species) which show a product to be toxic and/or carcinogenic. They are merely regulated and continue to be used. (Billions of dollars have been spent cleaning up preventable pollution after the fact, as in the case of dioxin.) This raises the question of whether the government really takes animal test results seriously. If it does not, why do they continue to be performed?

3. Even when positive human toxicity data are available, as in the case of benzene and DDT, chemicals are not withdrawn. Regulatory scientists habitually seek to confirm human findings in animals before regulatory steps are taken, thus delaying action further.

4. Toxic products are readily available in stores and supermarkets where consumers may buy them and use them liberally, since consumer behavior cannot be controlled. Labels do not list all potentially carcinogenic ingredients, nor warn consumers that the products they buy may pose cancer risks.

5. Enforcement of animal-derived environmental safety standards is ineffectual. Methods to gauge the merit or effectiveness of those standards have never been developed. (In reality, only with the 'immoral' but inevitable acquisition of human data can their

effectiveness be measured. Currently, because of the primary importance given to animal data and animal testing methods, such data
are lacking).

6. Legislation has continually been modified and weakened to favor
   polluters, due to intense industry lobbying. As in the case of the
   three employees out of 111,414 at the USDA researching alternative
   agriculture, federal initiatives to break our chemical dependency are
   virtually non-existent.

7. The animal tests have not been remotely successful in screening the
   backlog of over 75,000 chemicals currently in use. In fact, it appears
   that, because they are lengthy and inherently misleading, they have
   facilitated the growth of the chemical industry rather than helped to
   slow or impede it. The health and environmental consequences of
   such unbridled growth have already revealed themselves.

We cannot know how much more effective environmental regulations
might have been had animal testing been abandoned early on and
replaced by other testing methods. Some say that if animal testing
(which makes poisons appear safe in the eyes of the public) were
abolished and replaced with faster, less costly, reproducible methods,
such as *in vitro* assays, the identification and removal of harmful
chemicals from the marketplace would not take up to twenty years as it
does now.[110] SUPRESS, a California-based health advocacy group,
suggests that 'genuine pollution prevention measures would then consist
of laws and regulations that would ban the production of … poisons.
The limited number of absolutely "essential" poisons … would then
be used with caution and discretion, under laws that would be intended
to protect the environment, not its polluters.'[111] This alternative regulatory paradigm will be explored in more detail in the following chapters.

Some individuals like biostatistician Irwin Bross have suggested that
animal tests do not fulfill their intended purpose and are scientifically
fraudulent. Bross defines fraud as the intent to deceive, and describes
scientific fraud in three ways: (1) a scientific method continues to be
used even after the literature shows that it yields erroneous results, (2)
grants are awarded and accepted despite the lack of scientific merit in
the method, and (3) the spurious results from use of the method will
tend to support policies and programs of a granting agency, or will
add to the profitability of product lines of a corporate sponsor.[112]

Based on Dr Bross's criteria, many would claim that animal testing
for the purpose of human health risk assessment is indeed a fraud. If
so, several questions must be asked: are the animal tests legally sanctioned by the federal government, and if so to what extent?; who

benefits from the continuation of this scientific fraud?; and how can this fraud be eradicated? While the last question will be addressed in the conclusion to this book, the former questions will be addressed below.

The laws and guidelines governing animal testing requirements

'It is true that federal laws do not mandate the use of animals in confirming product safety. But it is equally true that the government regulators who are charged with interpreting and enforcing these laws continue to require these tests.' John Smale, President, Procter & Gamble, in a statement from an annual meeting, October 1989

The international control of potentially toxic substances is bogged down in a maze of legislation, much of it modeled after US programs. Since the National Cancer Institute began its animal carcinogen bioassay program in 1962, health agencies in various countries followed suit and began requiring an array of additional tests for carcinogenicity and chronic toxicity. European regulations like the EEC Dangerous Substances Directive dictate that a range of toxicological studies be on file for new chemicals; OECD Guidelines for the Testing of Chemicals mandate animal testing; and United Nations regulations have required corrosive substances to be tested on rabbits prior to shipment.

Most federal agencies in the US currently require product safety testing on animals or use the data that emanate from such tests as a standard, even though many companies are adopting research methods in-house that eliminate the need for animal testing. But current regulations governing animal testing for (non-medical) consumer products are unclear and inconsistent, both within and outside the US. For example, animal tests considered unnecessary in an exporting country may be required by an importing country.[113] In the US, there are specific regulations that require the animal testing of pesticides but not of cosmetics, though certain coloring agents in personal care products must be tested. There is confusion about which tests are required, which are merely guidelines or suggestions, and what alternatives to animal tests may be available.[114] A 'valid scientific argument' is sufficient to justify deviation from guidelines which encourage the execution of animal tests,[115] though it is unknown how many companies take the trouble to formulate such justifications.

Although the EPA, FDA and CPSC joined to form the Interagency Regulatory Alternatives Group (IRAG) in 1993 to further the use of non-animal testing methods, according to Carlton H. Nadolney, a toxicologist in the Division of Chemical Screening and Risk Assessment at the EPA, as of 1995, not a single *in vitro* toxicity bioassay has been listed as an option in the Code of Federal Regulations. Despite this fact, industry often submits test data from *in vitro* tests done in-house, and these are accepted by both EPA and FDA.[116] Policy statements about animal testing and regulatory acceptance of non-animal methods vary from agency to agency, change frequently, and have been interpreted in vastly different ways by different interest groups.[117] For a more detailed description of each federal agency's policy on animal testing, see the notes to this section.

The National Toxicology Program A 1992 report exemplifies the confusing nature of the NTP's animal testing policies. In it, the NTP Carcinogenesis Working Group declares (on p. 31723) that the NTP wishes to 'restrict the use of animals in future studies,' while simultaneously stating that the agency is 'heavily reliant on the use of inbred rodent strains for bioassays.'[118] A look at the agency's 1994 budget is revealing. That year, 75 percent of NTP's budget was devoted to classic animal tests (including chronic, sub-chronic, reproductive, immunological and respiratory studies), roughly 20 percent was allocated to 'methods development,'[119] and just 2–3 percent was spent on validation studies for non-animal methods—less than in 1991. In 1990, testifying before a Congressional subcommittee, then US Senator Paul Tsongas stated, 'NTP is an amalgam of three agencies: NIH, CDC, and FDA. It seems to us that that is the place where the validation process should take place in a much more aggressive fashion.'[120] In 1992, however, the NTP Working Group concluded that, although NTP coordinates and conducts much of the nation's toxicity testing, 'NTP should not be the national center for alternate test development, validation or application.'

In 1996, the results of an NTP workshop, 'Mechanism-Based Toxicology in Cancer Risk Assessment,' were published. The stated goals of the workshop were to find ways to test chemicals more efficiently, and to improve the scientific foundation upon which risk assessment is based. The recommendations proposed by individual working groups, however, made it clear that the NTP has no intention of abandoning animal testing—this despite the fact that in 1993, Kenneth Olden (director of the NIEHS, which directs the animal studies for NTP) acknowledged serious problems with the animal tests as predictors of human cancer risk.[121] Indeed, it was suggested that, in addition to the classic chronic and sub-chronic studies, 'multi-time' and 'multi-dose' studies be conducted to provide more information on dose–response relationships *in animals*. The use of transgenic mouse models was deemed to be a 'promising approach' for predicting carcinogenicity; in fact the NTP is placing emphasis on the development and use of such genetically modified mice. It was stated that the NTP 'should continue for the foreseeable future, long-term bioassays,' and that these should only be diminished when 'alternative methods are appropriately validated and accepted by all concerned parties' (a conclusion reached by the EEC three years prior in a 14 June 1993 Directive—93/35/EEC). It was stated that the NTP and other groups should be *encouraged* (though not required) to pursue the development of alternative methods.

Predictably, recommendations were made concerning reducing the uncertainty of inter-species extrapolation and enhancing understanding of inter-species differences; these included developing methods to measure biochemical, cellular and molecular endpoints in rodents and humans.[122] Ironically, such suggestions are likely to complicate existing testing protocols rather than simplify them. In 1980 Gio Batta Gori wrote that, 'the redundancy of these suggestions underlines their relative impotence, besides being incompatible with the limited testing resources now available.'

NTP still uses the controversial maximum tolerated dosing (MTD) strategy, and continues to work on finding numerous ways to refine classic animal tests and extrapolate their results to humans. It appears that although individuals within the NTP/NIEHS may want to move away from animal tests, the confusing language found in official policy statements, the nature of bureaucracies, and the lack of funds allocated to non-animal methods, makes it virtually impossible to achieve any real progress in this area. It is no wonder that other federal agencies have similar policies and research agendas.

The Food and Drug Administration   The Food and Drug Administration has no authority to require any testing procedures for the manufacturing, transportation and marketing of cosmetics;[123] though it does require animal testing for the registration of human drugs under the federal Food, Drug and Cosmetic Act.[124] For food additives and biologics (blood replacement products, tissue graft materials) FDA guidelines do outline animal testing procedures to establish safety standards. Study designs are similar to those listed for human drugs, which are extensive. Requirements depend, in part, on expected use and exposure potential.[125]

While FDA regulations do not specify the precise manner in which safety testing must be done, the agency's testing guidelines are revealing, and the FDA will reject data considered inadequate or incomplete. If the FDA deems that a reliable measure of a particular adverse effect can only be determined in animals, then the FDA will not accept the results of non-animal studies.[126] (Similar policies are in place in other countries, for example Japan.)[127] But the agency has issued conflicting statements regarding both the validity and necessity of conducting acute toxicity tests in general and the classical LD50 test in particular.[128] In 1987 the agency said that it would discourage the LD50 test in future guidelines for toxicological procedures. Despite the recognized problems with the LD50 test, so far the agency has not endorsed any non-animal test as a standard for corporations wishing to gain FDA approval for a product. In addition, the agency has not accepted data from non-animal methods when investigating product safety, according to a September 1988 letter to US Representative Barbara Boxer from Hugh Cannon, the FDA associate commissioner for legislative affairs.[129]

This confusing state of affairs is reflected in companies' public statements. In 1990 Kevin Loftus, a senior lawyer at Gillette, said that no food and drug law expert would claim that animal testing was not necessary, given the current state of federal regulations.[130] Gerald B. Guest, former director of the FDA's Center for Veterinary Medicine, was quoted in 1993 as saying, 'the FDA's position is that the use of animal tests by industry to establish the safety of regulated products is necessary in many instances, if not most, to minimize the risks from such products to humans.'[131]

In its 1994 annual report on the *Development, Validation and Legal Acceptance of Alternative Methods to Animal Experiments*, published in Brussels, the Commission of the European Communities stated that the FDA 'encourages the development of alternative methods but points out that no alternative test has yet been accepted by the entire scientific community ... ; [FDA] concludes that it is unlikely that animal tests can be completely dispensed with in the near future.'

An article about developments in *in vitro* technology in *Genetic Engineering News* (15 April 1995), however, revealed that the FDA's Office of Science Board is reevaluating its approach to toxicity testing and its current standards, primarily for animal tests.[132] If the agency begins accepting data from *in vitro* tests, and legally acknowledges their validity on paper, then progress may be within reach.

The Consumer Product Safety Commission Compared to the FDA, the Consumer Product Safety Commission, which regulates the use and labelling of hazardous products (for household use), has no authority to require animal tests to determine product safety under the Federal Hazardous Substances Act (FHSA) (15 USC 1261 *et seq.*). The

Federal Hazardous Labelling Act of 1960 details specific animal toxicity studies that are to be used in making agency decisions about the proper labelling and continued marketing of consumer products;[133] but the testing procedures and models are only guidelines.[134] The Act spells out label wording according to results of acute oral, dermal and inhalation LD50s and LC50s in rats and rabbits, rabbit eye irritation tests, and other irritation/sensitization tests in guinea pigs and hamsters.

The CPSC issued an official animal testing policy in September 1984 stating that 'animal testing is sometimes performed by the Commission or by manufacturers of products subject to the FHSA (15 USC 1261–1275) to determine hazards associated with such products.' But the policy also stated that the calculation of a classic LD50 value is not required by the FHSA, and manufacturers are encouraged to limit numbers of animals in tests, and reduce pain and distress.

Under the FHSA (and the Code of Federal Regulations for the CPSC, 16 CFR Ch. 11 (1.1.87 Edition)), a substance is deemed hazardous if it causes personal injury or illness during its handling, use or ingestion. The only hazard category to use animal toxicity data in the initial section (h)(1) is the 'highly toxic' ranking. Although human data, if available, are to take precedence over animal data, the statute deems that a substance is highly toxic if it kills rats and rabbits in oral LD50s, inhalation LC50s, and skin irritancy tests. The regulations also refer to another part of the FHSA that sets forth in detail the proper method to test toxic substances. The section describes acute dermal toxicity, primarily skin and eye irritancy experiments on rabbits.[135]

In its 1984 animal testing policy statement, however, published in the *Federal Register* 24 May 1984, the CPSC confusingly states:

> neither the Federal Hazardous Substances Act nor the Commission's regulations require any firm to perform animal tests. The statute and its implementing regulations only require that a product be labelled to reflect the hazards associated with that product. While animal testing may be necessary in some cases, Commission policy supports limiting such tests to the lowest feasible number ... the Commission and manufacturers of products subject to the FHSA, should whenever possible utilize existing alternatives to conducting animal testing. These include prior human experience, literature sources which record prior animal testing or limited human tests, and expert opinion. The Commission resorts to animal testing only when the other information sources have been exhausted.

Similarly to the FDA and EPA, in its animal testing policy statement of 1984, the CPSC states that alternatives will be accepted only 'when such techniques are accepted by the scientific community as adjuncts or alternatives to whole-animal testing.' While the CPSC urges the use of alternatives, which in scientific circles includes a reduction in the number of animals used, and refinement of classic animal tests, it makes no specific mention of *in vitro* tests.[136] Unfortunately, the CPSC appears to be paying lip service to its own animal testing policy with respect to the use of non-animal testing methods.

The Occupational Safety and Health Administration The Occupational Safety and Health Administration (OSHA) requires no animal testing;[137] paragraph (d) of 1910.1200 of the Hazard Communication Standard law states that manufacturers and importers may use 'available scientific evidence' to evaluate chemical hazards, which may include epidemiological and *in vitro* studies.[138] However, in a letter to Sara Amundson of the Doris Day Animal League (DDAL) in Washington, DC, dated 3 March 1994, Berrien Zettler, Deputy Director of OSHA's Compliance Programs, quoted the Hazard Communication Compliance directive (CPL 2–2.38C, Appendix C, p. 3) which states that *in vitro* studies, such as the Ames test, 'are ... not definitive findings of hazards.' Zettler stated that under the provisions of the law, 'the results of *in vitro* tests alone do not represent significant enough information to establish a health hazard for purposes of the HCS (Hazard Communication Standard), although the exception to this is the *in vitro* testing for corrosivity.'[139] This has motivated both the EPA and FDA to explore the possibility of writing *in vitro* corrosivity assays into their own guidelines wherever applicable, though as of late 1995 this had not yet happened. The agency thus accepts animal data as the standard for classification, labelling and toxicological safety evaluations, as do other federal agencies like the Departments of Labor, Agriculture and Transportation (even though nothing in the Hazardous Materials Transportation Act specifically requires animal testing). In addition, the agency does require a Material Safety Data Sheet (see Chapter 2) for any chemical to which a worker may be exposed. Data for these sheets have typically been obtained through animal studies, but human data have been used when available.

The Environmental Protection Agency Under the Toxic Substances Control Act (TSCA), and the Federal Insecticide, Fungicide, and Rodenticide Act (FIFRA), the EPA (which includes the Office of Pesticide Programs and the Office of Toxic Substances) is authorized to require the testing of all active ingredients (such as ingredients sprayed on food) as well as any formulations to be sold as final products (mixtures of chemicals common to many other products).[140]

A review of the EPA's current testing procedures found a heavy reliance on animal testing.[141] Under FIFRA guidelines (CFR 40, Part 158), the EPA cites no less than twenty different animal tests (including acute LD50s in rats and rabbits, Draize eye and skin irritancy tests, and chronic feeding studies in dogs), which are presumably required to fulfill data requirements for pesticide registration.[142] No non-animal methods are specifically listed. In its TSCA requirements for the registration of industrial chemicals (CFR 40, Part 772), the agency lists 15 different animal tests.[143] Ironically, again under TSCA, the EPA allows manufacturers to decide which tests to conduct for a new chemical or whether testing is necessary at all.

While the EPA does not have the authority to require specific tests, it can publish guidelines describing tests and test results it deems acceptable, and, similarly to FDA, can reject data that it considers inadequate. According to Holly Hazard, a lawyer with DDAL, the regulations under FIFRA (virtually unchanged since 1986) clearly encourage the continued use of the LD50 and other animal acute toxicity tests.[144]

Ironically there is evidence that, of all the agencies, the EPA has a more liberal policy concerning the use of animal tests for compliance with its acute toxicity testing guidelines; EPA has been one of the only agencies to openly discuss the shortcomings of various testing regimes including animal tests. In a memo released in 1984, the agency stated that 'the EPA does not encourage the use of animals solely for the calculation of the LD50.' The EPA's own Office of Research and Development supports basic research into cell, tissue and organ culture technology, which could replace whole animals in testing.[145] According to the *Journal of the American Medical Association* (22–29 December 1993: 2907), and *American Medical News* (6 May 1996, p. 31), the EPA would like to rely more on advances in microbiology, computer systems, mathematical modeling, and *in vitro* data.

In a statement concerning *Guidelines for Carcinogen Risk Assessment* published in the US *Federal Register* (24 September 1986, Vol. 51, No. 185, p. 33993), the EPA said that the guidelines, which are 'nonbinding policy statements' will 'accommodate new knowledge and new assessment methods as they emerge.' In several sections of the federal regulatory code, particularly in Section CFR 158.70 *Acceptable protocols*, the EPA Code clarifies that, 'failure to follow a suggested protocol will not invalidate a test if another appropriate methodology is used.'

Ten years later, the EPA has issued new guidelines for carcinogen risk assessment with the aim of redefining its policies in this area. The guidelines (published in the *Federal Register*, 23 April 1996, Vol. 61, No.

79, pp. 17960–18011 and which would not take effect until late 1997) essentially give more weight to epidemiological data, statistical analyses, and *in vitro* studies of human cells and genes. They acknowledge the problems with animal tests; nevertheless, EPA scientists state that if the data from 'new methods' are of poor quality and unless they pass 'rigorous scientific review,' the agency will continue to rely on animal testing data. It is hoped that the new guidelines will inspire industry to begin submitting non-animal data voluntarily; however, unless the guidelines become law, industry will not be required to adhere to them.[146]

Oliver Fordham, a chemist and National Program Manager of EPA's Economics, Methods, and Risk Assessment Division (EMRAD), stated that his office rejected the use of animal tests a decade ago because, 'no one wanted to do the rabbit tests.' He believes that the use of *in vitro* assays within the EPA in general would be a huge leap forward. In his opinion, the problem lies in changing antiquated regulations and having to respond to volumes of public comments when notices are posted in the *Federal Register*. He said the EPA simply does not have the resources to handle the process, or the money to challenge industry lobbyists who see regulations as burdensome and may fight any revisions. As a result, not only do many types of waste which pose environmental hazards go unregulated, but some EPA guidelines are so old, they refer to Department of Transportation regulations that don't exist anymore.[147]

There are scientists, like Fordham, within the EPA who would apparently like to see the agency move away from animal tests, if for no other reason than because industry itself is doing so. Moreover, while internal memos, private phonecalls, and proceedings from scientific congresses in which the EPA has been a participant, may reflect the willingness of individuals within the agency to move beyond animal tests, these points of view have not been incorporated into current regulatory codes and policy. In the past, the actions of one or a few politically powerful individuals have thwarted efforts to reform archaic regulatory practices and policies,[148] so that regulatory codes have continued to reflect the insulated and static world of federal bureaucracies, at the expense of true scientific progress. It is hoped that this state of affairs will soon change.

Most federal agencies seem to be using the same approach: emphasizing that they do not require animal tests but at the same time saying that they do not find non-animal methods acceptable measures of consumer safety. They largely resort to advocating a reduction in the numbers of animals used in classic animal tests. Federal Hazardous Substance Act and FIFRA regulations continue to define toxicity levels in terms of animals, and the EPA, CPSC, and FDA all publish guidelines/protocols for acute toxicity tests on animals including the LD50. (It should be noted here that the international OECD guidelines for the testing of chemicals—held up as the international standard for toxicity testing—also encourage animal testing (see for example OECD monographs 401, 404–6, 408, 414, 415, 417, 451, 474, 475, 478, 483–5). OECD guideline 404 for acute dermal irritation/corrosion (adopted 24 February 1987) sets forth in detail the proper way to test chemicals on albino rabbits, although a 29 July 1992 addendum to the guideline deems that alternative methods (such as *in vitro* tests) are acceptable even if not formally validated. The NTP is in close contact with European regulators, and the EPA works closely with the OECD to harmonize legislation in this area.)[149]

As a result, studies have shown that while some corporate laboratories have reduced their use of animals in acute oral and dermal toxicity testing, chemical, drug, and pesticide manufacturers continue to perform classical LD50 tests to comply with specific testing requirements and to satisfy governmental regulatory agencies in the US and other countries. While rodents are most widely used, dogs and primates are occasionally used if companies believe it to be 'absolutely required.'[150] It has been suggested that companies 'strenuously resist any US or international regulatory agency requests to provide classical LD50 values for acute toxicity tests.'[151]

Both the EPA and CPSC have indicated a preference for human data, and both have issued strong statements indicating their aversion to the use of animals if alternatives are available, although none of the federal agencies specifically outline acceptable non-animal tests in their policies. Companies like Proctor & Gamble, which continue to conduct animal tests, defend their policy by pointing the finger at regulatory agencies like the FDA which has not endorsed non-animal testing methods.[152] The degree to which federal agencies waive certain animal safety testing requirements or accept data from non-animal methods appears to vary, depending on the type of product, and the requirements of the regulatory agency involved. Companies have complained that currently, it is unclear whether regulatory agencies will accept data from alternative tests; they have expressed disappointment at the lack of collaboration between government and industry regarding the validation of replacement methodologies.[153]

Although there are glimmers of hope that the EPA, FDA, OSHA and DOT may be considering the merits of *in vitro* technology, the current state of affairs is a classic example of policy making which does not reflect changing times, or the concerns of consumers and businesses. This is particularly distressing because such policies influence the pace that new technologies are adopted. Regulatory agencies also rely to a large extent upon the advice of scientific experts, who do not seem able to agree on the potential of *in vitro* tests to determine carcinogenicity.[154] Until federal agencies make explicit regulatory announcements approving such methods, companies are not likely to adopt them for product testing. The status quo of animal testing will probably be maintained until professional disagreement, bureaucratic inertia, and political maneuvering within the scientific and regulatory communities are eradicated.

The business of animal testing: who profits?

'There's been a huge investment of time and money in understanding rats … It isn't going to change to another system overnight.' Thomas Sabourin, of the Battelle Institute, Columbus, Ohio, quoted in Barnaby J. Feder, 'Beyond White Rats and Rabbits,' *The New York Times*, 28 February 1988, Business section, p. 1

'The field of chemical carcinogenesis is a vast scientific enterprise, not only in the United States but throughout the world.' Joseph V. Rodricks, *Calculated Risks* (UK: Cambridge University Press, 1992), p. 114

It cannot be denied that as long as regulatory inertia is maintained, certain sectors of the scientific, regulatory and business communities, for whom animal testing provides a livelihood, will benefit. Who exactly has a stake in the continuation of animal testing?

Chemicals is a $1.3 trillion global industry. According to the (American) Chemical Manufacturers Association (CMA) figures from 1992, the chemical industry (which is the third largest manufacturing industry in the United States) exported $44 billion worth of merchandise, sold $16.3 billion to businesses in the US, and had profits of $24 billion.[155] In 1993, shipments reached $314 billion—a record, and a 4.1 percent increase over 1992 levels.[156] It has earned those assets through the sale of countless products deemed safe based on animal tests. For example, the market for agricultural herbicides in the US is over $3.5 billion per year.[157] Estimated annual sales of chlorine (which is used in 15,000 products) are $71 billion.[158] It is no wonder then that CMA has been an ardent advocate of risk assessment for decades.[159]

Since, as we have seen, animal testing can delay the removal of a chemical from the market, allowing manufacturers to reap a profit in the meantime, it could be hypothesized that industry would have a vested interest in the continuation of tediously slow animal tests. Because pre-market testing of a new product can take years and cost tens of millions of dollars, a company may be particularly eager to ensure that it recoups its investment, and turns a profit before a product is withdrawn.

Animal tests can also be used to stall regulatory reform by diverting attention away from a problem. For example, there is evidence that exposure to very low levels of chemicals, well below exposure standards set by regulatory agencies, causes an illness dubbed Multiple Chemical Sensitivity (MCS) in humans. Common symptoms include respiratory problems, headache, fatigue, flu-like ailments, mental confusion and short-term memory loss, gastrointestinal tract difficulties, cardiovascular irregularities, skin disorders, muscle and joint pain, irritability, depression, and eye, ear, nose and throat problems. Thousands of people have already filed lawsuits seeking disability or personal injury damages for chemically-related illnesses.[160] The chemical industry, and others that use chemicals in their operations, have been quick to criticize these claims and dismiss them as being the psychosomatic delusions of a minority. They say that even if the disease were officially recognized by the medical establishment, cutting back on chemical exposures for everyone would require 'revolutionary changes by society that would probably be technologically infeasible and economically disastrous.'

While the Chemical Manufacturers Association has not taken an official position on MCS, it intends to adopt 'the views of the traditional medical establishment on MCS' and has advocated 'well-conducted research in this area.'[161] Rather than make the necessary changes in society, or fund clinical (human) studies on the effects of low levels of chemicals on human health and immunity, which scientists say provide much more reliable conclusions,[162] experts at a National Academy of Sciences workshop recommended that 'animal models that mimic the human [MCS] syndrome be developed.'[163] Consequently, animals are beginning to be used in an endless variety of experiments which attempt to reproduce the symptoms of MCS observed in humans. Iris Bell—a psychiatrist at the University of Arizona who speculates that the limbic system, which is linked to the olfactory system, could be directly involved in the MCS syndrome—exposed rabbits to a high concentration of pollutants, followed by subsequent low concentrations combined with a rhythmic flashing light. Bell says this 'triggered abnormal paroxysmal activity in the olfactory bulb and a part of the limbic system called the corticomedial amygdala.' No human studies have yet been done to test the validity of the proposed limbic mechanism.[164]

Animal experiments are also being carried out to study the effects of 'environmental estrogens'—chemicals said to adversely affect fertility and fetal development. Mike Shelby, an NIEHS geneticist, hopes to open a Center for the Evaluation of Risks to Human Reproduction in late 1997, which he says would be based on the model of the International Agency for Research on Cancer in France[165]—a center notorious for its animal experiments. Scientists like Michael Zinaman, however, assistant professor of endocrinology and reproduction at Loyola University Medical Center in Maryland, maintain that it is 'not always possible to extrapolate animal studies to human fertility outcomes.'[166]

Nevertheless, new fields of research have been born. What relevance these animal experiments and others like them will ever have to humans is unknown and there is a strong likelihood, as is often the case, that questions about their practical application will remain unanswered. What is obvious is that such experiments will obscure the real problem at hand. They will serve to create more volumes of scientific papers filled with technical jargon understandable and interesting only to the scientists themselves, who will argue over the significance of certain doses of chemicals and their effects on rats;[167] hence the quest for a rapid solution to the real human problem—a solution which would probably entail banning entire classes of chemicals—is delayed. A method which prevents or delays regulators and the public from arriving at that conclusion is likely to be embraced by the chemical industry and the scientists who receive grants to do the research.

Others who stand to benefit from the continuation of animal tests include the contract laboratories, and scores of toxicologists, pathologists and so on, hired to perform the experiments now required by regulators. In 1991, Gio Batta Gori wrote of 'a regulatory machine' seeking to 'ensure continuation of public outlays for bioassay activities.' And in 1993 he wrote, 'regulatory agencies have incentives not dissimilar from any other industry: product development, marketing, and growth ... what the agencies must absolutely guarantee ... is the continuing prosperity of legions of employees and clients, and the political viability and fortunes of their managements ... advocates, and ... congressional backers.'[168]

Breeders and suppliers of animals, animal parts, and laboratory equipment also have much to gain. All would go out of business if alternative technologies were to replace animals. Items advertised in journals of the trade such as *Laboratory Animal Science* include feed, bedding materials, food dispensers and watering systems, transfer and rearing isolators, stainless steel cages—some of which cost $4,000 apiece—heaters, ventilation and sophisticated air filtration systems, syringes, measuring and weighing devices, diagnostic equipment, laboratory coats, and washable guillotines for decapitating mice, rats and other animals.[169] Animal breeders include the international (US-based) Charles River Breeding Laboratories (CRBL), Hazleton Laboratories in Vienna, Virginia, Harlan Sprague Dawley in Indiana, The Buckshire Corporation in Pennsylvania, The Coulston Foundation, a primate breeder and contract laboratory in Alamogordo, New Mexico (notorious for its animal welfare violations), and many others.

CRBL was described by *Fortune* magazine as 'the General Motors of its industry.' In 1983, sixteen CRBL facilities in seven countries 'produced' 22 million primates, rats, mice, guinea pigs and hamsters for sale to pharmaceutical companies, government agencies, the US Army, commercial testing laboratories and universities for a total of $45 million.[170] The company was acquired in 1984 for $135 million in stock by Bausch & Lomb, a giant in the field of consumer and industrial optics (such as Rayban eyeglasses, lenses and microscopes). Charles River Laboratories, which is awarded non-competitive contracts from the EPA, has now grown to include subsidiaries in the Czech Republic, The Netherlands, France, Italy, the UK, Germany, Hungary, Sweden, Spain, Belgium, and Japan.[171]

Charles River Research Primates, which breeds and imports primates from Africa, Asia and other countries, is the largest primate research facility in the world according to *Industry* magazine.[172] CRBL also owns Charles River Pharm Services (formerly East Acres Biologicals), a 350-acre research farm in the US which houses rabbits, chickens, geese, ducks, turkeys, horses, donkeys, ponies, cows, goats, sheep, and pigs. The facility does contract research with universities and pharmaceutical companies for whom it provides custom antisera and a range of blood products (sterile and non-sterile blood plasma, cells, tissues, organs and body fluids).[173] Consolidated revenues for Bausch & Lomb totaled $1,851 million in 1994 with 14 percent of that (or circa $260 million) derived from the sale of research animals by Charles River Laboratories.[174]

Biomedical research is a multi-billion dollar business; the biomedical research establishment's social and political influence is far-reaching and cannot be underestimated. Those who use and supply animals for research enjoy the support of a vast network of politicians, public and private granting agencies and academic institutions. Animal 'breeding and supplying establishments' are cited in EEC Directives (see 86/609/EEC, Articles 15, 18, 19(4)) and are awarded 'general or special exemptions' from requirements regarding the provenance, handling and treatment of 'laboratory animals.' The practice of using animals in research and testing is reinforced through all of these social and regulatory mechanisms, by the scientific community itself which continues to plead for the necessity of such research, and most importantly by the media which communicates the official party line to a public that rarely gets to hear both sides of a story. Some anti-vivisection groups have charged that the animal *welfare* groups have contributed to this state of affairs by accepting positions on 'animal research ethics committees,' thereby accepting the vivisection principle as bonafide.[175]

A challenge to this establishment is an enormous social and economic threat to those who profit from it. Financial, political and legal means have been used to silence alternative voices and disrupt the democratic process: by denying those voices equal time in the media (pharmaceutical companies are big sponsors of network television stations),[176] creating well-financed challenges to underfunded lobbying and legislative efforts, and so on. The extent of the biomedical establishment's influence, and the scientific community's constant public denigration of those who disagree with the official party line, has made it extremely difficult for dissenting individuals (including scientists) and advocacy groups to get their message through to the public. Many have encouraged investigative journalists to explore the issue; yet others have chosen to publish their own books and educational materials on the subject.

Irrespective of the profit motive, it is also probable that many scientists, regulators and heads of industry are simply used to the concept of animals as research tools and are uncomfortable with the idea of using unfamiliar technologies. According to Richard Griesemer, deputy director of the NIEHS, the number of scientists applying for federal grants and competing for contracts involving animal studies is increasing, not decreasing.[177] In *Animals and Alternatives: Present Status and Future Prospects* (Christoph A. Reinhardt, ed., 1991, p. 342), André McLean says that 'our power of intellectual analysis has improved enormously. Against that, our use of animals in toxicology appears very crude and old-fashioned, sometimes because we haven't thought of how to do things a different way.'

Product litigation charges have also become a serious problem, and consequently are a big barrier to change. Corporations are often skeptical of accepting a new testing method that could open them up to lawsuits if something were to go wrong, even though courts have increasingly questioned the validity of animal test data in worker compensation and product liability lawsuits. In *Johnson Controls v. The Natural Resources Defense Council* (NRDC), regarding a causal link between paternal exposure to lead in the workplace and consequent harm to offspring, NRDC challenged the Seventh Court of Appeals for rejecting animal testing data as 'speculative and unconvincing.'[178]

Nevertheless, according to Paul Wegner, director of marketing for the Clonetics Corporation, a company in San Diego which develops non-animal screens for toxicity testing, during the early stages of product development corporate toxicologists do not want anything in the records that might contradict the animal tests which are an approved method. Because animal tests are both more apt to ensure regulatory approval for new products, and to provide some measure of legal shelter, regulators and corporations alike may be reluctant to abandon them.

In this chapter I have shown that animal tests have not protected humans from exposure to harmful chemicals, nor have they been effective at slowing the growth of the chemical industry. I have described the burdensome nature of federal regulations which seem to encourage the perpetuation of a chemical testing system that is both inefficient and inhumane. Though many individual scientists would welcome a move away from animal testing, new ideas appear to be squashed by a bureaucracy seemingly more concerned with self-preservation than with genuine efficiency and scientific progress. Perhaps the most exasperating aspect of all, is federal regulatory agencies' refusal to incorporate non-animal testing methods into policy guidelines. The huge lobbying power of industry, which views new regulations as burdensome, cannot be discounted; and because chemical manufacturers have benefited from the long litigious consequences of ambiguous animal studies, they (along with other branches of business and science that have profited from the continued use of animals in testing) may lobby hard against efforts to change the system.

Despite such formidable obstacles, hundreds of non-animal testing technologies, or 'alternatives' as they are referred to, have been developed within the last two to three decades; the number of companies offering these technologies is growing. They have gained increasing acceptance by toxicologists and businesses alike because they are cost-efficient and easily reproducible. Regulatory agencies will be compelled, sooner or later, to come to terms with the inefficiency of the current system, and incorporate new technologies into their testing guidelines.

Some of these methods include computerized modeling and prediction systems (involving pharmacokinetic and/or mathematically-based programs), genetically engineered cell lines, X-ray assays, batteries of human skin and tissue cultures, epidemiological studies of populations, and carefully controlled clinical trials in which human volunteers agree to inhale, ingest or apply a particular substance under study.[179]

Non-animal technologies are being used by businesses, state and federal agencies in the US and elsewhere to determine mutagenicity, teratogenicity, and many forms of toxicity. Regulatory steps are being taken on an international level which are fueling efforts to replace animals.[180] While the merits of these technologies have been recognized, funding for the validation and implementation of existing non-animal methods by governments has been scarce and slow to be forthcoming. Most scientists say that the data from non-animal tests must be validated against existing animal data in order to be proven worthy; others believe this is counterproductive, and contrary to the aim of acquiring better data that is relevant to humans. In addition, while the animal tests themselves have never been scientifically validated, as was discussed in Chapter 3, animal advocates and some scientists believe that a double standard exists for non-animal technologies; the long, tedious validation process required for non-animal methods, mandated by scientists, is slowing down the implementation process and permitting the continuation of animal tests.

The debate about what constitutes 'an animal' will be examined briefly since many scientists who claim to be using 'alternative' methods are still using mammals and/or non-mammalian species in their laboratories.

Notes

1. Personal communication with David Sarokin, Director, Special Projects, Environmental Assistance Division, EPA, Washington, DC, 13 October 1995. Sarokin said that 0 percent was a result of 'rounding off to the nearest whole number.' Some success stories include mercury and lead in household paint, asbestos in floor tiling and insulation, chlorofluorocarbon coolants (CFCs), and polychlorinated biphenyls or PCBs. Grace Offen, *Greening Consumer Products Through Reformulation: Evaluation of Selected Strategies* (Tufts University, Medford, Massachusetts, 1996, unpublished).

2. Personal communication(s) with Brian Syms, Acting Chief of Toxic Substances Release Inventory Branch, and Jim Bradshaw, Information Management Division, of the Environmental Protection Agency, Washington, DC, 12 October 1995. Both conceded that different agencies may issue conflicting rulings, or there may be inter-agency overlap with respect to the regulation of chemicals.

3. Human data exist for only circa thirty substances, including benzene, asbestos, cigarette smoke, lead, and vinyl chloride. Joel Brinkley, 'Many Say Lab Animal Tests Fail to Measure Human Risk,' *The New York Times*, 23 March 1993, p. A16.

4. Ibid.

5. Thalidomide, the sedative given to pregnant women in the 1960s, which caused over ten thousand children in 46 countries to be born with crippling deformities, is now being marketed in Brazil and other developing countries as a 'cure' for cancer, AIDS, leprosy, and other disorders. Anne Underwood, 'A "Bad" Drug May Turn Out To Do Good,' *Newsweek*, 19 September 1994, p. 58–9. 'Thalidomide,' on *Sixty Minutes* (WCBS TV, USA) 28 July 1996, Burrelle's Transcripts.

6. Carl Smith, 'Countries Accept "Dirty Dozen" Pesticides From US Shippers Despite National Bans,' *Global Pesticide Campaigner*, newsletter published by Pesticide Action Network, San Francisco, California (September 1995): 3, 17. US Customs records indicate that between 1991 and 1994, at least eleven million pounds of pesticides including DDT, chlordane, paraquat, and parathion, were exported from the US to countries where their use is expressly banned.

7. Neal Barnard, 'Getting Chemicals Out of Our Environment: Tediously Slow Animal Tests Actually Prolong Human Risk,' *PCRM Update*, newsletter of the Physicians Committee for Responsible Medicine, Washington, DC (January–February 1990): 1; Richard B. Kurzel, 'The Effect of Environmental Pollutants on Human Reproduction, Including Birth Defects,' *Environ. Sci. Technol.* 15, no. 6 (June 1981): 638.

8. Vincent F. Garry, et al., 'Pesticide Appliers, Biocides, and Birth Defects in Rural Minnesota,' *Env. Health Persp.* 104, no. 4 (April 1996): 394–9.

9. Kaye H. Kilburn and John C. Thornton, 'Protracted Neurotoxicity From Chlordane Sprayed to Kill Termites,' *Env. Health Persp.* 103, no. 7–8 (July–August 1995): 690–4.

10. Leslie Lang, 'Mouse or Molecule,' *Env. Health Persp.* 103, no. 4 (April 1995): 334.

11. Frederick Kutz, et al., 'Ecological Research at EPA: New Directions,' *Environ. Sci. Technol.* 26, no. 5 (1992): 863.

12. Gina Kolata, 'New System of Assessing Health Risks is Urged,' *The New York Times*, 14 June 1996, p. A26.

13. Leslie Lang, 'Strange Brew,' *Env. Health Persp.* 103, no. 2 (February 1995): 142–5.

14. Al Meyerhoff, quoted in Mary H. Cooper, 'Regulating Pesticides,' *The Congressional Quarterly Researcher* (28 January 1994): 76.

15. Edith Efron, *The Apocalyptics: Cancer and the Big Lie* (New York: Simon & Schuster, 1984), p. 338.

16. Anthony Cortese, in *Critical Condition: Human Health and the Environment*, Eric Chivian, et al., eds (Cambridge, MA: The MIT Press, 1993), pp. 9–10.

17. Anon, 'Illegal Poisons in our Food,' *Rachel's Environment & Health Weekly* 493 (9 May 1996), published by the Environmental Research Foundation, Annapolis, Maryland, p. 1.

18. Richard Dahl, 'A National Proposition 65?,' *Env. Health Persp.* 103, nos 7–8 (July–August 1995): 672–4.

19. Environmental Working Group (EWG), Washington, DC, *Pesticides in Children's Food* (June 1993).

20. EWG press release, 'Tap Water Tests Find Weed Killers in 29 Cities: Herbicide Levels Routinely Exceeded Federal Safeguards,' 17 August 1995, courtesy of Richard Wiles, EWG, Washington, DC.

21. John H. Cushman, Jr., 'EPA is Canceling Pollution Testing Across the Nation: Budget Cuts are Blamed,' *The New York Times*, 25 November 1995, p. A1.

22. G. W. Suter and J. M. Loar, 'Weighing the Ecological Risk of Hazardous Waste Sites,' *Environ. Sci. Technol.* 26, no. 3 (1992).

23. 'Lab Given Permit to Dump Radioactive Water,' *The New York Times*, 15 October 1995, p. 36. Accidental spills wreak environmental havoc as well. Trains, trucks and boats have spilled toxic chemicals into the environment, killing wildlife and sometimes contaminating waterways for miles. Mary H. Cooper (28 January 1994): 79.

24. Richard Peto, 'Distorting the Epidemiology of Cancer,' *Nature* 284 (27 March 1980): 297–300. Methylene chloride and arsenic (a known human carcinogen) are still being used in the profitable computer chip industry despite a long history of concern over their use. Workers, who contracted brain, colon and testicular cancers, or whose loved ones died while working at computer chip factories, are suing the chemical manufacturers in a high-profile case which is likely to last for several years. William Glaberson and Julia Campbell, 'Ailing Computer-Chip Workers Blame Chemicals, Not Chance,' *The New York Times*, 28 March 1996, p. B1.

25. Curtis C. Travis, 'Determining an Acceptable Level of Risk,' *Environ. Sci. Technol.* 22, no. 8 (1988): 876.

26. M. S. Reisch, *Chemical & Engineering News* (9 April 1990), table, p. 12.

27. Marc Lappé, *Chemical Deception* (San Francisco: Sierra Club Books, 1991), pp. 45–6.

28. Eric Goldstein, 'N.Y. Air,' *The Amicus Journal*, published by the Natural Resources Defense Council, New York (Summer 1990).

29. Richard Dahl (July–August 1995): 673.

30. Mary H. Cooper (28 January 1994): 85. See *Regulating Pesticides in Food: The Delaney Paradox* (Washington, DC: National Academy of Sciences, 1987). The agri-chemical industry and EPA have historically ignored the Delaney Clause with respect to pesticides, relying instead on the Federal Insecticide, Fungicide and Rodenticide Act (FIFRA), which health and food safety advocates and environmentalists have for years criticized as being too weak.

31. Mike Weilbacher, 'Toxic Shock: the Environment–Cancer Connection,' *E Magazine*, June/July 1995, p. 30. A 1992 FDA study concluded that the average American family's supermarket grocery bags are laden with some 60–80 pesticides, herbicides, rodenticides and fungicides, several of them considered carcinogenic based on animal tests.

32. Associated Press, 'Food-Pesticide Overhaul Wins House Passage,' *The New York Times*, 24 July 1996, p. A18.

33. See note 18.

34. Jack Cooper, 'Update on Pesticide Laws and Regulations Affecting the Food Industry,' *Food Technology* (February 1992): 95; Sara Brudnoy, 'Pushing for a Paradigm Shift in Risk Assessment,' *The Scientist* (8 March 1993): 14.

35. *US Chemical Statistical Handbook* (Washington, DC: Chemical Manufacturers Association, 1994), p. 156. As of 1996, there were an estimated 30–40,000 hazardous waste sites in the US. Robin Meadows, 'Growing Pains,' *Env. Health Persp.* 104, no. 2 (February 1996): 148. Containers of nerve and mustard gas and other chemical poisons used by the military are buried at hundreds of other sites, and their potential threat to human health and the environment has not been assessed. It will probably take until the year 2034 at a cost of $17.7 billion to destroy all the chemicals and equipment (including storage and spray tanks) in these sites. 'Away From Politics' section, *The Herald Tribune*, 25 November 1992, p. 3.

36. John Robbins, *Diet for a New America* (New Hampshire: Stillpoint Publishing, 1987), p. 313; Mary H. Cooper (28 January 1994): 85.

37. Robin Meadows (February 1996): 146.

38. R. Clay and R. Dahl, 'Beyond Dobris,' *Env. Health Persp.* 104, no. 1 (January 1996): 32–4.

39. Mary H. Cooper (28 January 1994), 86.

40. *Chemical & Engineering News* (27 November 1989): 34.

41. Federal Civilian Employment Records, courtesy of April Bright, USDA, Human Resources Management, Washington, DC, 22 July 1996.

42. Personal communication with Robert Meyers, USDA, Office of Alternative Agriculture, Washington, DC, 22 July 1996. Some eight to ten employees in the USDA's National Organic Program have been assigned to implement national organic standards, but they are not involved in developing or promoting organic agriculture (OA). One long-time USDA employee who wished not to be identified said that it was not the USDA's mission to *develop* OA; that would have to be legislated. Meyers concurred and said that his department plays more of a supportive role by dispensing grants to OA and alternative pest control projects. While there is activity towards this end in universities, work within the USDA itself in this area is very fragmented, and grossly under-funded.

43. Eric M. Silberhorn, et al., 'Carcinogenicity of Polyhalogenated Biphenyls: PCBs and PBBs,' *Critical Reviews in Toxicology* 20, no. 6 (1990): 439–96; Rachel Carson, *Silent Spring* (New York: Houghton-Mifflin, 1994), p. 225.

44. Daniel H. Rosen, et al., 'Half-Life of Polybrominated Biphenyl in Human Sera,' *Env. Health Persp.* 103 (1995): 272–4.

45. Anon, 'Greenpeace and Human Health,' *Greenpeace Quarterly*, Washington, DC (Summer 1996), p. 9.

46. Arnold Schecter, a dioxin expert, reported that in samples of commonly consumed fast foods analyzed by his laboratory, there were 8 to 150 times more dioxins in them than the EPA feels would be a reasonable level. Cable News Network, transcript of *Network Earth* program, Sunday 25 June 1995.

47. A massive die-off of dolphins along the eastern shore of the United States in 1987 is presumed to have been caused by elevated levels of PCBs, DDTs and other pollutants found in the animals' blubber and tissue which are suspected to have caused immunoincompetence and susceptibility to a deadly bacterial infection. David Sarokin and Jay Schulkin, 'The Role of Pollution in Large-Scale Population Disturbances,' *Environ. Sci. Technol.* 26, no. 8 (1992): 1479. More recently, high rates of intestinal cancers in dead Beluga whales washed ashore in Canada's Gulf of St. Lawrence over the last decade have been attributed to toxic chemicals in the water, including dioxins, furans, PCBs, Mirex and mercury. Clyde H. Farnsworth, 'Scientists are Puzzled Over the Deaths of Whales in the St. Lawrence,' *The New York Times*, 22 August 1995, p. C12; 'Belugas in Danger,' *Greenpeace Quarterly*, Washington, DC (Summer 1996), p. 11.

48. Richard B. Kurzel (June 1981): 630.

49. Anon, 'Fear of Phenolphthalein?,' *Env. Health Persp.* 104, no. 3 (March 1996): 250.

50. F. Pott, et al., 'Tumorigenic Effect of Fibrous Dusts in Experimental Animals,' *Env. Health Persp.* 9 (1974): 313–15; J. Wagner, et al., 'Studies of the Carcinogenic Effect of Fiber Glass of Different Diameters Following Intrapleural Inoculation in Experimental Animals,' *Occupational Exposure to Fibrous Glass*, Proceedings of a Symposium sponsored by the National Institute for Occupational Safety and Health, University of Maryland, 26–27 June 1974, HEW Pub. No. (NIOSH): 76–151.

51. Robert Sharpe, 'Occupational Hazards,' *The AV Magazine*, Jenkintown, Pennsylvania (January/February 1995), p. 9.

52. Anon, 'Fiberglass is Possible Carcinogen,' *The New York Times*, 3 July 1994, p. 20. In 1991, OSHA decided that glass fiber products should be labelled as a potential cancer hazard. The decision followed studies of workers which showed an increased risk of lung cancer. In the 1950s, experiments with rats, guinea pigs, rabbits and monkeys produced no lung damage when the animals were forced to breathe the fibers. And an analysis in the 1980s revealed that hamsters, guinea pigs, mice,

monkeys, and baboons exposed to glass fibers, glass wool or mineral wool (in use since the 1950s) did not produce lung tumors following long-term inhalation. Ironically, experiments in which rats did develop cancer were dismissed as unlikely to have any relevance to the human condition because glass fibers were implanted into the tissue membrane lining the animal's lung, whereas people breathe in the fibers. It is well known that rats are especially prone to cancer when solid substances are surgically implanted in their bodies. In his book, *Occupational Lung Disorders*, Raymond Parkes concludes that 'the production of malignant tumors in animals by direct implantation experiments is unlikely to have any relevance to human exposure.' Robert Sharpe, *Science on Trial* (Sheffield, UK: Awareness Publishing, 1994), p. 106.

53. A. L. Kraus, et al., 'Benzoyl Peroxide: An Integrated Human Safety Assessment for Carcinogenicity,' *Regul. Toxicol. Pharmacol.* 21, no. 1 (1996): 87–107.

54. Joel Brinkley (23 March 1993), p. A16.

55. Robert Sharpe (January/February 1995), pp. 8–9.

56. Nedim C. Buyukmihci, 'Safety Testing of Products for Human Use ... ,' source: Internet address, http://www.envirolink ... arrs/avar/testing, as of July 1995. Carl Smith (September 1995): 3.

57. Dennis M. Maloney, 'Toxicity Tests in Animals: Extrapolating to Human Risks,' *Env. Health Persp.* 101, no. 5 (October 1993): 396.

58. L. B. Ellwein and S. M. Cohen, 'The Health Risks of Saccharin Revisited,' *Crit. Rev. Toxicol.* 20, no. 5 (1990): 311–26. Because of the way that regulatory laws are written, saccharin cannot be used as a food additive, but by a special legislative exemption, it can be used as an artificial sweetener with an accompanying warning as to its carcinogenicity in 'laboratory animals.' Sara Brudnoy, 'Pushing for a Paradigm Shift in Cancer Risk Assessment,' *The Scientist*, 8 March 1993, p. 14.

59. Dennis V. Parke, 'Ethical Aspects of the Safety of Medicines ... ', *Science & Engineering Ethics* 1 (1995): 291.

60. Ann M. Thayer, 'Alar Controversy Mirrors Difference in Risk Perceptions,' *Chemical and Engineering News* (28 August 1989), pp. 7–14.

61. Eric Dunayer, 'Testing Chemicals: Animal Testing Impedes Regulatory Action,' unpublished paper courtesy of The Physicians Committee for Responsible Medicine, Washington, DC (1992), pp. 9–10; Neal Barnard (January–February 1990): 1. Proponents of organic farming emphasize that food should be eaten where it's grown. This eliminates the need for preservatives and thus toxicity testing; in addition, transportation of produce to distant sites becomes unnecessary thereby conserving fossil fuels and reducing air pollution.

62. Joseph V. Rodricks, *Calculated Risks* (UK: Cambridge University Press, 1992), p. 213.

63. T. Tanimura, et al., *Arch. Environ. Health* 15 (1967): 609–13.

64. Parathion Fact Sheet, Federal CAS No. 56–38–2, courtesy of the Rachel Carson Council, Chevy Chase, Maryland.

65. Quinby et al., 'Parathion Residues as a Cause of Poisoning in Crop Workers,' *Journal of the American Medical Association* 166 (15 February 1958): 740–6; Rachel Carson, *Silent Spring* (New York: Houghton-Mifflin, 1994), p. 29.

66. Anne Schonfield, et al., 'PAN's Dirty Dozen Campaign – The View at Ten Years,' *Global Pesticide Campaigner* (September 1995): 8, see references 6–9.

67. Anon, 'Deadly Pesticide May Face US Ban,' *The New York Times*, 26 March 1991, p. A20.

68. This method of planting places specific plant species side by side to encourage beneficial insects, like ladybugs and wasps (who live on plant A), to eat offending pest populations (on plant B).

69. Mary H. Cooper (28 January 1994): 78–82.

70. Frank D. Schaumburg, 'Banning Trichloroethylene: Responsible Reaction or Overkill?,' *Environ. Sci. Technol.* 24, no. 1 (1990): 17–22.

71. Of six different gavage studies, two, using Swiss mice (Henschler) and Osborne-Mendel rats (NCI), found no significant increase in tumors; one by the NTP was considered inadequate to evaluate the presence of a carcinogenic response. A series of tests by Maltoni produced kidney tumors in male Sprague-Dawley rats and lung tumors in B6C3F1 mice; but the EPA Scientific Advisory Board judged the studies to be incomplete and of questionable value. Of seven different inhalation studies, two (by the MCA, using B6C3F1 mice and Charles River rats) were judged inadequate to evaluate carcinogenicity; one study by Fukuda found an increase in lung tumors in female ICR mice at high doses, but the incidence of total lung tumors did not significantly increase; another by Henschler found no increased tumors in male NMRI mice, but did see increased lymphomas in females which were not attributed to TCE. Another Henschler study with Wistar rats and Syrian hamsters produced negative results. And again, three Maltoni studies were deemed inconclusive. Trichloroethylene White Paper (Washington, DC: Halogenated Solvents Industry Alliance, April 1989).

72. Richard B. Kurzel (June 1981): 629. It has been known for years that *tetra*chloroethylene, a solvent similar to TCE present in dry-cleaning fluids, and used in anesthesia, causes spontaneous abortions, infertility and birth defects in humans. Ironically, the EPA approved trichloro*ethane* (TCA) and freon as alternatives to TCE in the mid-1970s. TCA is now on the EPA list of suspected carcinogens and freon is implicated in the destruction of the ozone. Frank D. Schaumburg (1990): 21.

73. 'Carcinogenesis Bioassay of Trichloroethylene,' CAS No. 79–01–6, NCI–CG–TR–2 (Washington, DC: National Cancer Institute, 1976).

74. In 1989 OSHA lowered the Permissible Exposure Levels (PELs) for TCE from 100 parts per million for an 8-hour exposure period to 50 parts per million; a short-term exposure limit (STEL) of 200 parts per million for a 15-minute exposure period was also approved. The EPA has set a Maximum Contaminant Level for TCE in drinking water of 5 micrograms per liter. TCE Tear Sheet (Pittsburgh: PPG Industries, Inc, undated).

75. TCE is currently regulated as a toxic priority pollutant under the Clean Water Act, and a hazardous air pollutant under the Clean Air Act. There are also reporting requirements of 1,000-pound releases into the environment under Sections 311–13 of the Emergency Planning and Community Right to Know Act (EPA's SARA Title III regulations).

76. Trichloroethylene Tear Sheet, CAS No. 79–01–6 (Washington, DC: Environmental Protection Agency, undated), courtesy of David Sarokin, EPA. Bedrich Molden, 'Czechoslovakia: Examining a Critically Ill Environment,' *Environ. Sci. Technol.* 26, no. 1 (1992): 16.

77. Frank D. Schaumburg (1990): 20.

78. E. Thorpe and A. Walker, 'Comparative Long-Term Oral Toxicity Studies in Mice With Dieldrin, … BHC,' *Fd. Cosmet. Toxicol.* 11 (1973): 433–42, cited in Eric Dunayer (1992), p. 11.

79. Eric Dunayer (1992), pp. 11–12.

80. US Congress, Office of Technology Assessment, *Identifying and Regulating Carcinogens* (Washington, DC: US Government Printing Office, 1987), cited in Eric Dunayer (1992), p. 11.

81. Eric Dunayer (1992), p. 12.

82. 'Fatal Lindane Contamination in India,' *Indian Express*, May 1990.

83. Environmental Protection Agency, *Suspended, Canceled, and Restricted Pesticides* (Washington, DC: US EPA, 1990). Six to twelve million children contract lice annually in the United States according to the National Pediculosis Foundation in Boston, Massachusetts. This figure is based upon sales figures for commonly sold delousing agents.

84. Anitra Frazier, *The New Natural Cat* (New York: Plume, 1990). Diana Post, 'Some "Modern" Pesticides Don't Know When to Stop Poisoning Our Pets,' in *Rachel Carson Council News* No. 86, published by the Rachel Carson Council, Chevy Chase, Maryland (October 1995), p. 1. Pennyroyal, a herb with insect repellant properties, has been suggested as an alternative, and several natural non-toxic anti-parasitic dips are available in specialty pet stores.

85. Personal communication with Deborah Altschuler, President, National Pediculosis Foundation (NPF), Boston, Massachusetts, 22 September 1995.

86. Ibid. According to NPF, the majority of users have followed directions when using the product, while in some cases pharmacists neglected to include directions on labels.

87. Cable News Network, 1 November 1994. The British National Formulary (1993) warns users to 'avoid contact with eyes' when using lindane preparations since they are known to cause excessive eye irritation and conjunctivitis in humans. In rabbits, on the other hand, the application of a far more concentrated solution of lindane produces minimal effects. W. M. Grant, *Toxicology of the Eye*, 2nd edn (Springfield, IL: Charles Thomas, 1974).

88. J. R. Davis, 'Family Pesticide Use and Childhood Brain Cancer,' *Arch. Environ. Contam. Toxicol.* 24 (1993): 87–92.

89. Personal communication with Erik Walum, Senior Researcher, Pharmacia AB, Biopharmaceuticals, Stockholm, Sweden, 15 October 1995. E. Walum, et al., 'Principles for the Validation of In Vitro Toxicology Test Methods,' *Toxic. In Vitro* 8, no. 4 (1994): 807–12.

90. Personal communication with Robert Sharpe, Sheffield, UK, 24 October 1995. Advanced Tissue Sciences in La Jolla, California is currently conducting such tests. See Chapter 5.

91. Personal communication with Phil Casterton, Amway, Michigan, 16 August 1996.

92. Humbart Santillo, *Natural Healing With Herbs* (Prescott, Arizona: Hohm Press, 1993), pp. 183–4.

93. Personal communication with Linda, National Pediculosis Foundation, Massachusetts, 10 October 1995.

94. J. R. LaPorte, 'Effects of Dioxin Exposure,' *Lancet* 1 (14 May 1977): 1049–50; G. Bogen, 'Symptoms in Vietnam Veterans Exposed to Agent Orange,' *JAMA* 242, no. 22 (30 November 1979): 2391. John McArdle, 'The EPA, Dioxin and Animal Testing: Here We Go Again?,' *The AV Magazine*, Jenkintown, Pennsylvania (January/February 1995), pp. 16–17. One 1991 government study blamed high levels of dioxin for numerous cancers in chemical workers. Sharon Begley, 'Don't Drink the Dioxin,' *Newsweek*, 19 September 1994, p. 57. Non-cancer effects such as developmental toxicity, reproductive and immunological effects have also been tentatively linked to exposure from minute doses of dioxin-like compounds in the food supply. Anon, 'EPA Affirms Health Dangers from Dioxin,' *The New York Times*, 13 September 1994, p. A14.

95. Joel Brinkley (23 March 1993), p. A16.

96. Warren R. Flint and John Vena, *Human Health Risks From Chemical Exposure: The Great Lakes Ecosystem* (New York: Lewis Publications, Inc, 1991), p. 34. John McArdle (January/February 1995), pp. 16–17. A five-and-a-half-page summary of a 2,000-page document released by the EPA in 1994, *Dioxin Facts: Scientific Highlights from Draft Reassessment*, contained no fewer than 75 qualifying words and adjectives, including 'may,' 'potential,' 'might,' 'likely,' and 'uncertain' in describing the relevance of animal test data for humans. In *The Apocalyptics* (1984, p. 217), author Edith Efron states, 'if one pays close attention to all the "mights" and "mays" one sees that these are all ways of saying that the mechanisms of carcinogenesis are still shrouded in ignorance.'

97. Dennis M. Maloney (October 1993): 398.

98. Gordon Graff, 'The Chlorine Controversy,' *Technology Review* (January 1995), p. 55.

99. Office of Communications, Education and Public Affairs, 'Dioxin Facts: EPA's On-Going Regulatory Program,' US EPA, Washington, DC, September 1994, pp. 1–5.

100. Greenpeace Action Report on Pesticides (Washington, DC: Greenpeace, 1990).

101. Herman Kraybill, 'Conceptual Approaches to the Assessment of Non-occupational Environmental Cancer,' *Advances in Modern Toxicology*, Vol. 3, Myron A. Mehlman, ed. (Washington, DC: Hemisphere, 1977), p. 37, cited in Edith Efron (1984), p. 269.

102. Lorenzo Tomatis, et. al, 'Studies on the Carcinogenicity of DDT,' *GANN Monograph on Cancer Research*, No. 17, O. Shigeyoshi, et al., eds, Japanese Cancer Association (Baltimore–London–Tokyo: University Park Press, 1975), p. 219, cited in Edith Efron (1984), p. 267.

103. H. P. Burchfield and Eleanor E. Storrs, 'Organohalogen Carcinogens,' *Advances in Modern Toxicology*, Vol. 3, *Environmental Cancer*, Myron A. Mehlman, ed. (Washington, DC: Hemisphere, 1977), pp. 355–6, cited in Edith Efron (1984), p. 269.

104. R. A. M. Case, 'Toxic Effects of DDT in Man,' *British Medical Journal* 2 (15 December 1945): 842–5.

105. Wayland J. Hayes, Jr., et al., 'Storage of DDT and DDE in People ... ,' *AMA Archives of Industrial Health* 18 (November 1958): 398–406.

106. H. P. Burchfield and Eleanor E. Storrs (1977).

107. Joel Brinkley (23 March 1993), p. A16.

108. Robin Meadows (February 1996): 148.

109. Patricia Hynes, 'The Unfinished Business of *Silent Spring*,' *Massachusetts Institute of Technology Environment* newsletter, Cambridge, MA (September 1992): 9–10. Under FIFRA, pesticides must be registered and the intended use of the product defined; but registration is not required for export, so that pesticides which have never been registered, whose registrations have been withdrawn, or whose uses have been highly restricted in the US may be exported for unrestricted uses to other countries. Chris Bright, 'Shipping Unto Others: Outlawed American Pesticides Find Markets Elsewhere,' *E Magazine* (July/August 1990), p. 30. A survey of 1991 pesticide exports by the Foundation for Advancements in Science and Education found that 96 tons of DDT were exported out of the US that year, twenty years after the ban on the chemical became effective. Carl Smith (September 1995): 3.

110. Carlton H. Nadolney, 'Alternatives to Whole-Animal Testing: Research Programs of the US Environmental Protection Agency,' in *Future Medical Research Without the Use of Animals: Facing the Challenge*, Proceedings of the Conference, 15–16 May 1990, Tel Aviv, Israel, published by Concern for Helping Animals in Israel (CHAI), Alexandria, Virginia, p. 158.

111. Hoorik Davoudian, 'Animal Experimentation: the Hidden Cause of Environmental Pollution? ... ,' a booklet published by SUPRESS, Inc. (Glendale California, 1993), p. 6. Rudolf Bahro, formerly with the West German Green Party, anticipated these sentiments in 1986 when he campaigned for an unconditional ban on animal experiments. Bahro believed that animal experimentation was the product of a misguided and corrupt scientific establishment. He suggested that science's unnatural partnership with industry was leading Western society into a profound environmental, spiritual and social crisis. Rudolf Bahro, *Building the Green Movement* (Philadelphia: New Society Publishers, 1986), pp. 196–209.

112. Irwin Bross, in *Future Medical Research Without the Use of Animals: Facing the Challenge* (1990), p.87.

113. A. Worden, et al., in *The Future of Predictive Safety Evaluation*, A. Worden, et al., eds (Boston, MA: MTP Press, 1986), p. 37.

114. Holly Hazard, Doris Day Animal League (DDAL), Memo to Congresswoman Barbara Boxer, Re: 'Confusion and Chaos Concerning Federal Regulatory Requirements for Acute Toxicity Testing on Animals by United States Corporations,' 2 December 1987, courtesy of Sara Amundson, DDAL, Washington, DC.

115. Patricia L. Lang, 'Product Safety Assessment: a Review of Animal Testing Requirements in the US,' Reference Paper (Fall 1991), Charles River Laboratories, Wilmington, Massachusetts.

116. Personal communication with Carlton H. Nadolney, Division of Chemical Screening and Risk Assessment, Environmental Protection Agency, Washington, DC, 1 June 1995.

117. For an overview of this issue, see Heidi J. Welsh, *Animal Testing and Consumer Products* (Washington, DC: Investor Responsibility Research Center Inc, 1990).

118. *Federal Register* (17 July 1992) Vol. 57, No. 138, pp. 31721–37. In a section of a 1992 report by the NTP Board of Scientific Counselors, entitled, 'Development of Alternate Assays to Replace or Complement Mammalian Studies,' (p. 31727), the NTP says that, 'the development and evaluation of animal and other models for toxicologic determinations is inherent to the mission of NTP.' The statement says that 'the NTP should foster the development and validation of new test systems' such as 'short-term assays, pharmacokinetic studies, structural analysis, mathematical modeling, ... *in vitro* studies and non-mammalian species.' The NTP also directs the National Institute of Environmental Health Sciences (NIEHS) to 'continue the exploration and validation of alternative systems including non-mammalian species.' The NIEHS is simultaneously directed to develop 'transgenic animals containing mutated positive oncogenes, deleted tumor suppressor genes and human oncogens.' The NTP considers transgenic mice to be valid alternatives to classic animal models. *National Toxicology Program: Fiscal Year 1994 Annual Plan*, Draft (North Carolina, NTP, May 1994). The report endorses a re-evaluation of high dosing practices but does not call for an abandonment of the Maximum Tolerated Dose (MTD) procedure. And, according to the NTP, 'at present there is no substitute for the [rodent] carcinogenesis bioassay.' That is perhaps why the so-called alternative methods the NTP proposes are not necessarily non-animal, why funding for the validation of non-animal methods steadily decreased from 1991 to 1993, and why three-quarters of the agency's budget is devoted to animal studies.

119. The US Office of Technology Assessment characterized 'methods development' as devising new approaches for extrapolating results from animals to humans, measuring uncertainty in test results, and developing new assay systems. Jan Ziegler, 'Health Risk Assessment Research: the OTA Report,' *Env. Health Persp.* 101, no. 5 (October 1993): 404.

120. House of Representatives, 101st Congress, Second Session, Hearings Before a Subcommittee of the Committee on Appropriations, Department of Labor, Health and Human Services, Education and Related Agencies, Appropriations for 1991, US Government Printing Office, Washington, DC, 1990, p. 327.

121. Joel Brinkley (23 March 1993), p. A16.

122. George Lucier, 'Mechanism-Based Toxicology in Cancer Risk Assessment,' *Env. Health Persp.* 104, no. 1 (January 1996): 84–8.

123. The submission of cosmetic safety testing information to the FDA on the part of cosmetic manufacturers is voluntary. Heidi J. Welsh (1990), p. 27.

124. L. P. Sanathanan, et al., 'A Blind Reanalysis of a Random Subset of NCI Bioassay Studies: Do Rats Predict Mice?,' *Fundamental & Applied Toxicology* 12 (1989): 191–201; Patricia L. Lang (Fall 1991).

125. Patricia L. Lang (Fall 1991).

126. Anon, 'Animal Research and Human Health: the Use of Animals in Product Safety Testing' (Washington, DC: Foundation for Biomedical Research, Undated).

127. The Japanese Ministry of Health and Welfare has refused to accept non-animal testing data from manufacturers. Personal communication with Hiromi Kamekura, Cosmetic Products Project, Japan Anti-Vivisection Association, Tokyo, 24 August 1996.

128. Holly Hazard, Memo to Congresswoman Barbara Boxer, 2 December 1987. In 1984, in a *Federal Register* statement concerning an amendment to antibiotic regulations which require LD_{50} tests to be performed prior to the marketing of a drug, the FDA critiqued the LD_{50} due to wide inter-species variability and consequently unreliable test results. The agency suggested a (non-animal) chemical potency assay that would be more reliable, cost-effective and precise. *Federal Register* (13 November 1984) Vol. 49, No. 220, p. 449919.

In a 1986 letter widely circulated by the FDA, Heinz J. Eiermann, Director of the Division of Cosmetics Technology, declared that the LD_{50} test had to be carried out to determine whether a cosmetic may be toxic when ingested by a child accidentally. In a letter to Senator Ida Mae Garrott of Maryland, 19 November 1987, Gary Flamm, Director of the FDA's Office of Toxicology Sciences, said, 'with respect to the classical LD_{50} test, use has diminished considerably over the past eight or so years. It is not required by the FDA at all.' Letter courtesy of Sara Amundson of the Doris Day Animal League, Washington, DC. Flamm asserted, however, that while there were a number of alternative procedures like the approximate LD_{50} and the limit test which could limit the numbers of animals used in tests, there were presently no 'non-animal alternative tests fully accepted by the scientific community;' Flamm maintained his support for the Draize and other refined versions of acute toxicity tests on animals.

129. Heidi J. Welsh (1990), p. 27.

130. Ibid., p. 81.

131. John R. Boyce, 'The Use of Animals in Testing: a Focal Point for Controversy,' *Journal of the American Veterinary Medical Association* 203, no. 4 (15 August 1993): 500.

132. Vicki Glaser, 'In Vitro Test Systems Getting a Close Look by Industry and the FDA,' *Genetic Engineering News*, 15 April 1995, p. 6. See also *The Scientist*, 28 October 1996.

133. See note 125.

134. Patricia L. Lang (Fall 1991), p. 2. Until 1984, regulations using animal data to define 'highly toxic' substances implicitly meant that companies had to test their products on animals to label their products properly. After the CPSC issued its policy statement, however, requirements became more ambiguous.

135. The protocol is set forth in the Code of Federal Regulations (1.1.1987 Edition) in sections 1500.3, 1500.40, and 1500.42. In section 1500.40, *Preparation of test animal*, experimenters are instructed to, 'make epidermal abrasions every two or three centimeters longitudinally over the area of exposure,' after which test liquids are applied onto the shaved and wounded skin of albino rabbits. Under section 1500.42, *Test for eye irritants*, experimenters are instructed to hold the albino rabbits 'firmly but gently until quiet' whereupon 'the test material is placed in one eye of each animal by gently pulling the lower lid away from the eyeball to form a cup into which the test substance [either solid, paste or liquid] is dropped.' Later in the regulations, the Act states that 'the number of animals tested shall be sufficient to give a statistically significant result,' without specifying that number.

136. In 1988, Andrew Ulsamer, CPSC's Associate Executive Director, in a letter to a Maryland legislator, wrote that animal tests such as the Draize and other acute toxicity tests were necessary due to the lack of adequate alternatives. [despite industry's widespread use of non-animal tests in-house] Heidi J. Welsh (1990), p. 31.

137. This was confirmed in August 1995 by Berrien Zettler, Deputy Director of Compliance Programs, who assured me that OSHA had no animal testing policy because it did not require such tests.

138. Letter to Sara Amundson of the Doris Day Animal League from Berrien Zettler, Deputy Director of Compliance Programs, OSHA, 3 March 1994, courtesy of Sara Amundson.

139. Ibid.

140. Patricia L. Lang (Fall 1991), pp. 2–3.

141. Anon, 'EPA Proposes New Screening of Chemicals,' *American Medical News*, 6 May 1996, p. 31.

142. See note 140. Gordon Graff reports that companies seeking to register, or reregister a pesticide must submit voluminous toxicity data. These typically include chronic rodent studies, generational teratogenesis studies on rabbits, and so on. Graff writes, 'such registration proceedings typically take years ... Beginning in 1989 for example, EPA started to reregister 800 active pesticide ingredients under tougher guidelines. As of April 1994, it had completed the process for only 60 compounds;' during that time, companies were allowed to sell their products. Gordon Graff (January 1995), p. 57.

143. Ibid.

144. In FIFRA, 40 CFR 158.135 under a section entitled *Kind of Data Required*, the toxicology data requirements listed are acute oral toxicity–rat, acute dermal toxicity, acute inhalation toxicity–rat, primary eye irritation–rabbit, acute delayed neurotoxicity–hen. And in the Federal Code of Regulations pertaining to requirements for compliance with EPA regulations, 40 CFR Ch. 1 (July 86 Edition) Section 162.3 (d), (e), (f) and (u), essentially summarizes experimental protocols and defines acute dermal and oral toxicity in terms of animal studies: (d) the term 'acute dermal LD_{50} means a single dermal dose of a substance ... that is lethal to 50 percent of the test population of animals under test conditions as specified in the Registration Guidelines.' Furthermore, in Section 157.22,(1),(2),(3),(4),(5), the EPA outlines *Toxicity criterion* 'based upon testing with an appropriate test species.' Specific LD_{50} and LC_{50} toxicity limits are given in relation to products sold in child-resistant packaging. Ocular irritation is discussed in terms of causing 'corneal ... irritation persisting for 21 days or more,' and dermal irritation is discussed in terms of a substance's ability to cause 'tissue destruction into the dermis and/or scarring ... at 72 hours.' In addition, pesticides must have 'warning,' 'caution' or 'poison' labels according to their toxicity which is to be measured by oral, dermal LD_{50} values,

inhalation LC50 values, and their ability to cause eye and skin effects, as per Section 162.10 of the regulations.

145. Carlton H. Nadolney, in *Future Medical Research Without the Use of Animals: Facing the Challenge* (1990), p. 159.

146. John H. Cushman, 'EPA Plans Radical Change in Calculation of Cancer Risks,' *The New York Times*, 16 April 1996, p. A1; Timothy Noah, 'EPA Will Rely Less on Animal Studies ... ,' *The Wall Street Journal*, 17 April 1996, p. B6; Gina Kolata, 'New System of Assessing Health Risks is Urged,' *The New York Times*, 14 June 1996, p. A26.

147. Personal communication with Oliver Fordham, National Program Manager, EPA, Office of Solid Waste, Economics, Methods, Risk Assessment Division, Washington, DC, 13 October 1995.

148. In 1991, the Paris-based OECD expressed its desire, at an international meeting, to replace the LD50 test with the 'fixed-dose procedure,' which uses *sub*-lethal doses of chemicals on a much smaller group of animals. Richard Hill of the EPA objected, claiming that the test gave no direct measurement of the minimum lethal dose of a substance; moreover the doses for the new test chosen by the OECD fit well with European classifications for whether a chemical is 'very toxic,' 'toxic,' or 'harmful' but less well with the US or Japanese systems. (EPA classifies chemicals similarly, but the divisions between the different categories are set at different doses.) At the US's behest, the OECD agreed to compromise and carry out preliminary 'sighting studies,' which involve testing female rats with varying doses of a chemical until a dose is found that will just kill. This move allowed US toxicologists to collect data on the minimum lethal dose of a chemical, even though these data are of dubious significance. Peter Aldhous, 'Tide Turns Against LD50,' *Nature* 353 (10 October 1991): 489.

149. *OECD Guidelines for Testing of Chemicals*, Vol. 2 (1987), Guideline 404 (Paris: Organisation for Economic Cooperation and Development, 1981). Angela Auletta, Director of the Health Effects Branch in the Health and Environmental Review Division at EPA, receives copies of all OECD guidelines and establishes the official US position on them. A testing strategy for ocular irritancy, which includes an *in vitro* test, was submitted by the European Union to the OECD's 25 member countries in 1995 who were to comment on the proposal by the Spring of 1996. Although forecasts for the bill's passage by the end of 1996 were good, William Stokes of the NIEHS reiterated that this does not mean *in vitro* tests will *replace* animals, but that they will be used as adjuncts. Personal communication with William Stokes, Environmental Toxicology Division, NIEHS, Research Triangle Park, North Carolina, 1 November 1995.

150. Myron A. Mehlman, et al., 'A Report on Methods to Reduce, Refine, and Replace Animal Testing in Industrial Toxicology Laboratories,' *Cell Biology and Toxicology* 5, no. 3 (1989): 349–58.

151. Ibid.

152. Personal communication with Proctor & Gamble, consumer relations department, 10 February 1997.

153. Personal communication with William Stokes, 1 November 1995.

154. Gerhard Zbinden, 'Alternatives to Animal Experimentation: Developing In Vitro Methods and Changing Legislation,' *TiPS* 11 (March 1990): 105; Barnaby J. Feder, 'Beyond White Rats and Rabbits,' *The New York Times*, 28 February 1988, Business section, p. 1.

155. Anon, 'Who We Are and What We Do,' brochure (Washington, DC: Chemical Manufacturers Association, 1992).

156. *US Chemical Industry Statistical Handbook* (Washington, DC: Chemical Manufacturers Association, 1994), p. 21.

157. Most weed scientists believe that the majority of herbicides are safe when used as directed, even though the surfactants and solvents added to herbicides to improve application are not considered in EPA toxicity tests. Sheldon Krimsky, *Agricultural Biotechnology* (Illinois: University of Illinois Press, 1996); Goldburg, et al., *Biotechnology's Bitter Harvest* (Washington, DC: Biotechnology Working Group, 1990).

158. Gordon Graff (January 1995), pp. 55–60.

159. Gina Kolata (14 June 1996), p. A26.

160. Anon, 'New Clinic for Chemically Related Illnesses,' *Env. Health Persp.* 104, no. 1 (January 1996): 14; Bette Hileman, 'Multiple Chemical Sensitivity,' *Chemical & Engineering News*, 22 July 1991, pp. 26–42.

161. Ibid. Similarly, in response to concerns over dioxin, which have prompted groups like Greenpeace to call for a ban of all chlorinated chemicals, the chlorine industry has retorted that every individual chemical should be tested and judged for its health effects separately. Cable News Network, feature story, 'Dioxin,' *Network Earth*, 25 June 1995.

162. Glenn W. Suter and James M. Loar (1992): 434.

163. Bette Hileman (22 July 1991), p. 40.

164. Ibid.

165. Anon, 'New Center to Study Environmental Impacts on Reproductive Risk,' *Env. Health Persp.* 104, no. 4 (April 1996): 376–7.

166. Anon, 'Environment and Infertility,' *Env. Health Persp.* 104, no. 2 (February 1996): 136.

167. Peter Montague of the Environmental Research Foundation in Washington, DC says that by making it impossible for the ordinary person to understand what they're up to, scientists, industry and government intentionally exclude the public from decision making. Interview with Peter Montague, in *Safe Food News*, published by Food & Water, Marshfield, Vermont (Spring 1993), pp. 11–14.

168. Gio Batta Gori, 'Are Animal Tests Relevant in Cancer Risk Assessment?,' *Regul. Toxicol. Pharmacol.* 13 (1991): 225–7; Gio Batta Gori, 'Whither Risk Assessment?,' *Regul. Toxicol. Pharmacol.* 14 (1993): 224–9.

169. Andrée Collard, *Rape of the Wild* (Indiana: Indiana University Press, 1989), p. 75; Bette Overell, *Animal Research Takes Lives: Humans and Animals Both Suffer* (Upper Hutt, New Zealand: Wright & Carman/New Zealand Anti-Vivisection Society, 1993), pp. 21–2.

170. Troy Soos, 'Charles River Breeding Labs,' *The Animals' Agenda*, December 1986, cover story.

171. Source: Internet address, http://www.criver.com, as of 28 May 1996.

172. Troy Soos (December 1986).

173. East Acres Biologicals, 1995 Catalogue, Southbridge, Massachusetts.

174. Bausch & Lomb, *The 1994 Annual Report*, Rochester, New York.

175. Bette Overell, 'A Catalogue of Recollections … ,' *NZAVS Mobilise* 43, published by the (now defunct) New Zealand Anti-Vivisection Society (November 1995), p. 12; Overell specifically names the New Zealand Royal Society for the Prevention of Cruelty to Animals (NZRSPCA).

176. Edward S. Herman and Noam Chomsky, *Manufacturing Consent: The Political Economy of the Mass Media* (New York: Pantheon Books, 1988), pp. 5–17. The authors write that the media has become integrated into a market economy; many of the large American media companies (ABC, NBC, CBS, Time Warner/Turner) have

assets worth billions of dollars. To maintain that wealth, and remain competitive, they have had to become beholden to their sponsors/potential funders: bankers, institutional investors, corporations. Corporate executives and bankers typically make up two-thirds of TV networks' boards of directors. These power brokers, who also provide monetary subsidies to the media, naturally gain special access to it. The networks themselves hold investments in stocks of major corporations (i.e. pharmaceuticals) and cannot transmit programs which could jeopardize that relationship or hurt their profits.

In New Zealand, the Government refused to register submissions and hear petitioners speak about the 'Petition to Abolish Animal Experimentation' presented to Parliament in 1989. Bette Overell (1993), p. 120.

177. Bill Breen, 'Why We Need Animal Testing,' *Garbage*, April/May 1993, p. 41

178. Anon, 'Animal Testing For Reproductive Harm,' *NRDC* newsletter (July/August, 1990): p. 11. See also J. Landau and H. O'Riordan, 'Of Mice and Men: The Admissibility of Animal Studies to Prove Causation in Toxic Tort Litigation', *Idaho Law Review* 25 (1989): 521–66.

179. Myra Sklarew, 'Toxicity Tests in Animals: Alternative Models,' *Env. Health Persp.* 101, no. 4 (September 1993); see also, Heidi J. Welsh (1990).

180. The EC has issued several directives since 1986 to promote alternatives to animal testing. Though the directives are not binding by law, they are allegedly enforced by national committees. A 1986 directive requires researchers from member countries to use non-animal methods if they are 'scientifically satisfactory and reasonably and practically available.' Anon, 'Message in a Bottle,' *The Economist*, 22 April 1995, pp. 83–5.

In 1990 the EC launched an initiative to evaluate alternatives to eye irritancy tests in rabbits. During this time the Japanese Society for Alternatives to Animal Experiments was established. In October 1991, the EC, upon the request of the European Parliament, instituted ECVAM (European Centre for Validation of Alternative Methods). Meetings of the scientific board began in January 1992. In 1993, Switzerland opened SIAT (Schweizerisches Institut fur Alternativen zu Tierversuchen), a center which promotes research into, and validation of, alternative methods. The Federal Health Office in Germany also opened the ZEBET center, which documents and evaluates alternative methods. *Impronte* (April 1994), p. 11, published by Lega Anti-Vivisezione, Rome, Italy. Nearly all of the industrialized countries (including the US, Canada, Japan and Europe) belonging to the OECD allegedly encourage the development, promotion and implementation of alternatives. Andrew Rowan, et al. (1995), p. 29. There have been several attempts (by federal agencies and non-profit groups) in the US to implement alternative testing programs. In October 1996 the second annual World Congress on Alternatives was held in Utrecht, Holland. Topics included alternatives in toxicology, validation and regulation, ethics, education, and information databases. For a detailed account of the conference see *The AV Magazine* (Alternatives Issue), Winter 1997, pp. 2–5.

5. Toxicological testing without using animals

'The standard carcinogen tests that use rodents are an obsolescent relic of the ignorance of past decades.' Philip H. Abelson, 'Testing for Carcinogens With Rodents,' *Science* (21 September 1990): 1357

As early as the eighteenth and nineteenth centuries, experiments on muscle physiology were carried out with muscle preparations *in vitro*. Since then, the use of cell and tissue culture techniques for toxicology testing and the study of physiological and biochemical processes has rapidly increased. Skeptics say that, 'extrapolation from cells and tissues to the complex human organism is difficult, [and] producing the complex physiological responses of the whole organism is not likely at this point.'[1] But scientists like John Harbell of Microbiological Associates in Rockville, Maryland point out that 'animal models provide ... limited data on the behavior of certain biologic compounds, such as ... antibodies, which react with species-specific molecules.'[2] Jeff Diner writes that, through the use of cell cultures, 'scientists can easily study cell processes [like] metabolism, hormone secretion, nerve organization and the mechanics of genetics without being concerned with complex and unknown variables in the whole animal.'[3] In 1974, researchers at Japan's Osaka University described how human tonsil lymphocytes could be used to investigate human immunologic phenomena *in vitro*;[4] others have recommended using human blood lymphocytes to detect mutagens and cancer-causing chemicals *in vitro*.[5] Some scientists believe that *in vitro* tests could assess the potential for damage to components of the nervous system.[6]

Today, virtually any cell from the human body, including brain cells, can be grown and kept alive (under *known* physical and chemical conditions) for days or even years *in vitro*.[7] Organ cultures can be used as models of a whole organ; for example, liver cells can represent the whole liver. In 1981, Philip Noguchi, a biochemist with the US Food and Drug Administration, demonstrated that organ culture tests to detect malignant carcinomas were far superior to the popular 'nude mouse bioassay' in both quantitative and qualitative terms. He voiced the hope that his results would stimulate other scientists to consider that 'responsible scientific inquiry can indeed be done without animals.'[8] Physiologists and pharmacologists, who traditionally work with human and animal tissues, are beginning to use these techniques, while pathologists have relied on them for several decades.[9]

According to William Stokes, Associate Director of Animal and Alternative Resources at the National Institute of Environmental Health Sciences (NIEHS), government agencies like the NIEHS are seeking methods that are faster, more accurate and less expensive.[10] It was acknowledged early on that animal tests were too slow and expensive; they could neither screen the backlog of the tens of thousands of chemicals in use, nor screen the thousand or more added each year for which there were no toxicological data available.[11] The competitive pharmaceutical market, which pressures companies to gather information about the toxicity and/or effectiveness of new compounds as rapidly as possible, has also spurred the quest. Contrary to the continually rising costs of maintaining laboratory animals, the costs of *in vitro* tests have dropped significantly over the past few years as a result of streamlining and the growing demand for the technology.[12] The Ames *Salmonella* (bacteria-based) test, for example, costs $300–$1,000 per chemical, a bargain compared to $2 million plus for the rodent bioassay.[13] Moreover, Frank Barile, Associate Professor of Toxicology in the Health Sciences Department at York College in Jamaica, New York, says that most cell tests today can be run in 24 hours. Some are even automated and can test some twelve different doses of a chemical at one time.[14]

The continued pressure from animal advocates over the last three decades, to abandon toxicity tests on animals, can be credited with having had an enormous influence on new technology development. Tens of millions of dollars of financial support for the development of non-animal methods, or 'alternatives' as they are called, has come from more than sixty sources worldwide, including humane societies, corporations, and governments.[15]

Several examples of these methods will be described below, and are summarized in Table 5.1, but it must first be noted that there are diverse criteria, within both the scientific/research and animal advocacy communities, about what actually constitutes an 'alternative.' This undoubtedly relates to both groups' goals with respect to the use of animals in research.

The 'alternatives' concept

In *The Principles of Humane Experimental Technique* (1959), W. M. S. Russell and Rex Burch first introduced the concept of the Three Rs (3Rs): Reduce (the number of animals used), Refine (the experimental techniques so as to minimize pain and distress to the animals), Replace (the use of animals with other technologies).

The 3Rs concept seems to be the most widely accepted definition of 'alternatives' among the scientific, regulatory, and corporate communities. Several mainstream animal advocacy groups such as the Humane Society of the United States accept these criteria as well, despite the fact that animals and/or animal parts are often used in so-called alternative tests.[16]

Examples of non-animal toxicological testing methods

'The research literature contains a large number of reports that conclude that *in vitro* methods could and should be used.' P. Knox in *The Future of Predictive Safety Evaluation*, A. Worden et al., eds (Boston: MTP Press, 1986), p. 173

In vitro/cell culture assays *In vitro* tests are typically used to answer one or several of the following questions. Will a substance destroy cells or alter human genetic material (DNA)? Will it impair organ function? Will it become more toxic once it has been metabolized? What will happen when the substance is applied directly to the skin or eyes, for example?

Materials used to conduct *in vitro* tests include both human and non-human organ-specific cells and fluids. With the help of clinical collaborators, some laboratories collect surgical discard specimens for human cell mutation assays.[17] Human tumor cells have been used to screen for sensitivity to anticancer drugs; and researchers have observed the effects of adding chemicals to beating heart cells in culture.[18] The human placenta, with its simple anatomy and circulation, yet many varied functions, is ideal for *in vitro* culture, particularly to study the physiological mechanisms by which chemicals damage DNA. Placenta has also been widely used to study teratogenic effects.[19] Due to the successful culture of human cells, extrapolation of these findings to humans is now scientifically plausible.

A commonly accepted premise within the cancer research establishment is that most carcinogens can damage DNA and hence have the effect of causing cells to mutate *in vitro*. It has been suggested that positive results in simple microbial test systems, which show an agent to be mutagenic and/or DNA-damaging in bacteria, provide strong evidence of carcinogenicity—and hence represent a toxic hazard. The occupational carcinogens benzene and vinyl chloride's DNA-damaging action was observed *in vitro*;[20] similarly, one class of airborne chemicals, the polycyclic aromatic hydrocarbons (PAHs), products of combustion, have been shown to be potent mutagens in human cell mutation assays.[21] Using these quick and simple tests, strong cases could be made for the speedy removal of toxic substances from the market, instead of waiting to see whether they cause cancer, developmental or other effects.[22] Toxicologist Gerhard Zbinden stated that early detection and elimination of chemicals that are transformed into toxic metabolites by human liver enzymes *in vitro* would lead to a considerable reduction of redundant animal testing.[23]

The Ames *Salmonella* mutagenicity test, developed by Bruce Ames in 1966, was one of the first *in vitro* tests to look at cell mutation, and is used by some 5,000 laboratories today for premarket testing and to identify the presence of toxins. Although the Ames test has its limitations since it cannot be used to assess the toxicity of non-DNA-damaging agents,[24] many toxicologists say that it would be asking too much of one assay to cover all aspects of toxicity; they have concluded that by using a battery of *in vitro* tests (as well as computerized structure activity analysis such as the COMPACT procedure discussed in this chapter), chemicals which are not identified as being toxic by one system can be identified by another.[25] In 1994, John Weisburger (former Director of the Bioassay Segment of the Carcinogenesis Program of the NCI, now at the American Health Foundation in Valhalla, New York), said that because of their complementary nature, positive results in three short-term tests—the Ames test, the Williams DNA repair test, and the p-postlabelling technique (see this chapter)—would provide strong and possibly certain qualitative evidence of carcinogenicity *in vitro*.[26]

Xenometrix—a company producing molecular toxicology products in Boulder, Colorado, including six new strains of the Ames *Salmonella* bacteria test—has developed cell-based assay systems to evaluate the cytotoxic, mutagenic and carcinogenic effects of chemical compounds. Its 'stress gene assay system,' containing bacterial or human cell lines, can tell not only whether, but also *how*, a given chemical harms a particular type of cell. After exposure of the engineered bacteria to a test chemical, an analysis of the activity of specific proteins sheds light on the mechanism of toxicity. The company's genotoxicity assays measure the potential carcinogenicity of compounds.[27] Microbiological

Associates in Rockville, Maryland, specializes in *in vitro* safety testing of pharmaceuticals, including tests for contaminants, and toxicologic studies to assess cellular toxicity and genetic damage.

While an *in vitro* test will never be 100 percent predictive, Björn Ekwall, cell toxicologist, professor of toxicology at Uppsala University in Sweden, and a key participant in the Multicenter Evaluation of In Vitro Cytotoxicity (MEIC),[28] says it will be better than an animal test. He says that at least three out of ten times an animal test misses a result that it should routinely measure in humans. Moreover, he claims that an *in vitro* battery test would cost a meager $100 per chemical, in comparison to over $2 million for an animal test, and could theoretically predict up to 90 percent of toxicity.[29] Toxicologist Frank Barile concurs and says that if a variety of (human) cell types and analytical methods were used, cell tests could predict up to 99.9 percent of toxicity.[30]

Ekwall and his colleagues at MEIC espouse the idea that, 'human gross toxicity can be broken down into a number of biokinetic, cellular and molecular events, each of which can be identified and quantified in appropriate *in vitro* systems. The various elements can then be used in different combinations to model various types of toxicity;' they are then validated against human data.[31] Ekwall, who has validated over seventy-five chemicals *in vitro*, using human data from autopsies and case reports, is currently trying to supplement existing *in vitro* tests by creating a battery of tests to measure acute, chronic, kidney, liver, skin and eye toxicity effects now accounted for in animal tests.[32] Whether it is productive to try to mimic *in vitro* the range of effects now produced in animals is a matter of contention, since this effort may prove to be as time-consuming (and misleading) as the animal tests. Indeed, Ekwall cautioned that there are two hundred specific cell types in the human body, and one cannot develop tests for each of these cells—it would simply be impractical. The question of how much knowledge is enough before action can be taken is a relevant one here. Ekwall conceded that, 'we should not imitate animal test systems [because] that is an old toxicology; in fact, simple cell line tests are much more revealing than people think, but it's difficult to sell the idea because it could be a threat, and the animal testing monopoly would be destroyed.'[33]

EDIT—the Evaluation-guided Development of new In vitro toxicity and kinetic Tests, was created by Ekwall to accomplish the above goals. By the year 2005, EDIT expects to have developed *in vitro* tests to cover the entire spectrum of toxicity for regulatory purposes. In addition, pioneering work is being done by Cecilia Clemedson and her colleagues at MEIC to simplify *in vitro* testing, and make it more precise and cost-effective.[34] Ekwall believes that if the American animal advocacy community (which allegedly has collective assets of circa $300 million)[35] pooled its resources to fund the MEIC project, batteries of inexpensive cellular tests could replace animals in product testing in a few years.[36]

Living tissue equivalents and pH Measurement: Skin², The Skinethic Laboratory, Epiderm, Testorgans, Irritection, Corrositex Efforts to reconstruct complex human tissues *in vitro*, particularly skin (with its layers of specialized cells, proteins and fats), have been very fruitful. Researchers at Advanced Tissue Sciences (ATS) in La Jolla, California developed Skin²—a commercially successful human skin substitute. In 1995, *The Economist* reported that researchers at ATS 'use cells from the off-cuts of routine circumcisions to construct sheets of fully differentiated, three-layered human skin on nylon scaffolds. By observing microscopic changes in tissue structure and measuring the rate at which cells release inflammatory substances, researchers can see whether compounds irritate the skin, as well as study wound healing.'[37] Currently, ATS's biggest customers are cosmetics companies like Helene Curtis, and European firms, but Procter & Gamble, S. C. Johnson Wax, Gillette, Exxon, and Bausch & Lomb are also clients.[38] Skin² has so reliably detected corrosive chemicals that, in 1994, the American and Canadian transportation departments approved its use in place of archaic and inhumane corrosivity tests on animals.[39] ATS will soon begin selling six additional culture systems including tissues from human oral mucosa, liver, lung, nerve, ocular tissues and tissues from the gastrointestinal tract.[40] ATS uses no animal by-products (for example collagen) in its formulation.[41]

Martin Rosdy, founder of the Skinethic Laboratory in Nice, France, has developed and patented an artificial skin technique created by culturing a donor's epidermal cells in a serum-free cell culture environment. In 1995, *Genetic Engineering News* (*GEN*) reported that 'the reconstituted epidermis [the outer protective layer of the skin] is standardized in terms of thickness, number of cell layers, culture time and sensitivity to known chemical irritants.' Rosdy says the skin cultures react just like human skin when treated with an active or irritant cosmetic product. Rosdy's technique is finding a market among European cosmetic firms like Chanel, L'Oreal, Lancaster and others who are phasing out animal testing due to EEC Directive 76/768 which would outlaw cosmetic testing on animals in Europe by 1998, provided that acceptable non-animal methods exist.[42] (Ironically, this Directive is facing opposition from COLIPA (the [European] Perfume, Cosmetics Products and Toiletries Industries Association) and the European Commission itself. Animal advocates doubt that the ban will take effect, despite widespread support for it from the European Parliament and millions of European citizens.)[43]

The MatTek Corporation in Ashland, Massachusetts developed Epiderm, an *in vitro* skin model derived from human epidermal proteins that is permeable like, and structurally and biologically analogous to, human skin. The company's three-dimensional EpiOcular corneal model also consists of human-derived epidermal proteins and is structurally similar to the human cornea.[44]

In 1989, Organogenesis Inc of Cambridge, Massachusetts used human cells to produce a line of 'living organ equivalents' called Testorgans (including Testlung, Testintestine, Testskin and a living artery analogue) capable of extending organ-like function *in vitro*. Robert Sharpe explains that Testorgans are useful in 'studying the effects of pharmaceuticals, pesticides, cosmetics, detergents and other substances on human organ systems.'[45] Testskin, a full thickness skin equivalent which was sold to Toyobo (a Japanese company) in January 1994, is already being used by some cosmetic companies. Ortec International, Inc in Queens, New York, and Integra Life Sciences in New Jersey, are manufacturing human skin substitutes. Ortec's patented process uses skin cells taken from routine circumcisions and is currently being used in clinical trials in the US. The FDA recently approved Integra's artificial skin for commercial use.[46]

The Microbics Corporation in Carlsbad, California developed the *Photobacterium Phosphoreum* assay for the detection of chemical irritants. In 1995, *The Economist* reported that 'during its normal metabolism, this luminescent bacterium converts part of its cellular energy to light. Certain classes of chemicals can interfere with this process and dim the glow, providing a way to measure their toxicity.' This assay is now being used in test batteries by companies such as Boots, the British drug firm.[47]

Two patented biomolecular technologies from In Vitro International in Irvine, California—Irritection (which actually comprises two assays: Skintex, a collagen barrier membrane and protein matrix, and Eytex, a synthetic protein matrix) and Corrositex—have a higher than 85 percent concordance level with human toxicity data.[48] In Vitro International's assay systems can evaluate the irritability and phototoxicity of chemicals on eye and skin tissue, predict absorption of chemicals through the skin, and study the interaction of chemicals in the liver, kidney, and heart, using tissue slices and primary cell cultures. Results can be obtained in 24 hours.

Application of a chemical irritant to the Skintex system causes the release of a membrane-linked dye. The test contains a protein reagent which changes in response to a chemical irritant, resulting in a detectable change in opacification. The Eytex test, which has a predictive value of 98 percent, and has been 'validated' (against animal data) with more than 10,000 substances, is used by more than one hundred and fifty laboratories worldwide, and toxicologist Virginia Gordon reports that it 'can screen insoluble, opaque and colored chemicals as well as final formulations for chemical irritancy.'[49] The Irritection assays are used in a variety of applications by over a hundred cosmetic, personal care, industrial chemical, paper and pulp, and photographic companies across the US.[50]

The Environmental Protection Agency and the Food and Drug Administration placed orders for the company's Irritection assays in 1995 and were still evaluating them in 1996. Scientists, animal advocates, and *in vitro* manufacturers all hope this is an indication of the agencies' willingness to explore the potential of *in vitro* technology and possibly sanction its use for regulatory requirements. A listing of these methods in the Code of Federal Regulations would make it official, but it is too soon to tell what the outcome will be. Public pressure would be needed to convince the agencies to act.[51]

The Corrositex assay has correctly identified both corrosive and non-corrosive solids, liquids and emulsions at a 90 percent accuracy level.[52] The test costs between $100 and $235 and can detect corrosivity in four hours; this compares well to the four to six weeks and $1,200–$1,800 required for an animal test.[53] On 28 April 1993, the US Department of Transportation accepted the Corrositex assay to establish corrosivity (and for classification purposes), in place of dermal irritancy tests with rabbits and the EPA has followed suit.[54] Furthermore, in March 1994, Berrien Zettler, OSHA's Deputy Director of Compliance Programs, stated that OSHA also accepts *in vitro* testing to establish corrosivity.[55] Certain EPA departments, such as the Office of Solid Waste, use measurement of pH to screen materials for corrosivity and/or dermal and ocular irritancy. A measurement of two or less (very acidic) or twelve or greater (very alkaline) precludes the need for further testing of any sort.[56] Additional suggestions have been made that skin patch tests for substances expected to be minor irritants be done on people, and that harsher irritants be tested on skin cultures, on human cadaver skin, or 'operation specimens.'[57]

The Neutral Red Assay, and Light-Addressable Potentiometric Sensor (LAPS) The Neutral Red Assay, developed at Rockefeller University in New York and marketed by the Clonetics Corporation in San Diego, screens for ocular and dermal irritation, and drug toxicity, and could easily replace the classic LD50 test; it categorizes a substance's toxicity on the basis of the damage it causes cell membranes. Cell cultures are exposed to varying concentrations of a chemical; cells that are damaged absorb a red dye. Unlike the Draize test, results can be read mechanically and precisely;[58] and the test was determined to be 'reproducible, sensitive, rapid, and economical,' by scientists Babich and Borenfreund in 1989.[59]

The Light-Addressable Potentiometric Sensor is a cell culture test developed by Molecular Devices of California, which uses a silicon chip biosensor to measure cellular recovery (or lack of it) from injury, as well as changes in cellular metabolism; when cells are exposed to a toxic compound, they release lactic and carbonic acids, thus acidifying the cell culture environment. This process is detected and monitored by the biosensor.[60] Cellular recovery tests such as these could be used to replace the Draize rabbit test for skin and eye irritancy.

Computer-based Structure-Activity Relationships (SARs) SARs are various forms of statistical or mathematical models fed into computers which seek to predict adverse biological effects of chemicals based on their molecular structure, weight and electronic charge. SAR data can be used to determine how a specific chemical produces a particular biological response, including toxicity, without recourse to animals. SARs have been used to design drugs by looking for more active, less toxic compounds, and they have shown 85–97 percent accuracy in predicting dermal sensitization, teratogenicity and carcinogenicity. Health Designs Inc of Rochester, New York's computer program TOP-KAT has been billed as a replacement method for the Draize eye test, as has the MULTI-CASE computer program.[61]

The COMPACT (Computer-Optimized Molecular Parametric Analysis of Chemical Toxicity) program identifies chemicals likely to be toxic, based on their molecular dimensions and electronic structures, and can identify carcinogens not identified in the Ames test. COMPACT has a 94 percent accuracy rate when 'validated' against the Ames *Salmonella* and rodent bioassays. (Similarly, TOPKAT has a 97 percent accuracy rate when 'validated' against rodent data.) The cost of conducting the COMPACT procedure (in 1993 dollars) is less than 1 percent of a rodent bioassay, and can be completed in days instead of years.[62] Both TOPKAT and COMPACT draw from animal data for comparison, however, and critics maintain that such software programs should only be considered as valid replacements for animal tests when they use human data.[63]

SAR models are currently used by regulatory agencies to determine the potential carcinogenic, teratogenic and generally toxic effects of chemicals for which insufficient data have been submitted. The FDA accepts SAR data to assess the potential risks of new drugs.[64] It has been suggested that SARs be used to prioritize testing or weed out dangerous chemicals from a group.[65] The establishment of an international databank to consolidate reliable SAR information from industry and the public domain would hopefully eliminate redundant animal testing.

Computer-based mathematical modeling and imaging of living systems

'Mathematical models can be developed ... at a number of levels: from the dynamics of subcellular effects to global models which consider the intact organism.' E. R. Carson, in *The Future of Predictive Safety Evaluation*, A. Worden, et al., eds (Boston: MTP Press, 1986), p. 212

Today, through the use of computers, mathematical/computer modelers have been able to build biological models of living systems, such as the human circulatory and respiratory systems, with numerous parameters that are rich and complete.[66] (The quality of the model naturally depends on the quality of the data.)

Physiologically based bio-kinetic models, or PBBKs, translate biological relationships into mathematical equations. They can be used to study the absorption, distribution, metabolism and excretion of a chemical by the body.[67] They can also be used to determine the relationship between the dose of a chemical and a particular metabolic effect. Maryland-based science writer Myra Sklarew reported that Melvin Andersen of the EPA works with these models 'to study biological processes at the molecular, biochemical, cellular and organ system levels.'[68] Cohen, et al. developed the ED01 model to study tumor production in response to chemical exposure; ED01 was so named because it can detect an increased tumor activity of 1 percent, and at doses of a chemical much lower than those customarily used in rodent studies.[69] While these models have mostly been used to facilitate calculations of inter-species extrapolations (from high doses in rodents to low doses in humans), they could conversely provide a method to extrapolate from *in vitro* studies, with human cells, to the human *in vivo* experience.

Computers have been able to transform complex data comprising hundreds or thousands of equations into three-dimensional visual representations of different organs, bones, muscles, and tissues. It is common for doctors in hospitals, biologists, and others to use computer graphics to study/visualize the human body as well as various cellular and biological phenomena.

Project Da Vinci at the University of Illinois is building a 3-D simulation of the human body. Matthew Witten (1993) explains that such life-size simulations of human beings (which are becoming a reality) require an assortment of clinical test and imaging data, as well as non-invasive measurements of a person's physiologic functions. Such models, in combination with structure/function and pharmacodynamic studies, could be used to predict toxicologic effects in humans for a comprehensive variety of endpoints.[70]

Some have suggested that by the end of the twentieth century, the genotoxicity of new compounds could be determined by entering a compound's molecular structure into a central databank, resulting in an instant toxicity profile.[71]

Non-invasive diagnostic techniques and modeling and sampling techniques

'You've got to find a means of getting inside people and seeing what's going on, firsthand, because extrapolations from animal studies or cell culture experiments are scientifically dubious.' William Thilly, Director, Massachusetts Institute of Technology's Center for Environmental Health Sciences, quoted in *Env. Health Persp.* 104, no. 2 (February 1996): 142

It is now possible to monitor the progress of a disease using a variety of imaging techniques including ultrasound, X-ray computerized tomography, positron emission tomography (PET), and magnetic resonance imaging (MRI), among others. Computerized tomography consists of scanning narrow tissue slices with X-ray beams, and can be used to assess early stages of organ damage.[72] William Thilly and his colleagues at MIT have devised a technique called mutational spectroscopy, which can identify DNA alterations inside human organs. This technique complements Thilly's experiments with live human cells, through which he identified the mechanisms by which nitrogen oxide damages DNA.[73] Magnetic Resonance Imaging and Spectroscopy (MRI/MRS) are technologies used, among other things, to monitor changes in human blood and soft tissues. John Yam and C. L. Alden (1993) say they are important in detecting and monitoring toxicity (such as cell death caused by poisoning), tumor growth, fetal development, clotting, and inflammation.[74] Maryland-based veterinarian Wendy Thacher writes that with the use of radioactive tracers, techniques like PET can be used over time to image blood flow, determine whether tumors are growing or dying, measure fluid levels in tissues and organs, monitor bodily activities such as oxygen metabolism, and changes in body pH. Flow cytometry and image analysis can measure toxicity at the cellular level or changes in cell function, using small blood or cell culture samples.[75]

Several modeling, sampling and biological monitoring techniques have been used by the EPA and the National Center for Health Statistics in Maryland, which have allowed environmental health scientists to measure humans' exposure to chemicals and estimate concentrations of chemicals in the air near factories. New analytical methods can ascertain whether certain chemicals are finding their way into the human body. Using a technique called passive dosimetry, chemical analyses of urine, blood, hair and saliva of workers in occupational settings have been measured over the years.[76] Color-indicating breathalysers are also used to monitor chemical exposure in the workplace. Radioactive and fluorescent tracer studies, followed by video imaging analysis, have allowed toxicologists, pharmacologists, and industrial hygienists to measure farm workers' exposure to pesticides; detect DNA damage in humans exposed to chemicals; and study the absorption, distribution, metabolism and excretion of chemicals in the body.[77]

Using the P-Postlabelling assay, in which radioactive phosphorus binds to damaged DNA, individuals can be monitored for high levels of DNA damage to see if they are being exposed to carcinogens in the workplace.[78] A popular technique for measuring human dermal exposure to a chemical involves attaching gauze, foam or cellulose pads to various parts of a person's body. The pads are removed at the end of the exposure period for residue analysis. Another method uses disposable overalls; after an exposure, they are removed for analysis.[79]

Human volunteer studies

'the recognition that animal studies ... have limitations for assessing safety for man suggests that ... there will be a gradual rise in the requirements for volunteer ... studies over longer periods of time.' E. L. Harris, in *The Future of Predictive Safety Evaluation*, A. Worden, et al., eds (Boston: MTP Press, 1986), p. 24

Human volunteer studies (which typically use healthy adults aged 18 to 65 years) are being used by an increasing number of corporations to assess dermal irritancy, penetration and allergic sensitivity. Such studies not only eliminate the need for inter-species extrapolation, but also technically eliminate the need for validation, since the human data that are sought are immediately acquired; they are in fact the true 'gold standard.' Toxicologist Virginia C. Gordon (1993) writes that while skin irritation is assessed visually, 'quantitative methods such as laser doppler flowmetry can measure blood flow and skin temperature ... Skin swelling can be measured with calipers or high-frequency ultra-sound.'[80] A number of other diagnostic and sampling techniques (described below) can be used to collect biological measurements, and assess DNA and organ system damage.

In tests measuring allergic sensitization to cosmetic substances and formulations, human volunteers are treated with a substance and al-lowed a two-week rest period; after the two weeks they are observed for effects. An initial study of twenty or thirty volunteers may be followed by a larger study involving up to a hundred people. If re-searchers record positive results or side effects from the use of the product, a larger test involving up to five hundred volunteers may be undertaken to determine the true significance of those results for the average consumer.[81] David Basketter, et al. of the Environmental Safety Laboratory at Unilever in Bedford, UK (a personal and household products company with operations in 90 countries and circa $50 billion in revenues in 1996) used a human four-hour skin patch test for dermal irritancy as a replacement for the Draize skin irritation and corrosion test on rabbits.[82] Similarly, Phil Casterton, Senior Scientist at Amway's Product Safety Department in Michigan, is directing human skin irrita-tion studies for the (American) Soap and Detergent Association as a valid replacement for the Draize test.[83]

Human studies involving the application of pesticides to the skin have been conducted, and some scientists have suggested that human dosing studies be undertaken with selected industrial chemicals.[84] In one study, picloram—an active ingredient in Dow Chemical's herbicide, Tordon—was both fed (in a liquid form) and dermally applied to six healthy male volunteers.[85]

British biochemist Dennis V. Parke explained that in the 1950s, he and other physicians who were under contract to industry used to establish 'safe doses' of pesticides for the general population by first doing preliminary toxicity tests *in vitro* and then proceeding with tests on themselves. Several pesticides (and drugs) were successfully marketed in this fashion. But the insurance companies stepped in and prohibited this practice because they were afraid of litigation. Now says Parke—who is a consultant to the US EPA on issues related to pesticides and other toxics—we are saddled with incomprehensible regulations which prohibit useful human studies, do not take advantage of existing *in vitro* and pharmacokinetic modeling methods, and require animal tests which do not produce clinically relevant data. He says that chemical companies like Dow Chemical are routinely searching for human data; they find it by going to pesticide manufacturing plants and paying factory workers and local residents for samples of their blood. When Parke sat on the World Health Organization's (WHO) International Pesticide Committee from the 1960s to the 1980s, it too recommended such a strategy to fill the need for human data.[86] Today, the WHO/Food and Agriculture Organization Joint Committee on Food Additives and Contaminants has established guidelines on the requirements for testing novel foods on humans. The guidelines prescribe single-dose studies, four-week studies, and follow-up procedures.[87]

Epidemiology

'The least controversial basis for regulation, when solid data exist, is epidemiology.' Thomas H. Maugh, 'Chemical Carcinogens:' *Science* 201 (29 September 1978): 1200

Epidemiology is the study of the cause and frequency of health-related events in a given population; it is an observational (as opposed to an experimental) science used in the evaluation of the cause, evolution, and control of human disease—both on an individual and a group level. Unlike animal experiments, in which there are typically a small number of genetically homogeneous subjects, epidemiological studies require a large sample size in order for results of a study to be considered statistically significant. There is general agreement that epidemiological studies provide the hard core of scientists' knowledge about the effects of chemical carcinogens on humans.[88] Critics say that human data can only be acquired either from humans who already have cancer, or by studying humans in the process of being exposed to carcinogens; hence they have acquired an aura of immorality. (Much of what we know about chemical effects in humans comes from accidents, as do most of the human dose-response data.) Yet without human data, scientists can learn nothing about disease and cannot calculate real risks. A scientific panel appointed by Kenneth Olden, director of the NIEHS, concluded in 1994 that the US government should redirect its efforts toward cell cultures and epidemiological studies on human populations that have accidentally experienced chemical exposure.[89]

The National Cancer Institute (NCI) is currently monitoring a population of individuals in Alabama exposed to enormous quantities of DDT between 1947 and 1971, to compare DDE residues in breast fat of women with breast cancer to residues in women without breast cancer. In a highly polluted area of China, the agency is conducting studies on how air pollution affects lung cancer risk. This year, with the EPA and NIEHS, NCI began a massive study of 100,000 farmers and their family members to try to determine reasons for their elevated risk of cancers of the brain, prostate, stomach, skin, and lip, as well as leukemia. Farmers are chronically exposed to pesticides, chemical solvents, engine exhausts, sunlight, and other substances common to the agricultural sector.[90] (It should be noted that the NCI has been criticized for allotting only 5 percent of its $1.8 billion annual budget to prevention, as opposed to diagnosis and treatment which critics say is much more profitable.)[91]

A recurring problem for epidemiologists is the lack of substantial data on the effects of chronic (long-term) exposure to contaminants at the low levels generally found in the environment.[92] Future directions in epidemiology, which will allow scientists to collect more detailed human data, lie in the use of biological markers—individual biological measurements of internal doses or body burdens of chemicals (for example blood lead levels). The most useful biological markers are urine, excrement, blood, nails, hair, breath, and fat. For example, the uptake of dioxin by Vietnam veterans was evaluated by analyzing the amount of dioxin in their blood up to twenty years after their initial exposure.[93] More use could also be made of the data from poison centers which are typically staffed by clinical toxicologists with expertise in acute toxicity and the problems associated with drug interactions.

X-Ray Technology The 'mutagen theory of chronic disease,' advanced by Rosalie Bertell, Gerald Lower, Charles Waldren and others, that most cancers are caused by chemicals in air, water and food that damage the DNA in our cells, opens the way to much simpler *in vitro* safety tests of environmental chemicals. Research by Waldren[94] and Puck indicates that cell mutations occur in humans at low, rather than high doses. Using human chromosomes, marker genes, and X-ray technology, Theodore Puck and his colleagues measured the rate of cell death and repair caused by agents as diverse as radiation, ultraviolet light, and certain chemicals. In one experiment, Puck, et al. chose to work with caffeine, a well-known mutagen. Human lymphocytes, with and without caffeine (for control purposes), were exposed to gamma irradiation for various periods at varying doses. A chromosomal analysis was carried out and the anomalies graphed on a dose-response curve; results indicated substantial mutagenesis by ionizing radiation when caffeine was present even in low doses in the test tubes, but not when it was absent. The important application of this research (which has been validated against human data), may be its use in identifying and screening chemicals for their capacity to cause cell mutations at the

Table 5.1 Non-animal methods for toxicological testing

Method	Uses
In vitro (human) cell culture assays including the Neutral Red Assay	Can be used in safety testing to screen potential toxins for general cytotoxicity, mutagenicity, genotoxicity, carcinogenicity, teratogenicity, neurotoxicity, dermal and ocular irritancy; to screen drugs for toxicity and effectiveness; to study cell processes like metabolism, hormone secretion, nerve organization, enzyme induction, the mechanics of genetics including DNA repair, and immunologic phenomena; could be used in hazard classification.
Living tissue equivalents including Skin², Testskin, EpiDerm/EpiOcular, Irritection/Corrositex,	Can be used to study and measure dermal and ocular irritancy; to screen for and study toxic effects of drugs, cosmetics, pesticides, detergents etc. on human organs, including chemical interactions; to predict absorption of chemicals through the skin; to identify corrosive and non-corrosive solids, liquids and emulsions.
pH measurement	Can measure dermal and/or ocular irritancy, and corrosivity.
Light-Addressable Potentiometric System (LAPS)	Can measure the metabolism, inhibition and recovery of cells; dermal and ocular irritancy.
Computer-based Structure Activity Relationships (SAR)	Can predict the toxicity (dermal sensitization, teratogenicity, carcinogenicity, etc.) of a substance based on its molecular structure, weight, and electronic charge.
Computer-based mathematical modeling and imaging of living systems	Can be used to study the ADME* of a chemical by the body at the molecular, biochemical, cellular and organ system levels and to predict toxic effects; can provide quantitative data on tissue solubilities; create 3-D representations of human organs, bones, muscles and tissues; visualize cellular, subcellular and supercellular phenomena.
Non-invasive diagnostic and modeling and sampling techniques	Can be used to detect and measure toxicity, including dermal exposure, and DNA damage at the cellular level through the analysis of blood, urine, hair, saliva, fat, nails, breath, cell culture samples; to monitor tumor growth, fetal development, the progress of a disease; to measure fluid levels, and DNA alterations, in tissues and organs and numerous biological activities; to study ADME.

Table 5.1 continued

Method	Uses
Human volunteer studies	Can be used to assess general toxicity, dermal and ocular irritancy, allergic sensitization, product efficacy.
Epidemiology	Can be used in the evaluation of the cause, evolution and control of human disease.
X-ray technology	Can be used to identify and screen compounds and agents for their capacity to cause cell mutations at low concentrations; to identify epidemiological threats.
Liquid chromatography	Can be used to screen drugs for toxicity.

*ADME = Absorption, Distribution, Metabolism, Excretion

low concentrations humans are exposed to in the environment, and without resorting to controversial inter-species extrapolations.[95]

Research into non-animal toxicological testing methods is continually evolving. Researchers at the University of Texas at Austin College of Pharmacy claim that some toxicity tests could be carried out entirely with a select group of fungi, *Cunninghamella elegans*, which they say metabolize a wide variety of drugs similarly to humans. They argue that a measurable toxic response can be obtained by recording the formation of toxic metabolites.[96]

Fanny K. Ennever, et al. at Case Western Reserve University School of Medicine in Cleveland, Ohio are developing plant-based carcino-genicity assays. All of the nine assays developed thus far appear to be highly sensitive, though their specificity has yet to be determined.[97] Heinrich P. Koch, et al. at the Institute of Pharmaceutical Chemistry, University of Vienna, Austria have developed a 'true alternative' which they say will replace the classic LD50 test. Koch found that ordinary yeast (baker's yeast, brewer's yeast) mixed with nutrients and trace elements (all non-animal ingredients) predicted toxicity for 160 chemicals in the same way as the classic LD50 in vertebrates.

Unlike the classic LD50 test, the yeast test is easy to standardize, there is only one mode of application, and results can be obtained in a few hours. (The yeast cells absorb chemicals similarly to the way the gastrointestinal tract absorbs drugs.) The authors claim that special transgenic yeast strains (similar to the well-known strains of mice and rats) could be developed to test environmental toxins, drugs, and the like. While the yeast test has not been validated against human data, there would be no excuse for rejecting this test to predict LD50 values, given the identical correlation between it and classic animal tests.[98]

According to Atkinson, et al., of the University of Nottingham Medical School in Nottingham, UK, over sixty *in vitro* tests have been proposed as replacements for the Draize rabbit eye test. A number of methods are currently being developed or modified in an attempt to provide *in vitro* methods for studying recovery from damage, something that neither the current *in vitro* tests nor the rabbit tests are able to do.[99] And in September 1996 in Uppsala, Sweden, at the annual meeting of the Scandinavian Society for Cell Toxicology, Björn Ekwall will unveil an *in vitro* battery to replace the LD50 test which will have been validated against human data.

R. H. Buck, et al. have proposed a liquid chromatography assay to replace animals in the testing of pharmaceutical preparations.[100] (See Table 5.1 for a summary of the non-animal methods and their uses, described in this section.)

The 'alternatives' scam: refinement and reduction vs. full replacement

'Experimental research with animals and the equally worthless 'alternative methods' (which for the most part are based on cell cultures derived from animals) are the greatest fraud in the entire field of science and medicine ... It is only through the use of truly scientific methods which are directly relevant to people (these include clinical studies of human patients, epidemiological investigations of human populations, autopsy and biopsy investigations, observations of human volunteers, and experiments with human cell, tissue and organ cultures) that we can hope to understand the causes of human diseases.' Christopher Anderegg, Chairman, Scientific Advisory Committee, SUPRESS, Glendale, California, July 1995

Despite the current wide variety of scientifically and economically viable 'alternatives' that have been marketed in the last two decades, scientists continue to use animals and animal parts in toxicity testing. These include non-human animal blood, mucus, calf or rabbit serum, and rat, hamster or mouse tissues and cells. Even the widely used Ames test, designed to identify mutagens and carcinogens, routinely includes cells from the rat's liver. Ironically, in 1979 Thomas H. Maugh stated in the journal *Science* (202, 6 October 1979: 38) that variations in the preparation of rat liver homogenates had been shown to alter *in vitro* experimental results; and in *Mutation Research* (vol. 85 (1981): 280),

M. McConville, et al., reported marked metabolic differences between the liver cells of different rodent species *in vitro*.

Dissected cow (or sometimes rabbit or chicken) eyeballs from the slaughterhouse are used as replacements for live rabbits in the Draize test. The eyeball is dropped into a chemical solution, rinsed, and examined for opacity and swelling.[101] The most widely adopted 'alternatives' have historically been methods which merely reduce the numbers of animals used, 'refine' existing tests, and/or use animal cells, tissues and fluids in *in vitro* tests, rather than avoiding whole animals or their parts completely. The Limulus Amebocyte Lysate (LAL) test, developed by the Endosafe company in Charleston, South Carolina (now owned by Charles River Laboratories), uses horseshoe crab blood to test whether drugs cause fever as a side effect. This *in vitro* test, which was 'validated' against rabbit data, was approved by the FDA as a replacement for the 'rabbit pyrogen assay.' That test, which is still performed by several European companies, uses an elevation in body temperature of rabbits injected with a test compound as a screen for fever-producing compounds. ECVAM and COLIPA have proposed that the OECD adopt an 'alternative' test for 'percutaneous absorption' (skin penetration) using the 'freshly excised, shaved and thinned skin of the pig,' which is apparently being used by numerous cosmetic laboratories.[102] Some research committees have advocated 'using the minimum number of animals necessary,' improving husbandry, and minimizing the discomfort and stress experienced by the animals (a difficult task in the context of lethal testing).[103]

The HET-CAM or CAMVA ('hen egg test-chorio-allantoic membrane' or 'CAM vascular assay') test, the FETAX (frog embryo teratogenesis assay-*xenopus*) and the *Drosophila* (fruitfly) assay, have all been touted as 'alternatives.' The CAM test, developed by J. Leighton, et al. (used by a number of companies including Colgate-Palmolive and adopted by the German government in 1994 to test corrosive materials), uses the heavily veined membrane under the outer shell of fertilized chicken eggs.[104] The test has been used to measure eye and skin irritation, to screen for teratogens, and to evaluate the effects of toxins like botulinum, diphtheria, aflatoxin, and snake-neurotoxin.[105] Researchers will look for signs of vascular swelling, haemorrhage, and cell death. The embryonic membrane allegedly has no nerve fibers for the sensation of pain; it also requires minimal care. However, while the newer HET-CAM assays use ten-day-old embryos, the original CAMVA test uses 14-day-old embryos which caused the method to be classified as an animal procedure in the UK; Martin Stephens of the Humane Society of the United States stated his belief that late-stage embryos are probably still being used in the US.[106] Birds, however, are not protected under the US Animal Welfare Act; embryos are excluded in France under the French Decree on Experimentation of 1987, and also from the EEC Animal Experimentation Directive of 24 November 1986 (Article 2A). The fact that the 14–day CAM has been used in Germany suggests that German law does not protect embryos.[107] More importantly, Charles River (Breeding Laboratories) UK, Ltd, as well as IFFA CREDO in France, and SPAFAS, Inc in Preston, Connecticut (USA) are just some of the companies supplying chicken eggs for these tests. The eggs must be 'germ-free' and less than one day old upon arrival. Hence SPAFAS for example, has its own farms of 'germ-free' chickens which supply the eggs, and the chickens themselves are also sold to laboratories,[108] most likely destined for neurotoxicity experiments.

The FETAX assay uses eggs from *xenopus laevis*—the South African clawed frog, or other defined frog species. The test begins when the embryos are 12 to 18 hours old and lasts until they are 96 hours old (tadpole size). While it is not necessary to kill the frogs to obtain the eggs, the adult male and female must be injected with human chorionic gonadotrophin (derived from human urine, though pregnant mare serum has also been used) into their dorsal lymph sacs to induce breeding every six to eight weeks. Eggs are removed by pressing the female's lower back.[109] NIEHS toxicologists say that the FETAX assay can be used to screen chemicals for their potential to cause birth defects, growth retardation, structural malformation, and behavioral and functional deficits. The US Army's Biomedical Research Laboratory at Fort Detrick, Maryland is evaluating FETAX as a method to detect hazardous agents in contaminated groundwater. It is also beginning tests with the human teratogen Thalidomide, now being evaluated as a possible treatment for AIDS. Robert Finch, a scientist at the Army's Fort Detrick laboratory, reported that FETAX has been validated against rat and rabbit data,[110] once again calling into question this assay data's relevance to humans.

Amphibians are not protected under the US Animal Welfare Act; in most European countries, the initial injection procedure to induce the frogs to breed is regulated as an 'animal procedure.' Moreover, the assay currently uses rat enzymes to activate chemicals (though William Stokes of the NIEHS said that human cells could also be used);[111] and breeder frogs are fed three times a week with pelleted frog feed or a ground mixture of beef organs—products of the slaughterhouse. In addition, frogs (and thus embryos) used in these experiments are sold by breeders/ suppliers like Xenopus Express in Homosassa, Florida, Xenopus 1 in Ann Arbor, Michigan (which has a large breeding colony), and NASCO in Fort Atkinson, Wisconsin. Xenopus Express imports its frogs from South Africa and recommends 'imported *xenopus*' for breeding.[112]

Organizations like the Ethical Science Education Coalition in Boston, Massachusetts have raised ethical and environmental concerns in this regard. Although *xenopus* are allegedly hearty frogs and females can lay hundreds of eggs at one time, the collection of wild frogs for scientific purposes has contributed to worldwide declines in frog populations (along with habitat destruction, pollution, acid rain, and ultraviolet radiation). Because the mortality of frog eggs and larvae are high in the wild (for each egg that survives to adulthood, over a thousand die) removing breeding adults from the ecosystem takes a heavy toll on the species. Moreover, humane transport regulations for the shipment of amphibians are severely deficient worldwide (particularly in exporting countries like Mexico, Chile, Indonesia and South Africa). Frogs are often packed with too many in a crate, sometimes upside down, and without sufficient food, water or ventilation. Not surprisingly, mortality rates in transit from some suppliers can be as high as 50 percent. Once in the laboratory, *xenopus* frogs are 'sacrificed' after one or two years, once their reproductive capacity has been exhausted and given the limited space available to house adult animals; they may also fall prey to one of many bacterial infections, including 'red-leg.'[113] Increased demand for FETAX could have a negative impact on wild frog populations, and given the nature of the procedures and materials used in the assay, a majority of animal advocacy groups would not consider FETAX to be an 'alternative.'

Similarly, the *Drosophila* assay uses fruitfly embryo cell cultures to screen for teratogens. The assay, which measures cell death and proliferation, reportedly correlates well with human epidemiological studies.[114] In all three cases, however, there are ethical concerns, old questions about the (un)reliability of inter-species extrapolation, and the concern about supporting suppliers of 'laboratory animals' who are now also profiting from the sale of these so-called 'alternative assays.'

Currently, many researchers like Roger McLellan, president of the Chemical Industry Institute of Toxicology in Research Triangle Park, North Carolina, are taking advantage of developments in computer modeling and *in vitro* techniques, as *complements* to animal tests.[115] Without regulatory testing schemes to encourage its use, *in vitro* technology has merely become a sub-discipline of *in vivo* research; *in vitro* methods are mainly being used for screening—exempting substances (primarily mutagens, eye and skin irritants, and corrosives) that give positive results *in vitro*, and/or using those results to evaluate the need for further animal studies. While this has had the positive effect of reducing the numbers of animals used in toxicity tests, it has done little to change the fundamental way the tests are carried out. As discussed in Chapter 4, judging from the results of a recent NTP workshop on mechanism-based toxicology (MBT) in cancer risk assessment, it appears that this mindset is not going to change in the immediate future since the workshop focused on ways of using MBT methods to refine animal tests, and reduce the uncertainty inherent in inter-species extrapolations, rather than move away from animal tests altogether.[116]

Several refinements of classic animal tests have been proposed and some have been adopted by both federal and private laboratories. None of the tests address the inherent problems with animal testing; according to Hugo Van Looy of the OECD Environment Directorate, these refinements were also accepted without validation.[117] Examples of refinements of classical animal tests include the limit test, the up-down test, the approximate lethal dose test, the acute toxic class test, the fixed dose procedure (which has been 'validated' against classic animal test data), the low volume eye test, the local lymph node assay, and the mouse ear swelling test (the latter three are used by Procter & Gamble, and the latter two were adopted by the OECD on 17 July 1992, Guideline 406). Tier testing is a combination of several of the above methods.[118]

As was discussed in Chapter 2, in many 'alternative' tests, smaller rodents such as mice (transgenic or otherwise) are considered to be valid replacements for larger mammals. Hence the definition of what constitutes an animal has become an issue of contention. The term 'non-mammalian' is used to describe species which are often used in 'alternative' tests. These include vertebrates such as fish (trout, mud-minnows), amphibians (frogs), reptiles (snakes, turtles, iguanas) and birds, and invertebrates such as octopi, squid, insects, and snails. The sea urchin has been used to screen chemicals for reproductive toxicity and mutations.[119] Snails have been used to study the neurotoxic side effects of anti-tumor agents.[120]

The NIEHS claims that non-mammalian species share a high degree of structural and physiological similarities with other vertebrate species; in addition, the agency claims that invertebrates' shorter lifespans and developmental periods allow scientists to obtain information from them in less time than from mammalian species.[121] However, if the aim of using animals is to use those animals which most closely resemble humans biologically, the justifications for using such 'lower' animals seem groundless. NIEHS's statement that 'lower species are often easier to handle and less expensive than most mammals' sounds much like the justification used by the IARC to justify the use of rodents, as opposed to larger animals, in cancer tests.

As discussed, non-human animal tissues and fluids are commonly used in toxicology laboratories. In 1990 in Britain, it was determined that only a small proportion of experiments using isolated tissues employed human material—84 percent used tissue from animals, mainly rats and guinea pigs. This revelation prompted animal advocacy groups in Britain to launch the Humane Research Donor Card which allows carriers of the card to donate organs and tissues to scientific research after death, in the hope of eliminating animal testing.[122] People for the Ethical Treatment of Animals (PETA) in Norfolk, Virginia also offers an organ donor card to its members. Many scientists have welcomed the idea since work with human tissues, parts or organs overcomes the problem of species variation and produces results directly relevant to people.[123]

In 1990 Carlton H. Nadolney, an EPA toxicologist, stated that legislative authority to allow the widespread use of fetal and placental tissue in (toxicology) research would allow human cell lines to be created which could replace the use of animal cells.[124] Then in 1992 US President Bill Clinton signed an executive order allowing, and approving federal funding for, the use of fetal tissue in research. Toxicologist Frank Barile revealed that he has been using a line of spontaneously aborted fetal cells for ten years in his laboratory; such human cells can be purchased (in the US) from organizations like the American Type Culture Collection in Rockville, and the National Institutes of Health in Bethesda, Maryland. Hospitals and individuals often donate cells and cell cultures to these cell banks/repositories.[125]

Many activists and some toxicologists claim that research on 'alternatives' is a charade designed to buy time for industries and investigators who have no real intention of giving up animal experiments.[126] Purists in the animal advocacy community argue that merely reducing the numbers of animals used in an experiment, or refining the experiment to alleviate pain and distress for the animals, does not constitute a true alternative and is anathema to the goal of replacing animals in research and testing. Some object on philosophical grounds to the use of animal parts and body fluids, including parts obtained from slaughterhouses, as they believe that their use perpetuates a life-destroying ethic in science, and supports other exploitative industries. Others, like Richard Steiner, former president of the World Society for the Protection of Animals, and Italian pathologist Pietro Croce, prefer to use the terms replacement or scientific method, rather than alternative, arguing that use of the word 'alternative' implies that non-animal methods are an *option* rather than a replacement for animal tests.[127]

At the other extreme, there are those in the scientific establishment who feel threatened by the very mention of the word 'alternative.' Louis Sibal, Director of Laboratory Animal Research at the National Institutes of Health (NIH), says that many scientists prefer to use the term 'adjuncts,' implying that *in vitro* and other technologies are used along with, rather than in place of, animal-based research. Clearly a large segment of the scientific community is uncomfortable with the alternatives concept.[128] Many scientists are ideologically entrenched, and have opposed the pressure of their peers and animal advocates' urgings to reduce or abandon traditional animal-based research methods in favor of non-animal technologies.[129] The signing into law of the (American) Animal Enterprise Protection Act on 26 August 1992, for example, reveals an establishment concerned about the growing threat of animal activism and its impact on scientific and regulatory reform. Rowan (1995) writes that 'the Act characterizes terrorism as the physical disruption of an animal enterprise'—a definition very different from the FBI's.[130] It is unclear how far-reaching the effects of the Act might be, but one must wonder whether it implies that American scientists working to replace animal testing with more appropriate scientific methods are also considered terrorists according to the Act.

In 1981, a bill (HR 556) was introduced in the US Congress for the purpose of establishing a National Center for Alternative Research into methods of research and testing that did not require the use of live animals. Although this bill was embraced by prominent regulatory scientists like John Weisburger, then at the NCI,[131] it did not pass. Subsequent attempts to enact legislation to restrict animal testing were blocked by industry and the biomedical research community.[132] The NIH, the major funding agency for biomedical research in the US (almost 40 percent of which is conducted with animals),[133] has attempted, on paper, to establish 'alternatives' programs several times: in 1985 under the Health Research Extension Act; in 1991 with a legislative amendment to the Public Health Service Act (HR 1532); and in 1993 under the NIH Revitalization Act (which is up for reauthorization at the start of 1997). The language in the last two bills was virtually identical. Though the NIH Revitalization Act of 1993, and the bill before it (1991), mandated the NIEHS to develop and validate alternative safety testing methods and protocols, the agency has not fulfilled that mandate.[134] In the Fall of 1993, Congress appropriated $12 million dollars to the NIEHS for the purpose of evaluating the potential of promising *in vitro* testing methods, and coordinating the adoption and implementation of such methods by different federal agencies. The agency received a three-year grant of $4.5 million in 1995 to develop and validate promising new methods.[135] Though NIEHS and inter-agency committees are busy holding workshops on alternative methods of research, nothing concrete has resulted from these efforts so far.

An 85-page draft report by the *ad hoc* Interagency Coordinating Committee on the Validation of Alternative Methods (ICCVAM) (dated 16 October 1995, and completed at the end of 1996), demonstrates an attempt to fulfill the mandate of the 1993 Revitalization Act through the establishment of a structured review process for the evaluation, validation and regulatory acceptance of alternative methods.[136] Bureaucratic inertia and the influence of special interests has stunted progress in this area before, which has been slow at best. Similarly, this report (which was first presented at an OECD workshop on toxicological test alternatives in Stockholm, Sweden in January 1996) sets up inequitable and arbitrary standards for the validation and acceptance of 'alternative' methods (defined as the Three Rs)—standards which were never required of the animal tests.

These include the requirements to state that an *in vitro* method cannot fully address *in vivo* metabolism (when it has never been shown that an animal model can fully address human metabolism); the requirement that the test method be 'relatively insensitive to minor changes in protocol;' that it be 'cost-effective;' that the 'time to conduct the test is not unreasonable in relation to the test results obtained' (though the animal tests do not meet any of these criteria); and that 'the method has been or is likely to be accepted internationally.' The report also directly maintains support for animal testing by requiring that new methods demonstrate 'a linkage' between existing test methods; furthermore, the performance of test methods is to be evaluated 'in relation to existing toxicity data and experience in the relevant target species.' An 18 March 1996 draft of the report (p. 9) states that a lack of 'good [reliable] in vivo data may drive the need for more animal testing in order to validate tests,' and (p. 11): 'new unforeseen questions' may arise 'that will require animal methods for answers.'

Perhaps the biggest hurdle is that new methods must be 'accepted by the scientific community,' when it is well known that it is *because* of ongoing debates within the scientific community about the merits of new technologies that they have not been accepted. In addition, the report demands inter-agency coordination on the assessment of validation programs, a feat which has never been achieved before and looks highly unlikely now, given the diverse priorities, budgets and mandates of the different federal agencies.

Skeptics believe that by setting up such a formal and demanding review process, ICCVAM is creating a bureaucratic obstacle which is bound to slow down broad acceptance of alternatives. They also believe the report is a response to certain agencies' usurpment of regulatory authority through the 'premature' adoption and use of *in vitro* methods like Corrositex and Skin²; and that it is intended to ensure that individual federal agencies do not act independently again, thereby humiliating the EPA and FDA who have been slow to adopt these methods.[137]

Although the 18 March 1996 draft of the ICCVAM report does state (p. 6) that federal regulations should be reviewed to ensure that they are not obstructing the adoption of 'alternative approaches,' it reveals (p. 11) that, ultimately, the power is left with the individual federal agencies 'without major changes in federal law' to decide how and whether 'alternative' methods will be used.

The 'alternatives' sector is, for the most part, an incestuous circle of government and industry scientists with a penchant for setting up organizations that have confusing acronyms, from ICCVAM to ECVAM and CAAT to SCAAT. All of these groups publish reports and virtually all reach the same wishy-washy conclusion that animal testing cannot be abandoned 'just yet.' In 1992, the Liaison Committee of European Associations of COLIPA set up the Steering Committee on Alternatives to Animal Testing (SCAAT). COLIPA works closely with ECVAM (ICCVAM's European counterpart), the Japanese Cosmetic Industry Association, and the (US) Cosmetic, Toiletry and Fragrance Association (CTFA) which supports the Johns Hopkins Center for Alternatives to Animal Testing (CAAT) in Baltimore, Maryland.[138] (According to Pam Logemann, Director of Worldwide In Vitro Lab Technology Sales at Advanced Tissue Sciences in California, CTFA has an Alternatives Task Force which received no funding in 1996 and has essentially been inactive.)[139] ECVAM's Scientific Advisory Committee is composed of representatives from COLIPA, the European Federation of Pharmaceutical Industries Association (EFPIA), the European Centre for the Ecotoxicology and Toxicology of Chemicals (ECETOC) and animal welfare groups.[140] Some scientists and animal advocacy groups have been cynical about these organizations' sincerity as well as certain corporations' commitment to the quest for replacements.

While there have been a handful of admirable efforts to develop and adopt alternatives, the majority have been criticized by animal advocates as being half-hearted. Several large companies that make household and personal care products, including Procter & Gamble (P & G), Revlon and Avon, have reduced their use of animals but have not ended animal testing altogether. Several raw ingredients used by the cosmetics industry are supplied by companies like Dow Chemical, Monsanto, and DuPont, who continue to do animal testing.[141] P & G still continues to use modified versions of classical Draize and LD50 tests with animals to assess the safety of various food and drug products, and contracts outside laboratories to perform animal tests, leading animal advocates to question how sincere the corporation is in its desire to stop testing. Some 'alternatives' under development at P & G, which are alleged to be faster and use 50 percent fewer animals than standard tests, include the 'mouse ear swelling test' to detect photo-allergic reactions, and mouse and guinea pig assays to measure irritancy and contact hypersensitivity.[142] Activists point to John Paul Mitchell, Aveda, and Tom's of Maine, as examples of mainstream 'cruelty-free' companies that use natural ingredients in their personal care products, or ingredients known to be safe and effective through years of human use, thereby eliminating the need for animal testing.

In addition, rather than funding the development of more 'alterna-tives,' some argue that it would be more useful to fund validation efforts for the myriad of true non-animal methods that already exist. Atkinson, et al. (1992) affirm that 'too many non-animal tests have been developed, without sufficient consideration of their intended use.'[143] Similarly, Barile (1994) claims that a multitude of tests continues to be developed though few are gaining general acceptance.[144]

On another level, criticism has been directed at the very organ-izations charged with developing 'alternatives.' The Fund for the Replacement of Animals in Medical Experiments (FRAME)—a British organization considered to be at the forefront in the development and promotion of 'alternatives'—advocates a careful examination of whether animal tests need to be conducted at all, but states that if they must be conducted, the animals in the laboratory should be 'properly cared for.'[145] Michael Balls (Chairman of the Trustees of FRAME and now Director of ECVAM—which was set up by the EC to foster the development and use of 'alternatives' in Europe) co-authored a paper with J. H. Fentem in 1992 in which the pair suggest an eight-stage scheme for predicting ocular irritancy testing.[146] Stage six is labelled 'essential tests in animals;' these should allegedly be done to confirm lack of irritancy rather than to demonstrate it. Nevertheless, one might wonder why the use of animals would be proposed at all by a group which claims to seek the *replacement* of animals in experimentation. Balls recently gave credence to animal-based research and testing in the Spring 1996 issue of a noted American animal welfare publica-tion.[147] Elsewhere, Balls stated that he thought animal testing could

potentially be abolished within fifty years;[148] such forecasts are bound
to keep industry, animal breeders and industry-beholden politicians
happy. FRAME has received corporate support from numerous
companies in the chemical, pharmaceutical and petroleum industries
including Shell and Imperial Chemical Industries (ICI).[149]

CTFA, which states that 'animal testing is necessary to ensure the
safety of the industry's products,'[150] (and whose European counterpart,
COLIPA, is allegedly lobbying against a European initiative to ban
cosmetic testing on animals by 1998),[151] provided support to establish
CAAT under the direction of Alan Goldberg. CAAT has received funds
from the NIH, an agency noted for its support of animal research.
Charles River Laboratories, Inc, the nation's foremost breeder of laboratory animals, has been a CAAT 'corporate sponsor.' Dow Chemical
and Shell have been 'corporate friends.'[152] CAAT's name is listed on
the back of a brochure produced by The Society of Toxicology called
'The Importance of Animals in the Science of Toxicology,' alongside
private foundations and federal agencies that openly promote the use
of animals in research.[153] In addition, Richard Hill of the EPA, and
Gerald Guest, a veterinarian formerly with the FDA—both of whom
have spoken out publicly about the necessity of animal testing[154]—
serve as scientific advisors to CAAT.

Goldberg, who has advocated using *in vitro* tests in conjunction with
standard animal tests in risk assessment,[155] and who conducted basic
research on animals himself into the mid-1980s,[156] stated that 'to eliminate animal testing at this time would constitute an abrogation of the
toxicologist's responsibility to ensure safety and will pose a risk to
human health that government, industry and the public will find unacceptable.'[157] He said that *in vitro* tests could be used to prioritize
animal testing,[158] and that the replacement of animals 'will require
significant scientific developments, particularly in the area of in vitro/
in vivo extrapolation before it becomes a reality.'[159]

For such defeatist and counterproductive statements (which may well
become self-fulfilling prophecies) to come from the director of a center
charged with developing alternatives is disheartening—particularly since
many toxicologists believe that it is precisely *because* of *in vitro/in vivo*
comparisons that alternatives have not been accepted more quickly.
Toxicologists like Björn Ekwall and Erik Walum of MEIC (whose
requests for financial assistance from CAAT and FRAME for MEIC
have consistently been rejected),[160] believe that *in vitro* and *in vivo* data
(from animal tests) cannot be meaningfully compared because they use
different endpoints, or toxicity criteria,[161] and that the *in vivo* data should
not be used as the standard because they are inherently flawed.[162]

One toxicologist, who did not want to be identified, stated that CAAT and FRAME were established largely to placate animal advocates' demands for progress in the 'alternatives' testing arena. P & G has given funds to CAAT in an attempt to appear interested in the development of 'alternatives', but that is a smokescreen. Although they appear to be working hard to bring about a revolution in testing methods, my source claimed that both CAAT and FRAME carry out activities which have produced more paperwork than progress. Most of their money has gone into sponsoring conferences and producing books and journals. Yet another scientist said, 'most of the people in CAAT are from industry and they have been working hard to prevent the development of alternatives.' The ongoing mechanistic research CAAT sponsors, much of which uses animal cells and tissues, is a token activity which never bears fruit; FRAME's validation studies, most of which have used animal data, have been conducted with so few chemicals that the results may have little value.

The validation issue: a barrier to a full and immediate ban on animal testing

'The LD50 method was never validated in the current sense but simply accepted by most countries and incorporated without validation into their guidelines. Somewhere someone should have the courage to do the same with alternative methods.' Lavinia Pioda, 'The Position of the Authorities,' in *Alternatives to Animal Testing*, Christoph A. Reinhardt, ed. (New York: VCH/Weinheim, 1994), p. 176

As discussed in Chapter 3, validation is the process by which the relevance and reliability of a test method are established for a particular purpose; in this case, validation methods must produce toxicological data that can be extrapolated to humans.[163]

The validation of alternatives has been the subject of both public and private, national and international research programs and conferences for over a decade now in the United States, Europe and Japan. Scientific institutes including CAAT in the United States, FRAME and ECVAM in Europe, and MEIC in Sweden, were established to bring together researchers working with *in vitro* and other methods in toxicology and pharmacology.[164] (MEIC is the only independent laboratory using human data from clinical case studies and autopsy reports in its validation programs.) So far, no unified standard for validating non-animal methods has come out of these groups' efforts.

In 1986, the journal *Science* reported that the NTP, through the

NIEHS, spent $70 million of public funds between 1981 and 1986 'to lay a basis for the validation of in vitro tests.' In 1988 the NTP spent $17.7 million (22 percent of its budget) on validation; in 1994, only 2–3 percent of the agency's budget was allocated to validation.[165] To date, no concrete validation schemes have been established. In fact, after having spent at least $100 million of public money on validation thus far, the NTP, which coordinates toxicity testing in the United States, has clearly expressed its desire *not* to be the national center for alternative test development, validation or application.[166] European industry spent 25 million European Currency Units (ECUs) in 1993 to develop *in vitro* methods (roughly US $30 million). But no agreement has been reached by the EC with respect to the use and/or validation of these methods. There has been little central coordination within governments and countries in this area.[167]

A majority of scientists believe that the use of animals in toxicology testing will only end when broadly accepted validation procedures are established.[168] EEC Directive 93/95/EEC claims that cosmetics testing on animals will only be banned by 1998 in Europe provided that acceptable validated alternatives exist. But scientists and regulators in the US and worldwide have yet to agree upon which evaluation standards they will employ to measure the usefulness of alternative tests, and they have yet to agree on the basic principles of validation. ICCVAM's report on the criteria for the validation and regulatory acceptance of alternative methods was allegedly written to resolve this, but the problems with the report have already been discussed. Moreover, conflicts of interest among the legislation's stakeholders will most likely serve to dilute the proposal so as to limit its effectiveness. Swiss toxicologist Gerhard Zbinden stated that widespread use and acceptance of alternatives by regulatory agencies would be a slow process because global consent on new concepts for consumer protection and product labelling is difficult to achieve, and because the standards and regulations for, and objectives of experiments vary from test to test, laboratory to laboratory and country to country. Consensus may well be impossible since the field of science does not typically function by consensus; rather, individuals' hypotheses or theories are presented to the scientific community at large and scrutinized—allowing for a democratic search for answers to what are often global questions. Consensus could very well represent a blockade to real progress since, first, it may simply not be achievable, and, second, because it could stifle creative thinking. In this vein Frank Barile (1994) stated that, 'progress relies on the continuous development of better strategies to evaluate new tests, rather than a set of inflexible guidelines for the inclusion or exclusion of protocols.'[169] Nevertheless, OECD procedures for adopting alternative methods require a consensus within the scientific community of over twenty-five member states and acceptance by regulatory agencies in North America and Japan—a process which could take years.

The fact that animal tests themselves have never been validated has been discussed. While critics charge that data from *in vitro* tests are not always predictive of human responses, data from animal tests are in reality just as arbitrary, yet they are the standard against which new methodologies are measured. An ongoing debate centers around the fact that the data generated from alternative tests are compared or validated against the existing animal data they are intended to replace. The EC, for example, insists that *in vitro* tests mimic *in vivo* toxic effects. The Cellular and Genetic Toxicology Branch of the NIEHS conducted a large-scale study to evaluate the utility of short-term *in vitro* assays for identifying carcinogens, by comparing the results from the study to rodent bioassay data.[170] Several validation schemes for potential alternatives to the Draize eye test have also been undertaken which compare *in vitro* data with *in vivo* data from animal tests. But Atkinson, et al. (1992) retort that 'few *in vitro* toxicologists take account of the variability of the animal data [so that] ... a maximum average Draize eye test score becomes "true" and an *in vitro* score which fails to match that value is labelled "false."' This norm is maintained in spite of extensive criticism in the scientific literature of the use of the rabbit eye to measure ocular irritancy in humans.[171] In addition, as in the area of animal-to-human extrapolation discussed in Chapter 2, the number of statistical methods used to compare *in vitro* with animal or human (*in vivo*) data are manifold, and each may produce a different result.[172]

The issue of validating *in vitro* tests against animal tests has long been an obstacle for replacing the latter. In its 1986 report entitled *Alternatives to Animal Use in Research* (Chapter 8, p. 190), the US Office of Technology Assessment stated that,

> the implementation of alternatives [in testing] is hindered by various forms of institutional inertia such as regulatory schemes, product liability law, and general resistance to change. *Important impediments are the large body of existing information—derived from animals—that is relied on for the interpretation of new data and the lack of sufficient information [validation] to support the use of alternatives.* (Emphasis added.)

Scientists like Ekwall, Scaife, Barile, and Koeter (of the OECD's Environmental Safety and Health division), believe that the validation of *in vitro* systems which predict human toxicity is necessary and important, but they contend that an ideal validation scheme should use human rather than animal toxicity data as the sole reference. If animal data are used as a reference, says Ekwall, the imprecise animal data will be compared against possibly meaningless *in vitro* data.[173] In echoing Ekwall's concerns, British scientist N. J. Van Abbé in Surrey said, 'there is little merit in assessing an innovative approach by making comparisons which in effect, only perpetuate the problems of interpretation associated with its forerunner. To be specific, a new skin sensitization test really needs to be compared with … human skin sensitization and a proposed eye irritancy test against human eye irritancy.'[174] Similarly, Diane Benford of the University of Surrey wrote in 1987 that 'the value of LD50 data is limited and the relevance of LD50 replacement tests is therefore also questionable.'[175] Offering a similar conclusion, Thomas Sutter, a researcher at Johns Hopkins University in Baltimore, Maryland said that, 'without the incorporation of human *in vitro* data into the risk characterization process, biologically based risk assessments will simply represent improved models for the interpretation of data generated by animal experiments.'[176] In an issue of *Reproductive Toxicology* (vol. 7 (1993), Supplement 1, p. 121), Herman Koeter says that, 'the *in vitro* test should not seek for high correlations with an existing *in vivo* assay, but mimic as well as possible a particular aspect of the real event for which the hazard should be assessed, e.g. human fertility.'

Such statements are all the more compelling when it is revealed that laboratories and companies that conduct human dose-response studies and compare them with historical animal data during validation, find that not only do the animal data correlate poorly with the human data, but they are riddled with false negatives and false positives![177] Barile (1994, p. 194) writes, 'it is generally accepted that these correlations are not good … due to species differences.' Amway's Phil Casterton recently said, 'we're not making any attempt to relate [our human data] to rabbit data because rabbit data are highly variable. They're subject to interpretation of the lab person looking at them, especially in the area of mild to moderate irritation. It's worthless as far as I'm concerned. When you're trying to predict what the response is going to be in humans, you should use humans.'[178] The problem, contends Barile, is the perennial lack of available human data for validation (most of which is currently obtained from poison centers, emergency rooms, autopsies and human volunteer studies). Although this information has not been systematically compiled into one global databank, it still represents the most reliable source of data for toxicologists since human data are 'less susceptible to misinterpretation than animal data.' He correctly points out that, if animal results are used as the gold standard in validation studies, 'the species gap [is] also unnecessarily included in the evaluation of the new in vitro test.' The comparison of the animal data to human data (when they exist) constitutes the 'validation of animal tests paradoxically forced upon cytotoxicologists.'[179]

Some companies, and independent laboratories like Advanced Tissue Sciences (ATS) in California, Amway in Michigan, Unilever in the UK and MEIC in Sweden, are taking it upon themselves to conduct human dose-response studies and/or use human data in *in vitro* validation programs. Frazier (1990) and Balls (1990) both wrote that validation programs are not only time-consuming but very expensive, exhausting the budgets of the funding parties (generally foundations, non-profit organizations, and some governmental bodies). It should be noted that, typically, the burden of validation falls on *in vitro* manufacturers. Indeed, ATS spent $30,000 to test three compounds for a final validation study which compared human irritancy data against data from its Skin^2 product. The company also funded and conducted a worldwide validation study using its Skin^2 technology. The study, which began in October 1995 and was completed in April 1996, compared the *in vitro* dermal irritancy of several commercial surfactants (soaps, detergents), against data from concurrent *human* dose-response studies. ECVAM is completing the European leg of the validation trials and is supposed to present the results to the EC and OECD. ATS plans to generate a large database of human and *in vitro* information based on this and future research. Once Skin^2 is validated, the company plans to lobby regulatory agencies to accept the technology as a valid replacement for dermal, ocular, and corrosivity testing on animals.[180] Similarly, under Phil Casterton's direction, the (American) Soap and Detergent Association aims to establish a human database of reactions to generic product formulations. The data will be published in toxicology journals and made available to other laboratories. It is hoped that more companies will initiate such studies and begin to share information, thus increasing the pool of human (and *in vitro*) data to replace the animal data for validation purposes.

Currently, there are more than seven international *in vitro* toxicology databases containing information on *in vitro* methods, toxicity data and ongoing validation projects.[181] In 1992 the Galileo Data Bank was established in Pisa, Italy (with the help of the European Community) as an internationally recognized data retrieval system. It was created to classify chemicals as to their toxicity, predict risk, and above all speed up *in vitro* validation programs; its criteria demand a uniform system for naming, measuring, classifying and determining the toxicity of chemicals. The premise behind the project is that a chemical's toxicity can be understood by an analysis of its molecular characteristics. The bank is consulted by researchers, universities, regulatory bodies and corporations all over the world that are involved in the development of non-animal testing methods and in toxicological evaluations. Individuals can scan data for over 21,000 alternative tests, read toxicological profiles of over 2,000 chemical substances tested with several diverse non-animal methods, and identify appropriate non-animal methods for any given need.[182] Similarly, the TOPCAT worldwide databank in Bethesda, Maryland, provides data on the prediction of chemical toxicity using molecular/structural analysis.[183] Others have suggested the establishment of agency or institute-linked databases that would allow regulatory bodies to have mutual access to the same information and coordinate validation and technology development in this area, with the aim of reforming legislation.[184] The creation of ICCVAM in the US and ECVAM in Europe would suggest that the potential for the success of such a plan exists if both committees' intentions are sincere.

A critical observer might conclude that the more than decade-long, often bureaucratic, technical, and increasingly complex discussion about the validation of non-animal methods has merely served to stall the abandonment of animal tests. Countless papers and technical reports have been published in peer-reviewed toxicology journals which discuss the feasibility of, and/or critique, various validation programs. Simple schemes, such as one proposed by Herman Koeter of the OECD[185] or Björn Ekwall of MEIC for example,[186] have yet to be adopted widely. As discussed in Chapter 3, Pam Logemann of ATS in California challenges the myth that validation studies must take several years to complete, citing ATS's completion of six validation studies (with Skin²) in six years.[187]

This situation has compelled toxicologists like Lavinia Pioda to call for more radical proposals. Pioda, who is responsible for regulating toxic chemicals at the Federal Health Office in Berne, Switzerland, believes that it is up to regulatory authorities to begin accepting—and even requiring—non-animal testing methods as part of international guidelines. Pioda says that, especially now, with the current network of international agreements, 'no producer willingly conducts two different tests when one of them is internationally accepted.' And because animal tests were accepted without having been validated, so too should non-animal methods be accepted without being subject to rigorous and lengthy validation schemes (which place a huge burden on companies and dissuade them from choosing new methods). Pioda states that someone should have the courage to take the first step.[188] Animal advocates and others need to force this debate. Author Edith Efron goes further and says:

> no one can say whether a substance that mutates a bacterium or causes cancer in an animal is causing cancer in man. No one can predict from such data. No one can quantify the probability of a potential of risk let alone quantify the risk ... the Sinister Molecule ... is a moral fiction devised to permit regulatory action in the absence of epidemiological knowledge.[189]

If one subscribes to this premise, that neither animal tests nor *in vitro* tests can truly predict cancer in humans, and that this knowledge will only ever be gained from human beings, then from a purely moral perspective the animal tests should be abolished immediately.

In order to fulfill the need for human toxicity data, the cooperation of poison centers, hospitals, industry, and insurance companies would be imperative. As discussed, a handful of laboratories and companies are compiling such data, albeit on a very limited scale due to financial constraints. This lack of funding has created obstacles for meaningful validation studies, and has led to the fragmentation of research by several different sectors; it has made the establishment of a truly useful and comprehensive international database (and hence the global sharing of information), difficult. Realistically, only government bodies or agencies like the US National Toxicology Program could amass the resources necessary to fund such research, and so far they have been unwilling to do so. Whether an international regulatory authority like the EC, OECD, or United Nations could solve these problems is also unclear since these entities issue animal testing regulations themselves. Moreover, both the EC and United Nations Educational, Scientific and Cultural Organization (UNESCO) have revealed themselves to be less than cooperative in such matters. When UNESCO was called upon by the UK-based International Association Against Painful Experiments on Animals (IAAPEA) to set up an independent commission to assess the validity of animal tests and investigate the potential of non-animal testing techniques, UNESCO (which is heavily supported by the US) rejected the request. Instead, the agency offered to establish a dialogue between IAAPEA and bodies such as the International Council for Laboratory Animal Science that are inextricably linked to the animal research industry.[190]

As the dilemma over the funding of validation studies is discussed, it should be remembered that no such criteria or prerequisites were ever deemed necessary for the animal tests themselves. Scientists clearly do not want equal science, they want better science; Amway's Phil Casterton says that non-animal methods are being held to a higher standard than the animal tests. He stated his belief that the Draize test, for example, could be abolished immediately.[191] Olivera Markovic, a clinical chemist, believes that only scientifically sufficient data proving that alternative methods can decrease the risk to humans below the level achieved with animal testing will produce legislative changes.[192] Perhaps that is an admission that the current system is not as virtuous as proponents claim. It is ironic that such a double standard exists for 'alternatives' and one must wonder why the animal testers have never been challenged on these points, since the validation issue—and the additional time-consuming and expensive research, paperwork, fund-raising, lobbying, and scientific and regulatory dissent it creates—is one of the bureaucratic obstacles holding up the replacement of animal tests with non-animal methods.

Despite the frustrating inertia within the scientific community and the US federal government (among others) with respect to the validation issue and the refusal to abandon animal-based toxicology, numerous corporations and state agencies have taken it upon themselves to use non-animal methods for their purposes without waiting for the results of official validation schemes. Due to the absence of clear *industry* standards for validation, and continued lack of guidance from federal regulators, companies have relied on their in-house toxicology departments to define their own validation standards when choosing non-animal methods.

For example, in the past Avon has chosen *in vitro* tests which demonstrated good correlation with *in vivo* studies with animals. The company's decision to adopt Eytex to screen for eye irritancy, and to use human skin patch testing in conjunction with its computer database for product safety evaluation, has been silently accepted by the US government.[193] As was previously mentioned, European companies like Chanel and l'Oreal have taken it upon themselves to use *in vitro* technologies to test cosmetics. Estée Lauder, Yves Rocher, Rhône-Poulenc, and Mobil also use them. A few examples of similar initiatives will be described below.

Some success stories

The New Jersey Department of Environmental Protection The New Jersey Department of Environmental Protection (NJDEP) has been using the Ames assay as a screening tool to detect potentially toxic discharge problems in New Jersey waters for over a decade. Test labs have also conducted Ames assays on wastewater samples for the agency, to obtain a comprehensive assessment of toxins—mostly industrial effluents and/or mutagens—associated with chronic disease. NJDEP requires industrial facilities to use the Ames test on a specific schedule using specified sample collection techniques and assay protocols. Each facility is required to report the results of the tests and, when mutagenic results are obtained, graph dose-response curves with linear slopes. Thomas Atherholt of the NJDEP says that by using the Ames assay the agency has identified industries with mutagenic effluents, and obtained information on a broad array of mutagens—that would otherwise have remained undetected—in a timely and cost-effective manner. The assay has also been used to help substantiate the need for, and monitor the success of, toxicity reduction programs.[194]

Tom's of Maine Instead of using rats to test its products—by brushing their front incisors with cotton swabs, killing them, and cutting their jaws off so their teeth can be viewed under a microscope—Tom's of Maine has used human volunteers and extracted human molars to test its products since 1970.[195] In July 1995, The American Dental Association (ADA) granted its official seal to the company's non-animal tested toothpaste. The seal certifies that the toothpaste not only cleans teeth but actually rebuilds them due to the fluoride contained in it. The awarding of the seal is highly likely to increase the company's distribution and sales; when Crest became the first toothpaste to get the ADA seal, its sales tripled.

Avon, Revlon, The Body Shop and Aveda Although they still rely on data from previous animal tests and have been criticized for accepting animal test data from their raw ingredient suppliers, Avon and Revlon, the two most profitable cosmetic companies in America, have stopped testing products on animals *in-house*, though their contract laboratories and suppliers may still test on animals. Noxell, which makes Noxzema skin creams and Cover Girl cosmetics, has used a non-animal eye irritancy test since 1989 claiming it is 100 percent effective.[196] (It should be noted, however, that Procter & Gamble, which continues to do animal testing, bought Noxell in 1992.) Amway stopped testing on animals in June 1989, preferring to rely on human and practical experience; though Phil Casterton also conceded that the company's raw material suppliers probably still conduct animal tests to comply with federal regulations.[197] The Body Shop, a 'cruelty-free' cosmetic company with mass appeal and over 1,100 retail stores in 46 countries, has never conducted animal tests; the company has been criticized for using ingredients that have been tested on animals in the past, despite founder Anita Roddick's public crusade against the practice (see this section).[198]

Aveda, a more 'upscale' personal products company, goes a step further. The company will pay a premium for ingredients that are certified as having *not* been tested on animals, as well as those that have been grown organically (without pesticides, herbicides or fungicides) and harvested sustainably. Aveda uses botanical ingredients known to be safe through years of human use, including henna for hair dyes, essential oils, and Bixa—a plant ingredient grown especially for the company by a tribe in Brazil, which is used in the company's lipsticks and has never been tested on animals. Aveda's profits have grown by 30 percent since 1994.[199] Many of Aveda's and other 'cruelty-free' companies' ingredients are sourced in Asian, African and South American countries where the indigenous peoples' knowledge about medicinal and cosmetic properties of plants has been passed down through the generations.

There are currently over five hundred cruelty-free cosmetics, household, companion animal, office supply, and personal care products companies in the United States that do not do any animal testing.[200] The Coalition for Consumer Information on Cosmetics, formed in 1993 and composed of nine animal advocacy organizations, representing millions of members across the United States and the world, is submitting a questionnaire to cosmetics companies to gauge the potential for an industry-wide move away from animal testing—a move which is long overdue. Members of the group plan to lobby the US Congress to encourage this transition and make it a reality.[201] In addition, the Coalition has developed consistent standards by which to measure cruelty-free cosmetics/personal care products companies;[202] for example, companies who conduct or commission, or whose contractors and suppliers conduct or commission animal tests cannot be called 'cruelty-free.'

This is timely given that in 1995, the (American) National Consumer's League filed a petition with the US Federal Trade Commission seeking to prohibit companies from making 'cruelty-free' claims on product labels.[203] (This move contradicts public sentiment on this issue. A recent Associated Press poll revealed that two-thirds of Americans believe it is wrong to test cosmetics on animals.)[204] A similar measure would take effect in Europe in 1998, despite overwhelming consumer opposition to cosmetics testing on animals, and consumers' desire to buy non-animal-tested products. The UK's Department of Trade and Industry recently published guidelines on the implementation of the European Union's Cosmetics Testing Directive which could lead to a ban on 'cruelty-free' logos on cosmetics, thereby preventing consumers from making ethical choices in the marketplace. The guidelines require companies to state whether any of their ingredients or final products have ever been tested on animals. Because virtually all of the 8000 or more cosmetic ingredients on the market have at some point been tested on animals, companies like The Body Shop that do not conduct animal tests but may use common cosmetic ingredients that have been tested on animals in the past would be prohibited from marketing their products as 'cruelty-free.' Meanwhile, Gillette and Procter & Gamble, both of which continue to perform and commission animal tests, would not be required to state this on their products.[205]

A lawsuit forcing regulatory agencies to require the labelling of all animal-tested products might be needed to resolve this issue, though it would naturally face immense opposition from cosmetics (and chemical) companies. British toxicologist Iain F. H. Purchase issued another challenge to this new regulatory proposal which threatens freedom of choice: animal data are often used for labelling and classification purposes—for example, to formulate user warnings on products; however, given that the data are irrelevant to the human situation, such animal-based user warnings should be forbidden on labels and product packaging.[206] This would compel companies to acquire the human data necessary for relevant user warnings. Similarly, in 1986 J. Remfry made the case for a law/consumer education campaign requiring the labelling of goods with a full listing of the ingredients, and an explanation of how those ingredients were developed and/or tested.[207]

According to British biochemist Dennis V. Parke, the scientific case for a move away from animal tests is unassailable. He says that the use of alternative procedures, coupled with low dose human toxicokinetic studies (which were more common in the 1950s before the threat of litigation raised its head), could eventually lead to the complete abandonment of animal testing. Parke says that a shift from an emphasis on animal experiments to pharmacokinetic studies in humans would likely provide employment opportunities. Mass spectrometry physicists would replace cage cleaners, and molecular toxicologists would replace animal dissectors—both of which Parke considers to be changes for the better.[208]

Such Utopian ideas are inspiring, but the truth is that signs of progress are still distant. Although the use of *in vitro* techniques in toxicology research and testing has become more common, its application in regulatory toxicology and in the industrial sector has been limited. Animal advocates in Europe fear that if the European cosmetics testing ban, proposed for 1998, is delayed (or abandoned) by unyielding regulatory agencies, there will be little chance of making progress in other areas of testing. Both US and international toxicity testing regulations continue to encourage the performance of animal tests. This has had a negative impact on the *in vitro* industry. Some companies have been forced to close their product development divisions, focus on more profitable products like biologicals for the medical sector, or sell existing technologies to other companies; others do not have the funds to pursue promising research projects;[209] and those still in the business are worried.

According to Pauline Ryan—Associate Director of Business Development at Organogenesis, Inc, producers of the now defunct Testorgans line, in Canton, Massachusetts—pressure from animal advocates in the early 1980s created a big push for *in vitro* technology development. But she said drug, cosmetic and chemical companies never really believed in 'alternatives,' saw the technology as an additive cost, and did not sink any real money into its development. Instead, they gave money to organizations like CAAT and FRAME in the hope that animal advocates would simply 'go away' and they could resume business as usual.[210]

It appears that animal advocates *were* placated and lulled into believing that progress was being made in the 'alternatives' industry, according to my source who wished not to be identified. They are not on the offensive anymore and this has created a backlash. Industry is now investing less in 'alternatives' than it ever has, and is going back to standard animal tests. In 1993, Edward M. Jackson, editor of the *Journal of Toxicology*, wrote, 'the public relations aspects of the search for alternatives to animal testing have kept activists virtually at bay and stalled any state or federal legislation for the most part.'[211]

When pressure from animal advocates died down in the late 1980s, the market for *in vitro* products shrank accordingly. According to Pauline Ryan, in 1995 *in vitro* technology represented a meager $5 million share of the testing market worldwide, a figure confirmed by Diane Birely, In Vitro International's Marketing Services Manager. Interest in the technology is predominantly relegated to academia; and because rigid federal regulatory guidelines prevent companies from breaking ties with convention, there is little incentive for *in vitro* companies to develop or market new technologies.[212] According to Mark Benjamin, Director of Scientific Affairs at Xenometrix in Boulder, Colorado, the future of the *in vitro* field hinges on regulatory agencies' acceptance of these new methods; but industry will have to drive federal agencies to accept them.[213]

Diane Birely agrees. It is true that regulatory acceptance of *in vitro* technology would play a big part in bringing about change; if regulatory agencies were to abolish animal testing and only require *in vitro* tests, industry would not have a choice as to which methods it could use. In this sense, a revolution would be required to change the way federal agencies do business. But only industry has the financial and political power necessary to force government to change.

Toxicologist Gerhard Zbinden noted that non-animal safety tests might be reliable from a scientific point of view, but they are not viewed as carrying as much weight as the animal models in the defense against product liability claims which are so pervasive today.[214] The idea that industry uses animal tests to protect itself from litigation is valid only to a degree, says Birely. The legal repercussions of a $5-10 million settlement for a company like Procter & Gamble, which had $1.5 billion in profits in 1994, are negligible. In addition, consumer lawsuits can drag on in the courts for years; most would financially wipe out the average citizen before they ever came to fruition, and industry is let off the hook. In Birely's opinion, because industry has relied, and continues to rely, upon animal-derived toxicity databases, and because scrapping these databases and rebuilding *in vitro* ones from scratch would be extremely costly and risky, industry is reluctant to change. That view has been echoed by Dagmar Roth-Behrendt, a German Member of the European Parliament (MEP) who in 1994 received 150,000 letters protesting against animal testing for cosmetics. She said that industry is hoping the debate will 'go away' and says the public must continue to force the issue into the public arena.[215] Frank Barile agrees; he says, 'the pharmaceutical and chemical companies continue to say one thing and do another;' but he says that 'industry are followers—they do what regulators tell them to do; companies are interested in profit—there's no reason for them to "go out on a limb" for alternatives. The regulations will only change when enough pressure is applied.' Amway's Phil Casterton believes that a combination of industry leadership and public pressure will be needed to end animal testing. Intense pressure, in the form of lobbying, boycotts, letter-writing campaigns and demonstrations, must again be applied by animal advocates, scientists and others.

Toxicologist Björn Ekwall believes that now, more than ever, federal and private resources are needed to fund legitimate and promising *in vitro* validation efforts like the MEIC and EDIT projects; funds should also be allocated to scientific research efforts devoted to perfecting existing *in vitro* techniques. And finally, legislation must change in order for true progress to be achieved. Barile, who believes that educating young people may be the key to change, has been demonstrating *in vitro* methods to high school students.

The following and final chapter pulls together the arguments articulated in this book, and attempts to present solutions to this politically charged and very complex problem. Although the issue of toxicity testing on animals has, for decades, provoked heated debate and disagreement between scientists, industry, federal regulators, and environmental, health and animal advocates, it is imperative that a singular solution be found. Policy recommendations will be made which may seem radical; but given the ineffectiveness of the current animal-based testing system which has been described in this book and acknowledged by so many mainstream scientists, given remarkable developments in technology which make the testing of chemicals quick, cheap, reliable and humane, and given the threat to our health and environment from mounting industrial pollution, such recommendations are necessary. The role that activists interested in this issue must play to bring about change will be discussed.

Notes

1. Myra Sklarew, 'Toxicity Tests in Animals: Alternative Models,' *Env. Health Persp.* 101, no. 4 (September 1993): 291.

2. Vicki Glaser, 'In Vitro Test Systems Getting a Close Look by Industry and the FDA,' *Genetic Engineering News*, 15 April 1995, p. 6.

3. Jeff Diner, 'A Compendium of Alternatives to the Use of Live Animals in Research and Testing,' brochure, publication sponsored by the American Anti-Vivisection Society, Jenkintown, Pennsylvania (December 1989), p. 3.

4. T. Watanabe, et al., *Journal of Immunology* 113 (1974): 608–16.

5. See *Mutagenesis* 4 (1989) for several examples; M. T. Skaanild and J. Clausen, *ATLA* 16 (1989): 293–6. Toxicologist Björn Ekwall said that, 'now, with knowledge of human blood concentrations, we can bypass animal tests. Through analytical chemistry, or biopsy with a small needle, one can measure how much of a particular chemical or pesticide is in a person's blood. One can then compare actual concentrations of chemicals in human cells with the values from in vitro cytotoxicity tests. If the values match, then a substance could be deemed toxic.' Personal communication with Björn Ekwall, Uppsala, Sweden, 6 June 1995.

6. Iain C. Campbell, et al., *ATLA* 24 (1996): 339–47.

7. Anon, 'Message in a Bottle,' *The Economist*, 22 April 1995, pp. 83–5; Judy Siegel, 'BGU Honors Psychiatrist Who Contradicted Science by Getting Brain Cells to Duplicate,' *The Jerusalem Post*, 15 May 1990.

8. Philip Noguchi, 'Alternatives to Animals in Cancer Research: A Personal Experience,' in *Non Animal Research Methodologies*, Proceedings of a Symposium, George Washington University Ethics and Animals Society, Washington, DC (18 February 1981).

9. Gerhard Zbinden, 'Alternatives to Animal Experimentation: Developing In Vitro Methods and Changing Legislation,' *TiPS* 11 (March 1990): 104.

10. Myra Sklarew (September 1993): 288.

11. H. Bartsch, et al., in *The Predictive Value of Short-Term Screening Tests in Carcinogenicity Evaluation*, Gary M. Williams, et al., eds (Amsterdam/New York: Elsevier, 1980), pp. 269, 286.

12. Vicki Glaser (15 April 1995), p. 6.

13. Personal communication with Pauline Gee, Vice President of Research and Development, Xenometrix, Colorado, 25 October 1995.

14. Personal communication with Frank Barile, 18 August 1996.

15. Anon, *The Economist* (22 April 1995), pp. 83–5. There are several sectors involved in funding the development of non-animal testing methods. These include federal governments, the European Community which represents 15 international governments (as of 1996), and private foundations such as The American Fund for Alternatives to Animal Research (AFAAR) in New York. AFAAR is a small organization which, since 1977, has issued 30 grants totaling $1 million to finance a variety of research and validation efforts like the Multicenter Evaluation of In Vitro Cytotoxicity (MEIC) project in Sweden. Personal communication with Ethel Thurston, 23 March 1995, New York City. Trade associations like the Soap and Detergent Association have also invested in the development of non-animal methods. In Vitro International in Irvine, and Advanced Tissue Sciences in La Jolla, California are just two corporations actively involved in developing these technologies. The Body Shop, a British-based personal care products company, has donated money to universities and projects like MEIC. The Neutral Red Assay (see pp. 158–9) was developed with funding from the Revlon Corporation. Procter & Gamble, which had $30 billion in revenues and $1.5 billion in profits in 1994 (Procter & Gamble Annual Report, 1994), has allegedly spent several million dollars on the development of alternatives over the course of the last decade; but the company continues to conduct animal tests and, as of February 1997, is still being boycotted by In Defense of Animals, an animal advocacy group in Mill Valley, California.

16. Heidi J. Welsh, *Animal Testing and Consumer Products* (Washington, DC: Investor Responsibility Research Center, 1990), p. 72.

17. Steve Nadis, 'On the Trail of Mutations at MIT,' *Env. Health Persp.* 104, no. 2 (February 1996): 143.

18. Myra Sklarew (September 1993): 289.

19. P. Beaconsfield and C. Villee, *Placenta—A Neglected Experimental Animal* (London: Pergamon Press, 1979).

20. Robert Sharpe, 'Occupational Hazards,' *The AV Magazine*, published by the American Anti-Vivisection Society, Jenkintown, Pennsylvania (January/February 1995), p. 8.

21. Steve Nadis (February 1996): 143.

22. J. H. Weisburger and G. M. Williams, 'Carcinogen Testing: Problems and New Approaches,' *Science* 214 (23 October 1981): 401–7.

23. Gerhard Zbinden (March 1990): 106.

24. J. Ashby and I. F. H. Purchase, 'Reflections on the Declining Ability of the *Salmonella* Assay to Detect Rodent Carcinogens as Positive,' *Mutation Research* 205 (1988): 51–8.

25. Frank A. Barile, *Introduction to In Vitro Cytotoxicology* (Florida: CRC Press, 1994), p. 206; Thomas Maugh, 'Chemical Carcinogens: The Scientific Basis for Regulation,' *Science* 201 (29 September 1978): 1205; Neal Barnard, 'Getting Chemicals Out of Our Environment,' *PCRM Update*, newsletter of the Physicians Committee for Responsible Medicine, Washington, DC (January–February, 1990): 3. See also C. C. Travis, et al., *Mutagenesis* 5, no. 3 (1990): 213–19 and *Mutation Research* 241 (1990): 21–36; C. Clemedsen, et al., *ATLA* 24 Suppl. (1996): 273–311.

26. J. H. Weisburger, 'Does the Delaney Clause of the US Food and Drug Laws Prevent Human Cancer?,' *Fundamental & Applied Toxicology* 22, no. 4 (May 1994): 489.

27. Vicki Glaser (15 April 1995), p. 6; Anon, *The Economist* (22 April 1995), p. 84.

28. MEIC is an ongoing international project involving 97 laboratories from the US, the UK, Belgium, Japan, Sweden and other countries in Europe; it was begun in 1989 to evaluate the relevance for human toxicity of various *in vitro* toxicity and toxicokinetic tests.

29. Personal communication with Björn Ekwall of MEIC, Uppsala, Sweden, 6 June 1995 and 18 October 1995.

30. Personal communication with Frank Barile, 18 August 1996.

31. Björn Ekwall, 'Basal Cytotoxicity Data in Human Risk Assessment,' in *Proceedings of the Workshop on Risk Assessment and Risk Management of Toxic Chemicals*, T. Miura, et al., eds (Japan: National Institute of Environmental Studies, 1992), 137–42.

32. On 6 June 1995, Björn Ekwall discussed with me the need to develop 'missing tests' for his battery. (1) A test for chronic toxicity. (In the test which is being developed, varying concentrations of chemicals are added, over time, to cell cultures that have been grown *in vitro* for approximately three months. The culture vessel is changed periodically and a new chemical dose is added, until there are several flasks containing varying concentrations of chemicals. The flasks are followed for four months and cell death is measured at one day, two weeks, four weeks and so on. Chronic toxicity is present if cells continue to die.) (2) A mechanistic understanding of how and why human cells get sick and die. (Using an electronic microscope, chemically injured/damaged and dying cells can be studied. Twenty years ago, Walton and Buckley systematically investigated the potential of electron microscopy but their work has not been followed up. Using this advanced technique, Ekwall said one could determine, in a living human, how and why cells were sick and dying. In this way, a useful *human* toxicity database could be established. Using a less powerful technology—light microscopy—Ekwall said he was able to ascertain at a glance whether acid pH was killing cells.) (3) A test for 'differential cytotoxicity.' (Presently, simple cell lines cannot account for cell killing by toxic metabolites—products of metabolism. Ekwall explained that in 20 percent of cases people are not killed by the original chemical molecule; through a process called biotransformation, the liver transforms the original molecule into a toxic metabolite and they are poisoned by that metabolite. A test for cell toxicity with human liver cells, and ordinary cells for metabolites, should be developed. Ekwall said this problem is easily resolvable by culturing human liver cells from autopsies, surgeries or biopsies—two MEIC members have already tested 50 substances with human liver cells—the liver cells are combined with target cells from different organs *in vitro*. Isolated target cells are used as controls. If the cells in the flask containing both liver and target cells die faster at lower concentrations, that is a sign that a substance is operating as a metabolite and is hurting target cells.) (4) A test to observe and measure absorption in the gut with cultured human gut cells. (Such a test is useful to determine how substances pass the mucous linings of the intestine, and is currently being developed and used by Ciba-Geigy, a Swiss-based pharmaceutical company.) (5) An ordinary cytotoxicity test, in place of the Draize test, to observe and quantitatively measure cellular recovery and reversibility of injury. (This test was recently developed by Russian toxicologist Anatoly Lukyanov; the test measures whether, and how much, cells in the body recover from a chemical assault or injury. Ekwall explained: 'if you get a chemical on your skin or in your eye, it might do temporary damage and then be eliminated. Other chemicals have a mechanism whereby they continue to cause toxicity even after they have been eliminated.' A pioneering *in vitro* test has now been developed by Imai in Osaka which consists of exposing cells to a chemical,

assessing cells after two days, washing the cells/removing the chemical, putting them in a fresh medium without the chemical and observing how the cells recover. It should be noted that dozens of non-animal tests to measure eye and skin irritancy have already been developed, but few have been accepted by regulatory authorities as valid replacements to the Draize rabbit test.) (6) Toxicokinetic tests to determine how substances are absorbed, distributed, metabolized and eliminated by the body. (This would consist of a test to measure the rate and degree of accumulation of chemicals in cultured human cells. Toxicokinetic tests *in vitro* generally do not cover excretion which, overall, are poorly developed tests and will probably require five to ten more years of research according to Ekwall. Renal excretion (from the kidney) would be especially useful. No test has been developed to mimic this phenomenon which is now measured, albeit poorly, in animal tests at autopsy.) (7) A test to measure (a) absorption in the intestine, (b) biotransformation, (c) critical time in target organs, (d) distribution, and (e) elimination, or how chemicals are distributed in the body. Though similar to test 6, this test would explain how dose and response are related in human beings. (Such a test would examine how a dose in the human being is related to concentrations in the blood, how a chemical accumulates in specific cells, how it binds to blood, protein, fat and bone, and whether a substance passes from the blood to the brain (the blood–brain barrier). Ekwall said that this is similar to an intestinal passage test which is already done *in vitro* now at pharmaceutical companies like Ciba-Geigy with cultured blood–brain barrier cells. Here again, post-mortem examinations of animals subjected to toxicity tests have given measurements of a, b, c, d, and e. Researchers calculate that the toxic dose = a + b + c + d + e, but they cannot know, says Ekwall, which factor is contributing to toxicity. Using *in vitro* tests, separate mechanistic tests could measure (a) (using human gut cells), (b) (using human liver and target cells), (c) (using different target cells c_1, c_2, c_3 ...), (d) (using any human cell) and (e) (using human clinical data like urine and blood samples). He stressed that we must also know the elimination rates from local sites like the skin and the eyes. The results from each separate analysis would be combined to get a toxic dose that was relevant to humans.) (8) A test to gather data on excitatory toxicity/injury, to detect and measure seizures from drug side effects, for example. This test has been developed by Ekwall in Sweden (see B. Ekwall, 'Toxicity to Hela Cells of 205 Drugs as Determined by the Metabolic Inhibition Test Supplemented by Microscopy,' *Toxicology* 17 (1980): 273–95). Braunbeck and others are carrying out similar work at Heidelburg University in Germany under the auspices of Ekwall's MEIC/EDIT programme. (There are two types of injury—depressive and excitatory; most *in vitro* tests measure data for depressive toxicity—where the cells are inhibited. The excitatory or cellular stimulation state is typically seen before the depressive state but no one has bothered to isolate it and measure it until now. Ekwall believes that, using such a test, excitatory reactions such as seizures from drug side effects could easily be represented *in vitro*.) (9) A test to measure 'organizational toxicity'— toxicity to transmitters and hormones connected to the receptors of cells. (While most toxicity occurs at the cellular level, a small percentage is toxicity to transmitters and hormones connected to the receptors of cells. For example, curare is not poisonous to cells but to the transmitter between the cells and the muscles (nerve disorders). There is a relatively common test to measure the disturbance of receptor transmission in muscles and nerves (pharmaceutical companies use it to measure direct and indirect interference with receptors, nervous connections); but the technology has not been standardized or made to be compatible with other cellular tests and this must be done.) (10) A test to measure the excretion of chemicals from the kidney, lung and liver; (this is the most difficult test to develop *in vitro*, though Ekwall raised the possibility of using artificial kidney technology for such testing. He explained: 'we are dealing with a delicate balance of highly dynamic forces *in vivo*. High blood pressure pumps blood through a kidney at high speed and varying concentrations. If you have a little less salt, or higher blood pressure, results of an experiment will be altered. The *in vitro* system is static and cannot reproduce this dynamic quality.')

33. Personal communication with Björn Ekwall, Sweden, 6 June 1995.

34. C. Clemedsen, et al., 'MEIC-Evaluation, Part II,' *ATLA* 24 Suppl. (1996): 273–311.

35. Sally Satel, 'Animal Crackers,' *The Women's Quarterly*, Virginia (Summer 1996), p. 19.

36. Ekwall determined that each new test would require the labor of ten scientists over a three-year period. Naturally this would depend on the equipment that would be required, the expertise of an individual laboratory, and the complexity of the test. The budget for a proper validation study of these tests (using human data) costs circa $100,000 per year.

37. Anon, *The Economist* (22 April 1995), p. 84.

38. Personal communication with Tracy Donnelly, Applications Coordinator, In Vitro Lab Technology, Advanced Tissue Sciences, La Jolla, California, 24 October 1995.

39. Anon, *The Economist* (22 April 1995), pp. 83–5.

40. Personal communication with Tracy Donnelly, California, 24 October 1995.

41. Robert Sharpe, *Human Tissue: A Neglected Experimental Resource*, published by The American Anti-Vivisection Society, Jenkintown, Pennsylvania (1993), p. 13.

42. Joel Stratte-McClure, 'Skinethic Laboratory Perfects Human Epidermal Cell Culture Technique,' *Genetic Engineering News* (15 April 1995), p. 7.

43. Reuters, 'EC Animal Testing Ban Dismissed As a Farce,' 15 June 1993; Anon, 'Insight Into Alternatives to Cosmetics Tests,' *BUAV Campaign Report*, published by the British Union for the Abolition of Vivisection, London (Winter 1995/1996).

44. Vicki Glaser (15 April 1995), p. 6.

45. See note 41.

46. Claudia Carpenter, 'New Human Skin is in on Wall Street,' *The New York Post*, 5 March 1996, p. 25.

47. Anon, *The Economist* (22 April 1995), p. 84.

48. F. Kruszewski, et. al., 'Application of the Skintex System to the Evaluation of Cosmetic Products,' in A. M. Goldberg, ed., *In Vitro Toxicology: 10th Anniversary Symposium of CAAT, Alternative Methods in Toxicology, Vol. 9* (Larchmont, NY: Mary Ann Liebert, 1993), p. 210.

49. Virginia C. Gordon, 'Applications of *In Vitro* Methods for the Cosmetic, Household Products, and Pharmaceutical Industries,' in Michael B. Kapis and Shayne C. Gad, eds, *Non-Animal Techniques in Biomedical and Behavioral Research and Testing* (Florida: Lewis Publishers, 1993), pp. 11–25.

50. Personal communication with Diane Birely, In Vitro International, 15 October 1995.

51. Ibid., 26 August 1996.

52. 'Proposed Update III for the SW–846 Methods Manual (Third Edition),' January 1995, *Environmental Compliance Reporter, Inc,* Washington, DC, pp. 1120–8, courtesy of Diane Birely, In Vitro International, Irvine, California.

53. Christopher Byrnes, 'Consumer Product Safe Testing Revisited,' *Our Animal Wards*, published by Wards, Inc, Vienna, Virginia (Spring 1996), pp. 12–15.

54. 'In Vitro Science Comes of Age,' brochure (Irvine, California: In Vitro International, Undated).

55. Letter to Sara Amundson of the Doris Day Animal League, Washington, DC, from Berrien Zettler, Deputy Director of Compliance Programs, OSHA, dated 3 March 1994, courtesy of Sara Amundson.

56. Heidi J. Welsh (1990), p. 72.

57. Ibid., p. 76.

58. Barnaby J. Feder, 'Beyond White Rats and Rabbits,' *The New York Times*, 28 February 1988, Business section, p. 1.

59. Vicki Glaser (15 April 1995), p. 6. The Clonetics Corporation markets normal human cells and cell culture media. Glaser reported that Clonetics' cell types include 'epithelial cells—from dermal, breast and airway cells, endothelial cells—from the dermis, lung, umbilicus, and coronary or pulmonary arteries, and six types of muscle cells.'

60. Heidi J. Welsh (1990), p. 73; Vicki Glaser (15 April 1995), p. 6.

61. G. Klopman, et al., 'Multiple Computer Automated Structure Evaluation Methodology ...,' *ATLA* 21, no. 1 (January 1993): 14–27.

62. David F. V. Lewis, et al., 'Validation of a Novel Molecular Orbital Approach (COMPACT) for the Prospective Safety Evaluation of Chemicals ... ,' *Mutation Research* 291 (1993): 61–77.

63. Antonio Metrangelo, 'Riflessioni Sui Metodi Cosiddetti Alternativi,' *Comitato Scientifico Antivivisezionista*, Supplement to no. 2/53, Rome, Italy (April 1996), p. 24.

64. Shayne C. Gad, 'SAR Approaches as an Alternative to Animal Testing for Predicting Toxicity in Man,' in M. B. Kapis and S. C. Gad (1993), pp. 62–71.

65. Eric Dunayer, 'Testing Chemicals: Animal Testing Impedes Regulatory Action,' 1992, Unpublished paper courtesy of the Physicians Committee for Responsible Medicine, Washington, DC, p. 24.

66. See Peggy Carlson, ed., *Alternatives in Medical Education: Non-Animal Methods* (1995), available from the Physicians Committee for Responsible Medicine, PO Box 6322, Washington, DC, 20015, USA.

67. Myron A. Mehlman, et al., 'A Report on Methods to Reduce, Refine and Replace ... ,' *Cell Biology and Toxicology* 5, no. 3 (1989): 355.

68. Myra Sklarew (September 1993): 289. Sklarew says the models provide 'quantitative data on tissue–toxicant interactions, rates of metabolism and concentration response *in vitro*.'

69. S. M. Cohen, et al., *Toxic. & Appl. Pharmac.* 104 (1990): 79–93.

70. Matthew Witten, 'Computational Modeling of Biological/Medical Systems,' in M. B. Kapis and S. C. Gad (1993), pp. 115–43.

71. H. S. Rosenkranz, et al., 'Prediction of Environmental Carcinogens,' *Environ. Mutagen* 6 (1984): 231–58.

72. W. Howe, et al., in A. Worden, et al., eds (1986), p. 72.

73. Steve Nadis (February 1996): 144.

74. John Yam and C. L. Alden, in M. B. Kapis and S. C. Gad (1993), pp. 35–6.

75. Wendy Thacher, 'Noninvasive Techniques Improve Human Research,' *Good Medicine*, published by the Physicians Committee for Responsible Medicine, Washington, DC (Spring 1994): 6–7.

76. David J. Severn, 'Exposure Assessment,' *Environ. Sci. Technol.* 21, no. 12 (1987): 1161.

77. R. Fenske, et al., *Am. Ind. Hyg. Assoc. J.* 47 (1986): 764–70.

78. K. Randerath, et al., 'P-Labelling Test for DNA Damage,' *Proc. Natl. Acad. Sci. USA* 78 (1981): 6126–9.

79. David J. Severn (1987): 1161.

80. Virginia C. Gordon, in M. B. Kapis and S. C. Gad (1993), p. 16.

81. Ibid.

82. D. A. Basketter, et al., 'The Identification and Classification of Skin Irritation Hazard by Human Patch Test,' *Food and Chemical Toxicology* 32 (1994): 769–75; D. A. Basketter, et al., 'Identification of Irritation and Corrosion Hazards to Skin: An Alternative Strategy to Animal Testing,' *Food and Chemical Toxicology* 32 (1994): 539–42.

83. Personal communication with Phil Casterton, 16 August 1996.

84. W. Howe, et al., in A. Worden, et al., eds (1986), pp. 63–78.

85. R. J. Nolan, et al., 'Pharmacokinetics of Picloram in Male Volunteers,' *Toxicology & Applied Pharmacology* 76 (1984): 264–9.

86. Personal communication with Dennis V. Parke, Surrey, UK, 25 October 1995.

87. E. L. Harris, in A. Worden, et al., eds (1986), p. 24.

88. Phillip Shubik, 'Needed: Better Studies to Predict Cancer Risk,' *Chemical Week*, 14 February 1979, pp. 39–40.

89. Elissa Wolfson, 'Testing for Toxins,' *E Magazine*, January/February 1994, pp. 14–15.

90. National Cancer Institute, 'Highlights of NCI's Carcinogenesis Studies,' 23 June 1993, Bethesda, Maryland. Whether these studies will help to prevent the future release of the chemicals under study remains to be seen.

91. Michael Colby, 'Losing the War on Cancer,' *Safe Food News*, newsletter published by Food & Water, Marshfield, Vermont (Spring 1992), p. 6.

92. Don Putman of Microbiological Associates in Rockville, Maryland says that databases linking hospitals and insurance companies exist which report human illnesses and injuries as a result of workplace exposures for example, but they are not used to their full potential. Personal communication with Don Putman, Rockville, Maryland, 10 June 1993.

93. A. Lynch, *Methods in Biological Monitoring* (New York, John Wiley & Sons, 1987). A 1991 *Wall Street Journal* article reported that Germany and many other countries do far more extensive monitoring of human tissue to measure the public's ingestion of toxic chemicals than the United States. A National Research Council study found an EPA fat screening program to be outdated and flawed. The report suggested that a blood screening program would be more appropriate. Barbara Rosewicz, 'US Urged to Test Blood Instead of Fat to Gauge Ingestion of Toxic Chemicals,' *Wall Street Journal*, 7 May 1991, p. B5.

94. C. Waldren, et al., 'Measurement of Low Levels of X-Ray Mutagenesis in Relation to Human Disease,' *Proc. Natl. Acad. Sci. USA* 83 (July 1986): 4839–43.

95. Theodore T. Puck, et al., 'Caffeine Enhanced Measurement of Mutagenesis by Low Levels of Gamma-Irradiation in Human Lymphocytes,' *Somatic Cell and Molecular Genetics* 19, no. 5 (1993): 423–9.

96. Anon, 'Researchers Study Microbes as Substitute for Animal Testing,' *Texas Medicine* 88, no. 12 (December 1992): 29.

97. F. K. Ennever, et al., 'The Ability of Plant Genotoxicity Assays to Predict Carcinogenicity,' *Mutation Research* 205, no. 1–4 (May–August 1988): 99–105.

98. Heinrich P. Koch, et al., 'The Yeast Test: An Alternative Method … ,' *Meth. Find. Exp. Clin. Pharmacol.* 15, no. 3 (1993): 141–52.

99. K. A. Atkinson, et al., 'Alternatives to Ocular Irritation Testing in Animals,' *Lens and Eye Toxicity Research* 9, no. 3–4 (1992): 247–58.

100. R. H. Buck, et al., 'Animal Test or Chromatography?, … ' *Journal of Chromatography*, no. 548 (1991): 335–41.

101. Joanne Zurlo, et al., 'Current Concepts in In Vitro Toxicity Testing,' *Lab Animal* (March 1993), p. 28.

102. Commission of the European Communities, *Development, Validation and Legal Acceptance of Alternative Methods to Animal Experiments*, Annual report 1994 (Brussels), p. 15. See also *The AV Magazine* (Alternatives Issue), Winter 1997, pp. 2–5.

103. Andrew Huxley, 'Animal Procedures: Funding of Research into Alternatives,' *The Veterinary Record* 128, no. 5 (2 February 1991): 114–15.

104. K. A. Atkinson, et al. (1992); Heidi J. Welsh (1990), p. 72; C. A. Reinhardt, ed., *Alternatives to Animal Testing* (New York: VCH/Weinheim, 1994), p. vii.

105. John M. Bowen, 'Chick Embryo Biology Information System,' *Animal Welfare Information Center Newsletter* 3, no. 2 (April–June 1992), p. 10 (published by the National Agricultural Library, Beltsville, Maryland).

106. Personal communication with Martin Stephens, HSUS, Washington, DC, 9 August 1996.

107. Personal communication with Krys Ungar, FRAME, Nottingham, UK, 25 July 1996, and with Carol Newman, Dr Hadwen Trust, Hertfordshire, UK, 23 July 1996.

108. Personal communication with phone attendant, SPAFAS, 31 July 1996.

109. Wendy J. Davies and Stuart J. Freeman, 'Frog Embryo Teratogenesis Assay,' in S. O'Hare and C. K. Atterwill, eds, *Methods in Molecular Biology*, Vol. 43 (New Jersey: Humana Press, Inc, 1995): 311–16.

110. Personal communication with Robert Finch, US Army, Biomedical Research Laboratory, Fort Detrick, Maryland, 9 August 1996.

111. Anon, 'NIEHS and the Use of Alternative Methods in Toxicological Research and Testing,' brochure (North Carolina: NIEHS, Office of Communications, 1993); personal communication with William Stokes, NIEHS, North Carolina, 1 November 1995.

112. See Xenopus Express homepage on the Internet. Other species—like the Blomberg toad, which lives 28 years in the wild—survive eight months in the lab. American species like the Leopard frog and Bufo toad, which have been considered for the FETAX assay, do not breed successfully in captivity. Xenopus 1 claims to have some 20-year-old *xenopus* females in its breeding colony, though Finch believes those are exceptions.

113. Personal communication with Robert Finch, 9 August 1996.

114. Nicole Bournias-Vardiabasis, '*Drosophila Melanogaster* Embryo Cultures: An In Vitro Teratogen Assay,' *ATLA* 18 (1990): 291–300.

115. Myra Sklarew (September 1993): 291.

116. MBT involves using knowledge of disease mechanisms and of biological effects better to predict the toxicological potential of chemicals. It is being used with increasing frequency by toxicologists in an attempt to estimate risk at low doses, to extrapolate between species, and to understand species, strain and individual differences in response.

117. Hugo M. Van Looy in C. A. Reinhardt, ed. (1994), p. 18.

118. John Yam and C. L. Alden, in M. B. Kapis and S. C. Gad (1993), pp. 27–33. The Fixed Dose Procedure, first advocated by the British Toxicology Society over a decade ago as an 'alternative' to the LD50 test, relies on the observation of clear signs of toxicity (convulsions, weight loss, bleeding from the genitals, eyes and mouth) developed at one of a series of fixed dose levels, for example 5g/kg, 10g/kg. When the animals are near death, they are killed and their tissues examined. The test uses 10 to 20 animals instead of 200. M. Van den Heuvel, *Human and Experimental Toxicology* 9 (1990): 369–70. The Acute Toxic Class test, originally proposed by German toxico-

logist Gerhard Zbinden, also uses morbidity as an endpoint, but employs a tiered testing strategy that requires, at each dose level, a decision either to stop testing or to proceed to a higher or lower dose level. This procedure uses 7.5 animals per test; *Nature* 357 (11 June 1992): 432. It was recently incorporated into British toxicity testing guidelines. Personal communication with William Stokes, NIEHS, 1 November 1995.

119. Anon (North Carolina: Office of Communications, NIEHS, November 1993).

120. Myra Sklarew (September 1993): 289.

121. See note 111.

122. Robert Sharpe, 'Tissue Shortage,' *Nature* 354 (12 December 1991): 427.

123. F. Zucco, *Toxicology* 17 (1980): 101–4; S. Yoshitomi, et al., *In Vitro Cell Dev. Biol.* 23 (1987): 55; D. A. McCormick, *Trends in Pharm. Science* 11 (1990): 53–6. Ironically, scientists at the NCI have used human cells in an attempt to validate animal findings. Thomas Maugh (29 September 1978): 1201.

124. Carlton H. Nadolney, in *Future of Medical Research Without the Use of Animals: Facing the Challenge*, Conference Proceedings, 15–16 May 1990, Tel Aviv, Israel, published by Concern for Helping Animals in Israel (CHAI), Alexandria, Virginia, p. 159.

125. Personal communication with Frank Barile, 18 August 1996.

126. Paul Cotton, 'Animals and Science Benefit From ... ,' *Journal of the American Medical Association* 270 (22–29 December 1993): 2907; personal communication with Björn Ekwall, Sweden, 18 October 1995.

127. Richard Steiner in C. A. Reinhardt, ed. (1994), foreword; Pietro Croce, *Vivisection or Science: A Choice to Make* (Switzerland: CIVIS, 1991), p. 137.

128. Anon, *The Economist* (22 April 1995), p. 83. According to Pauline Ryan, Director of Business Development at Organogenesis, Inc in Canton, Massachusetts, *in vitro* research is increasingly being carried out in academic laboratories in universities; graduate students often order *in vitro* kits for Masters theses. Personal communication with Pauline Ryan, 18 October 1995.

129. American Medical Association White Paper on Animal Research (1989).

130. Andrew Rowan, et al., *The Animal Research Controversy* (Massachusetts: Center for Animals & Public Policy, Tufts University School of Veterinary Medicine, 1995), p. 148.

131. Edith Efron, *The Apocalyptics: Cancer and the Big Lie* (New York: Simon & Schuster, 1984), p. 402.

132. Heidi J. Welsh (1990), pp. 33–4.

133. Edward H. Ahrens, *The Crisis in Clinical Research: Overcoming Institutional Obstacles* (New York: Oxford University Press, 1992).

134. Personal communication with Sara Amundson, 1 November 1995.

135. Personal communication with William Stokes, NIEHS, North Carolina, 1 November 1995.

136. Anon, 'Validation and Regulatory Acceptance of Toxicological Test Methods,' a report of the *ad hoc* Interagency Coordinating Committee on the Validation of Alternative Methods (Draft) (North Carolina: NIEHS, 16 October 1995).

137. Personal communication with Sara Amundson, Washington, DC, 7 November 1995. It should be noted that the Committee will inevitably receive comments back from stakeholders, including federal research and regulatory agencies (Committee members), industry, interest groups (like humane societies and biomedical research organizations), academia, and labor unions (who don't want to see testing requirements diminished for safety reasons); it must then process the comments, respond, and decide how to move ahead.

138. Douglas C. McGill, 'Cosmetics Companies Quietly Ending Animal Tests,' *The New York Times*, 2 August 1989, p. A1.

139. Personal communication with Pam Logemann, 14 August 1996.

140. Commission of the European Communities (1994), pp. 12–13.

141. Anon, 'ECVAM's Director Discusses Validation,' *CAAT newsletter*, Vol. 13, no. 1 (Fall 1995), online edition.

142. John Yam and C. L. Alden, in M. B. Kapis and S. C. Gad (1993), p. 33.

143. K. A. Atkinson, et al. (1992): 247–58.

144. Frank Barile, *Introduction to In Vitro Cytotoxicology* (Florida: CRC Press, 1994), p. 203.

145. Heidi J. Welsh (1990), p. 60.

146. Michael Balls and J. H. Fentem, 'The Use of Basal Cytotoxicity and Target Organ Toxicity Tests in Hazard Identification and Risk Assessment,' *ATLA* 20 (1992): 368.

147. Michael Balls, 'Use of Animals in Laboratories: Scientific and Ethical Issues,' *HSUS News*, published by the Humane Society of the United States, Washington, DC (Spring 1996), pp. 19–20. Balls stated for example that, 'the length and quality of our lives have been enhanced by discoveries made in the past through animal experiments.'

148. Anon, 'Alternatives in Animal Testing,' *Env. Health Persp.* 104, no. 3 (March 1996): 252.

149. Personal communication with Ethel Thurston, American Fund for Alternatives to Animal Research, 18 October 1995.

150. Andrew Rowan, et al. (1995), p. 101.

151. Personal communication with Amy Morgan, Coordinator, Caring Consumer Campaign, People for the Ethical Treatment of Animals, Washington, DC, 26 October 1995. Amy discussed with me the contents of the minutes from the 27 April 1995 meeting of the Coalition for Consumer Information on Cosmetics in Washington, DC. During that meeting it was revealed that COLIPA, the European counterpart of the CFTA, attempted to impede industry from responding to a questionnaire submitted by the coalition of animal advocates, to gauge industry interest in non-animal methods. COLIPA submitted its own questionnaire, which it advised industry was the only legitimate one; COLIPA's questionnaire was allegedly aimed at encouraging the continued use of animals in toxicity testing.

152. *The Johns Hopkins Center for Alternatives to Animal Testing* newsletter, vol. 7, no. 2 (Fall 1989), back page.

153. These include The Foundation for Biomedical Research (Washington, DC), the National Institute of Mental Health (Rockville, Maryland), and The Scientists Center for Animal Welfare (Bethesda, Maryland), which provides guidelines on the 'proper treatment' of animals in research.

154. See Chapter 4, 'Are the animal tests required by law?'

155. Alan M. Goldberg and John M. Frazier, *ATLA* 18 (1990): 65–74.

156. Alan M. Goldberg, et al., 'A Kinetic Study of the In Vivo Incorporation of 65ZN Into the Rat Hippocampus,' *J. Neurosci.* 4, no. 6 (June 1984): 1671–5; Alan M. Goldberg, et al., 'Perturbation of a Hippocampal Zinc-binding Pool After Postnatal Lead Exposure in Rats,' *Exp. Neurol.* 85, no. 3 (September 1984): 620–30; Alan M. Goldberg, et al., 'Alterations in Consummatory Behavior of Mice Produced by Dietary Exposure to Inorganic Lead,' *Dev. Psychobiol.* 8, no. 5 (September 1975): 389–96.

157. Heidi J. Welsh (1990), p. 79.

158. Alan M. Goldberg and John M. Frazier, 'Alternatives to Animals in Toxicity Testing,' *Scientific American*, August 1989, pp. 24–30.

159. Alan M. Goldberg, *ATLA* 18 (1990): 65–74. It appears as though CAAT is training students to advance its doctrine. After spending three weeks at a CAAT laboratory in May 1995, one student wrote, 'now I see why there is not yet a way to completely replace animal use in research.' Jaina Hirai, 'A Student's View of the Laboratory,' *CAATALYST* (CAAT student newsletter), vol. 1, no. 3 (1996), p. 1.

160. The American Fund for Alternatives to Animal Research, a small organization in New York which receives no funding from the chemical industry, has provided Ekwall with $20,000 a year since 1990.

161. *In vivo* tests have a much less precise gross endpoint. Dr Ekwall explained that in toxicology, there is a spectrum of at least fifteen toxicological effects, including eye and skin irritancy, allergic sensitization, acute toxicity, chronic toxicity, subchronic toxicity, teratogenicity, neurotoxicity, carcinogenicity, and so on. All of these factors are not measured *in vivo* individually; only the 'lump sum' of effects is measured. So that a toxicologist may say that a chemical is acutely toxic *or* carcinogenic *or* teratogenic in an animal as measured by the death of the animal for example. In reality, death is a measure of more subtle forms of toxicity which cannot be gauged in one animal test. Separate animal tests would have to be performed to measure each toxicological endpoint separately. *In vitro* tests, on the other hand, can measure all of these toxicological endpoints individually *at one time*; the pieces can then be put together like a jigsaw puzzle to get a more accurate understanding of toxicity and which factors cause it. According to Ekwall, the toxicity of a substance could be measured using just 15 test tubes. If 15 separate animal tests were performed for each toxicological endpoint, using the standard 50 animals in each test (and assuming the tests would not have to be repeated), at least 750 animals (15 × 50) would be required to do what can be accomplished with 15 test tubes.

162. Erik Walum, 'Identification of Neurotoxicity by In Vitro Methodology …,' in *Future Medical Research Without the Use of Animals: Facing the Challenge*, Conference Proceedings, 15–16 May 1990, Tel Aviv, Israel, published by Concern for Helping Animals in Israel (CHAI), Alexandria, VA, pp. 137–55. Both CAAT and FRAME have been accused of refusing to publish the work of noted scientists like Roland Nardone, J. C. Petricciani and Björn Ekwall, many of whom have not been allowed to present papers on their work at CAAT-sponsored conferences. Essentially, say critics, CAAT wants to maintain a monopoly of scientific opinion—opinion which supports the position that animal testing is still necessary. Personal communication with Ethel Thurston, AFAAR, New York City, 18 October 1995.

163. M. Balls, et al, 'Report and Recommendations of the CAAT/ERGATT Workshop on the Validation of Toxicity Test Procedures,' *ATLA* 18 (1990): 313–37.

164. The first *in vitro* validation program was proposed in 1982 in Nottingham, UK by FRAME—the Fund for the Replacement of Animals in Medical Experiments. Around the same period, the European Research Group for Alternatives in Toxicity Testing (ERGATT) was established. Flavia Zucco, 'Le Alternative Praticabili,' *Impronte*, April 1994, p. 11, published by Lega Anti-Vivisezione, Rome, Italy.

The Center for Alternatives to Animal Testing (CAAT) at Johns Hopkins University, founded in 1981 with money from the Cosmetic, Toiletry and Fragrance Association, also has a Subcommittee on Validation and Technology Transfer. ECVAM, the European Centre for Validation of Alternative Methods, founded in 1993, and which maintains the INVITTOX database, aims to 'facilitate and coordinate activities designed to evaluate the relevance and reliability of non-animal tests and test batteries designed for use for particular purposes.' Michael Balls, 'The Foundation of ECVAM: A Significant Step Towards the Replacement of Animal Tests?,' *ATLA* 21 (1993): 123–4.

In 1986, the Multicenter Evaluation of In Vitro Cytotoxicity began its validation program in Uppsala, Sweden. Björn Ekwall, et al., 'The Work With the MEIC Human Database,' *Alternatives Research*, Proceedings of the 8th Annual Meeting of the Japanese Society for Alternatives to Animal Experiments, 28–29 November 1994, Tokyo, pp. 119–20.

165. Heidi J. Welsh (1990), p. 81.

166. Anon, *National Toxicology Program, Fiscal Year 1994 Annual Plan*, Draft (North Carolina, NTP, May 1994).

167. Erik Walum, et al., 'Principles for the Validation of In Vitro Toxicology Test Methods,' *Toxicology In Vitro* 8, no. 4 (1994): 807–12.

168. In the pro-animal testing literature, the general toxicology literature, and the 'alternatives' literature, there is unending discussion about the need to validate non-animal methods.

169. Frank Barile (1994), p. 206.

170. Raymond W. Tennant and Errol Zeiger, 'Genetic Toxicology: Current Status of Methods of Carcinogen Identification,' *Env. Health Persp.* 100 (1993), p. 308.

171. See references in Robert Sharpe, *Food & Chemical Toxicology* 23 (1985): 139–43.

172. K. A. Atkinson, et al. (1992).

173. Erik Walum, et al. (1994): 808.

174. N. J. Van Abbé, in A. Worden, et al., eds. (1986), p. 146.

175. Heidi J. Welsh (1990), p. 69.

176. Myra Sklarew (September 1993): 290.

177. Personal communication with Pam Logemann, 14 August 1996.

178. Personal communication with Phil Casterton, Senior Scientist, Amway, Michigan, 16 August 1996.

179. Frank Barile (1994), pp. 194–5.

180. Personal communication with Pam Logemann, 14 August 1996, and with Tracy Donnelly, Applications Coordinator, In Vitro Lab Technology (ATS), La Jolla, California, 24 October 1995. ATS is currently conducting human dose-response skin patch testing with 21 surfactants (soaps, detergents) using 100 volunteers across North America. Based on these trials, ATS will determine the severe, moderate, and mild effects of various concentrations of a variety of substances on human beings. Data from *in vitro* irritancy tests using Skin² will be validated against the human data. The company will conduct pre-validation studies with six surfactants. Criteria for the acceptability of the data will be established by outside statisticians who will determine whether the data are within an acceptable range. The database will be available to ATS's clients; the results of the research, as well as ongoing research related to such projects, will be published by the company. The studies will be made available to the general public at a later date.

181. C. F. M. Hendriksen, 'The RIVM Center for Alternatives to Animal Testing … ,' in C. A. Reinhardt, ed. (1994), p. 68.

182. Gregorio Loprieno, 'La Banca Dati Galileo,' *Impronte*, April 1994, p. 13, published by Lega Anti-Vivisezione, Rome, Italy. Though many of the 'previously published data' in the bank are animal data, and, as has been discussed, it is not ideal to compare alternative data with animal data, it is hoped that such a bank would prevent the unnecessary duplication of animal tests.

183. Horst Spielmann, et al., 'ZEBET: Three Years of the National German

Center for Documentation and Evaluation of Alternatives to Animal Experimentation at the Federal Health Office in Berlin,' in C. A. Reinhardt, ed. (1994), p. 79.

184. Erik Walum (1994): 809. A similar project was established by Bagley, et al. (1992) who published a reference bank of validated alternative procedures to the Draize rabbit eye irritation tests. D. M. Bagley, et al., *Toxicology In Vitro* 6 (1992): 487–91. FRAME's INVITTOX databank contains information on alternative experimental protocols in the academic literature.

185. Herman B. W. M. Koeter, 'Test Guideline Development and Animal Welfare: Regulatory Acceptance of In Vitro Studies,' *Reproductive Toxicology* 7, Supplement 1 (1993): 117–23.

186. Björn Ekwall, *In Vitro Alternatives to Animal Pharmaco-Toxicology* (Madrid: Farmaindustria, 1992), pp. 361–90.

187. Personal communication with Pam Logemann, 14 August 1996.

188. Lavinia Pioda, 'The Position of the Authorities,' in C. A. Reinhardt, ed. (1994), p. 176.

189. Edith Efron (1984), p. 420.

190. Anon, 'Cruelty or Progress? Why Does UNESCO Fear an Independent Inquiry Into Animal Testing?' *International Animal Action* 36, published by IAAPEA, Hertfordshire, UK (Spring 1996), p. 1.

191. Personal communication with Phil Casterton, 16 August 1996.

192. 'Q/A Interview: Dr Olivera Markovic Promotes Reduction of Chemical Testing on Non-Human Animals,' *National Anti-Vivisection Society (NAVS) Bulletin* (Chicago, Illinois) no. 3 (1988): 16–17.

193. Heidi J. Welsh (1990), p. 81.

194. Thomas Atherholt, et al., 'Analysis of New Jersey DEP's Ames Assay Requirement in Selected Industrial New Jersey Pollutant Discharge Elimination System (NJPDES) Wastewater Permits,' 1991, Division of Science and Research, New Jersey Department of Environmental Protection, CN409, Trenton, NJ.

195. Frank Ahrens, 'Why is This Rat Smiling: The Toothpaste That's Not a Brush With Death,' *The Washington Post*, 17 August 1995, p. C1. Tom's will donate $5,000 to an animal charity on behalf of the next company that stops animal tests. PETA's *Animal Times*, Spring 1997, p. 5.

196. Douglas C. McGill, 'Cosmetics Companies Quietly Ending Animal Tests,' *The New York Times*, 2 August 1989, p. A1.

197. Personal communication with Phil Casterton, 16 August 1996.

198. Eric Utne, et al., 'Beyond the Body Shop Brou Ha Ha ... ,' *The Utne Reader* 67 (January/February 1995), p. 101.

199. Personal communication with Jim Hulbert, Coordinator of Ecological Affairs and Sustainability, Aveda Headquarters, Minnesota, 24 July 1996.

200. Amy Morgan, ed., *The Shopping Guide for Caring Consumers* (Summertown, Tennessee: Book Publishing Co, 1995).

201. Personal communication with Amy Morgan, People for the Ethical Treatment of Animals, Washington, DC, 26 October 1995.

202. Coalition for Consumer Information on Cosmetics, 'Standard', courtesy of Karen Purves, Animal Protection Institute, Sacramento, California, 14 November 1996.

203. Ibid.

204. David Foster, 'Animal Rights Tenets Are Gaining Support in US, Poll Shows,' *The Seattle Times*, 3 December 1995, p. A4. According to a Biennial Science Indicators Survey, commissioned by the US National Science Board in 1991, public support for

animal research dropped between 1985 and 1990. Anon, National Science Board, *Science and Engineering Indicators 1991* (Washington, DC: US Government Printing Office, 1991).

205. Anon, 'Logo Ban?' *BUAV Campaign Report* (Winter 1995/1996), published by the British Union for the Abolition of Vivisection, London. Gillette instituted a moratorium on animal testing for its cosmetic products in 1996. However, the company does not ask its suppliers to refrain from animal testing, as of early 1997, it has not given any written assurance that it will not resume animal testing, and it continues to test its pharmaceutical products on animals to meet regulatory requirements. Personal communication with Jason Baker, People for the Ethical Treatment of Animals, Norfolk, Virginia, 13 January 1997.

206. Iain F. H. Purchase, 'In Vitro Methods in Risk Assessment,' *ATLA* 24 (1996): 328.

207. J. Remfry, in A. Worden, et al., eds. (1986), p. 38.

208. Dennis V. Parke, 'Clinical Pharmacokinetics in Drug Safety Evaluation,' *ATLA* 22 (1994): 207–9.

209. Personal communication with Joe Rininger, technician, Paracelsian, Ithaca, New York, 23 October 1995.

210. Organogenesis has been forced to discontinue the marketing of its highly effective Testskin product in the United States; in 1994 the company sold the rights to the product to Toyobo, a Japanese company in Osaka, Japan. It has discontinued its other Testorgans products. Personal communication with Pauline Ryan, Associate Director of Business Development, Organogenesis, Inc, Cambridge, Massachusetts, 18 October 1995. In late 1996, Advanced Tissue Sciences halted further development of alternative technologies. *The AV Magazine*, Winter 1997, p. 5.

211. Edward M. Jackson, 'Ten Years and Still No Alternatives to Animal Testing,' *J. Toxicol.—Cut. & Ocular Toxicol.* 12, no. 4 (1993): 261–3.

212. Personal communication with Pauline Ryan, 18 October 1995.

213. Vicki Glaser (15 April 1995), p. 6.

214. Gerhard Zbinden (March 1990): 106.

215. Reuters, 'Ban on Cosmetic Tests at Risk,' 17 November 1994.

6. Reclaiming our health and our humanity: strategies for change

'It should not be forgotten that real alternatives are in essence revolutions, and revolutions cannot be incorporated into an existing structure. All our laws are based on animal experiments. Therefore it should be acknowledged that the existing structure will have to be changed.' Lavinia Pioda, in C. A. Reinhardt, ed., *Alternatives to Animal Testing* (New York: VCH/Weinheim, 1994), p. 176

'We ought to aim for a redirection of all the monies lavished on subsidizing laboratory research into finding ways to decontaminate the Earth and its atmosphere from harmful pollutants ... The monies poured into the manufacture of food additives, cosmetics, plastics and endless new chemicals ... should be channeled into banning all such products ... Ultimately ... the responsibility lies with individuals to seek a wholesome way of life.' Andrée Collard, *Rape of the Wild* (Indiana: Indiana University Press, 1989), p. 98

' ... the public's sensitivity to environmental destruction ... and its anxiety over the apparent inability or unwillingness of government, industry and mainstream environmental groups to "solve the problem" ... is likely to increase support for more "radical" solutions, if not radical means.' Rik Scarce, *Eco-Warriors* (Chicago: Noble Press, 1990), p. 261

'We must always go further, even if by doing so we are making excessive demands ... As in all other sensitive areas of radical cultural change, minimal consensus tactics are ... counter-productive.' Rudolf Bahro, *Building the Green Movement* (Philadelphia: New Society Publishers, 1986), p. 204

'Public pressure is essential if we are to eliminate experiments on animals and achieve a completely ethical system of scientific research and healthcare.' Robert Sharpe, 'Out of the Dark Ages,' *International Animal Action*, journal of the International Association Against Painful Experiments on Animals (IAAPEA), Hertfordshire, UK (Fall 1986): 3–7

Fear of disease is a natural symptom of rampant industrialization. The practice of toxicity testing on animals is rooted in this fear and hence is a product of the latter, as detailed in Chapter 1. The way in which animal tests are performed, and the way animal data are used within a regulatory framework has been described in Chapter 2. The secrecy in science, and lack of government agencies' fiscal accountability to the public, ensures that Americans and citizens in other countries remain uninformed about the kind of science they are funding. We have seen that there are essentially two testing approaches in animal-based toxicology research: (1) testing animals at doses that attempt to mimic those to which humans are exposed, and (2) testing animals at doses that exceed anything to which humans are exposed. Both methods are admittedly unrealistic and problematic. Scientists and regulators concede that animal tests are not only unreliable, but also expensive and time-consuming. They compensate for this by continually trying to 'improve' them by any means possible; and so the tests continue to be performed. Animal test data are used to establish environmental safety standards, and to predict cancer and other health risks for humans by means of (controversial) extrapolations. The inherent problems with inter-species extrapolations, and the use of non-human animals in general, to predict cancer and other toxic effects in humans have been exhaustively discussed in Chapter 3.

Because animal tests invariably produce ambiguous results, as illustrated in Chapter 4, and because this is used to industry's advantage, their net effect has been to delay regulation rather than accelerate it. The array of chemicals that humans have become exposed to has grown exponentially since the end of the nineteenth century. According to Joe Thornton, Greenpeace's research coordinator, the US EPA's current chemical evaluation system—thorough investigation and regulation of one compound at a time—is far too slow to protect humans and wildlife.[1] Dangerous products, such as the pesticides captan, lindane and parathion, have been allowed to remain on the market as a result—harming humans, wildlife and the environment. Some believe that if different testing methods were used which could eliminate the ambiguity associated with animal tests, delays in regulation could, potentially, be greatly diminished. Currently, however, chemicals typically remain on the market for decades before they are even tested; and regulators often ignore the results of their own animal tests. The majority of chemicals found to be carcinogenic in animals continue to be sold (and many products are inadequately labelled). Often, as in the case of benzene and arsenic (used in the computer chip industry), chemicals which undeniably cause cancer in *humans* are also left on the market.

Rarely, if ever, are chemicals banned outright; instead, cost–benefit decisions dictate that they be regulated. The science (or 'art') of risk assessment was basically devised to gauge the risks that all of these regulated chemicals posed to humans. Methods to evaluate the utility and/or effectiveness of toxicological risk assessment programs have never been developed. Moreover, the current animal-based chemical evaluation system is not capable of testing the backlog of chemicals already in the environment, and so cannot gauge the long-term effects of past chemical pollution. Unfortunately, the lack of corresponding human data ensures that we will never really know the answer to those questions. Unless the focus of research returns to epidemiology and other forms of clinical (human-based) research, this barrier will never be overcome.

It has been demonstrated that animal testing is part of a larger problem involving a regulatory system which caters to industry rather than carrying out its mission to protect human health. Current national and international toxicity testing guidelines, many of which are over a decade old, encourage manufacturers to perform animal tests; under present policies, any company seeking to register or reregister a pesticide for example, must submit voluminous animal data on its toxic effects. Yet, federal regulations simultaneously allow companies to pollute, undermining concurrent attempts to protect the public health. The enormous financial, legal and political power of the chemical industry, the biomedical research establishment, and other vested interests like animal breeders who profit from the continuation of animal testing, has stunted efforts to replace animal tests with more efficient technologies. Aside from the political influence of vested interests, the unimaginable bureaucracy inherent in federal policy-making insures that if progress is made at all, it is made at a snail's pace.

As we have seen in Chapter 5, more accurate, less costly (and humane) technologies *do* exist and should be implemented now. Forward-thinking toxicologists believe that a battery of *in vitro* tests could easily predict toxicity; in fact such tests are often more revealing than industry would care to admit. Many of these methods have been validated by manufacturers in-house, though they have not been formally accepted by regulators. While the animal tests themselves have never been validated, the rigorous double standards for the validation of non-animal methods are clearly delaying their implementation. Endless scientific debate about the merit of these methods (which hinges on the ongoing debate about the mechanisms of toxicity and carcinogenesis) has also slowed down the process. Other reasons include the inflexibility of scientists and regulators, anxiety about the costs and legal repercussions of changing to new methods, bureaucratic inertia, political apathy, and lack of public awareness of, and involvement in, this issue.

Proponents of animal tests state that we cannot wait for absolute proof of carcinogenicity in humans before acting to protect human health. Indeed, if protecting human health is truly our goal (as well as protecting the health of animals and the environment, and reducing research and health care costs), we should discard the rodent bioassay. Toxicologists should not be tricked into developing *in vitro* tests which seek to mimic the plethora of pathological processes currently observed in animal tests, for that will continue to stall regulatory reform. We should be willing to heed the results from a battery of simple *in vitro* tests for mutagenicity, carcinogenicity, reproductive effects, and general cell toxicity. Cecilia Clemedsen, et al., of the MEIC project are working to simplify *in vitro* batteries to this end. In 1995 Gordon Graff reported that 'most European environmental agencies have adopted the strategy of screening compounds early in the review process to see if they harm cultured, cellular DNA.'[2] A battery of such cell-based tests could prevent the marketing of carcinogens and otherwise toxic chemicals. If human cells were used in these tests, in combination with human dose-response and SAR data, the problem of inter-species extrapolation would vanish.

The need for a new paradigm

'Many would-be reformers feel compelled to work "within the system." Indeed, this is the usual advice ... given to activists by their ... "friends" who have establishment connections. The formula suggests the futility of working within a system controlled by an establishment: the machinery can sometimes be changed but the values cannot. In the end it is the values that determine the critical decisions. Fortunately however, the general public is not constrained to work inside the system ... The public has the advantage of numbers and numbers do count.' Irwin D. Bross, 'A Formula to Make Animal Activists More Effective,' Unpublished paper, 1990, p. 17

Clearly a new regulatory, scientific, and socio-ethical paradigm is needed. A wedge must be driven between government and corporate interests; federal regulatory bureaucracies should be dismantled, or at the very least stripped of their complexity. There are essentially two strategies that can be employed to change things: (A) working within the current governmental, scientific and corporate structure to achieve incremental changes in policies, attitudes and practices—a centralized approach; or (B) working outside the current structure for radical change by applying social, political and economic pressure on these various sectors—a 'grass roots,' decentralized approach. Following either of these approaches would give rise to a particular set of circumstances, here dubbed Scenario A and Scenario B.

Scenario A In Scenario A, animal, health and environmental advocates would adhere to the CAAT and FRAME doctrine which states that 'in vitro toxicity testing cannot replace animal testing in a single quantum step because regulatory mechanisms do not yet exist to review and approve new methodologies,' and that 'insisting on comprehensive bans on animal testing will only jeopardize the adoption of in vitro technology.'[3] Those who adhere to this philosophy would accept a gradual phasing out of animal testing; they might consider the reduction and refinement of classic animal tests as an acceptable step towards eventual replacement.[4] Under Scenario A conditions, the use of invertebrates and other non-mammalian animal species would be accepted as a concession for a reduced reliance on larger mammals like dogs, monkeys, and so on. Scientists and regulators' demands for lengthy and resource-intensive validation schemes would be granted, thus assuaging their fears of adopting new methods too quickly.[5] Scenario A advocates might accept the pace at which NIEHS and other international regulatory agencies continued their exploration of 'alternatives,' and established review processes to evaluate non-animal methods; they might lobby for more funds to be allocated towards those agencies' efforts. They would work *with*, rather than against, companies like Procter & Gamble and Gillette who continue to test on animals as they develop 'alternatives;' they would support government coordination of the many private initiatives to develop, validate and implement 'alternatives,' and, given the globalization of markets, would probably encourage US research agencies to collaborate with their European counterparts like ECVAM as other countries have done.[6]

Rack and Spira (1989) have suggested giving even more responsibility to the very organization that has shirked its responsibilities in this area. The authors suggest that the National Institutes of Health (NIH), the organizational nerve-center of US biological research (whose 1994 budget was circa eleven billion dollars),[7] establish a series of cell technology centers around the country that would serve as resources and stimulation for progress in cell and molecular biology and toxicology. In this way, they say, 'the search for alternatives will become integrally part of the mainstream.'[8] Another suggestion was made by Coenraad F. M. Hendriksen (1994) that agency/institute-linked centers for alternative methods be established within governments, so that work on the Three Rs would be regarded as a matter of course.[9]

Before Scenario A's proponents placed any more faith in federal agencies to make progress in this area, however, it would be judicious to assess the effectiveness of the vast number of programs and projects already in existence, to gauge whether agencies are complying with previous initiatives.[10]

As discussed in Chapter 4, current US guidelines for toxicity testing do not take scientific advances of the last decade into account, and they are not reflective of the changes mandated by the 1993 NIH Revitalization Act. The NIEHS was directed by the Act to establish criteria for the validation and regulatory acceptance of alternative assays for safety testing. Only in late 1995 were attempts made to fulfill that mandate on paper through the drafting of the ICCVAM report, the fate of which remains uncertain.[11] Without a Congressional mandate to implement the recommendations made in the report, it will have little impact. So far, no *in vitro* methods have been listed in the US Code of Federal Regulations, despite the fact that companies often submit *in vitro* data to regulatory agencies.[12] Progress in Europe has been similarly slow. Pam Logemann of Advanced Tissue Sciences (ATS) believes that federal agencies should be forced by law to require the submission of *in vitro* over animal data, particularly because testing laboratories involved in human trials are finding that their human data do not correspond with animal data—the gold standard used for validation trials.[13] Because the key lies in changing legislation, those who adhere to Scenario A should ideally challenge governments to overhaul federal policies and guidelines, honor legislative commitments, and commit to funding programs for human trials, *in vitro* research, development, and (simple) validation programs—programs now being funded by *in vitro* manufacturers at great expense.

In essence, Scenario A embraces the 'Three Rs' philosophy; it takes small, incremental baby steps towards the eventual replacement of animals in toxicity testing, and places faith in institutions or bureaucracies to 'do good.' It trusts that industry will honorably continue developing more 'alternatives,' and that governments will dutifully carry out mandates to implement these methods; it seems to ignore the influence that special interests have in shaping regulatory agendas. But because bureaucracy in government is notorious, and because resistance to 'alternatives' has been shown to exist within science, industry *and* government (particularly within the NIH, the EC, OECD, and the UN),[14] one could expect that, at best, cosmetics testing on animals (which is not a legal requirement anyway) might be phased out eventually. However, animal testing for carcinogenicity, teratogenicity, neurotoxicity and general toxicity would probably not be phased out for a very long time, if at all. Even toxicologists working on alternatives are in general agreement about this.[15] Indeed, a recent EC report claims that *in vitro* tests may be able to replace animals in tests for eye irritation, skin absorption, mutagenicity, and phototoxicity 'in the near future,' but those tests account for only 22% of all animal testing.[16]

Scenario B Public pressure would be an essential component of the second and more radical scenario, Scenario B, of which I am an advocate. This scenario essentially calls for a ban on animal testing, an idea that has been advanced before by former German Green Party leader Rudolf Bahro, and proposed in Canada and some European countries by way of referendums. In his book, *Building the Green Movement* (1986, p. 207), Bahro said, 'only a position of complete abolition ... will permit us to draw attention to the essence of the issue.'

Making such a ban a reality would require a groundswell of public involvement in the political/legislative process, similar to the successful campaign led by the San Francisco-based Earth Island Institute to make tuna fishing 'dolphin safe;' it would be up to animal advocacy groups and progressive scientists to ensure that that requirement was met. Contrary to animal testing proponents' claims, a comprehensive ban on animal testing would become the mother of invention; scientists would be compelled to use their ingenuity to find new research methods, and a new ethical paradigm would be fostered as a result. Regulations would have to be rewritten to be simple and straightforward; the laws, guidelines and policies of the various international regulatory agencies would be brought into harmony with one another; they would promote the use of non-animal technologies that are rapid, cost-effective, humane, and relevant to human beings. An across-the-board listing of these assays in the US Code of Federal Regulations and in EC and OECD guidelines would finally legitimize them in the eyes of lawsuit-weary companies that must supply toxicity data to federal agencies.

William Stokes of NIEHS confirms that the key is not the development of more alternatives, but regulatory acceptance of the methods that already exist. Once a non-animal method is accepted by a country, it is up to that country, or corporations using the technology, or investors, to lobby for the incorporation of the methods into OECD testing guidelines. This would legitimize the technology and pave the way for other countries to use it.[17] Experience shows that when non-animal methods are made available under regulatory mandates, their use becomes widespread, as in OSHA's acceptance in 1993 and 1994 of In Vitro International's Corrositex assay and Advanced Tissue Science (ATS's) Skin^2 product in place of the Draize corrosivity/irritancy test with rabbits. The Corrositex assay is now used by some four hundred and twenty companies in the US (corporations, contract laboratories), and certain agencies within the US government, to establish corrosivity.[18] As Tracy Donnelly of ATS stated, 'government agencies, as well as industry, need to learn how to look at the data from *in vitro* tests and use them.'[19]

A renewed focus on epidemiology and (responsibly conducted) human volunteer studies would also be emphasized as scientists came to terms with the fact that only human data can fill the knowledge gaps in their understanding of the effects of chemicals on human beings. As the British biochemist Dennis V. Parke states, animal studies are essentially an elaborate, but far from foolproof, system for detecting any potential hazards of chemicals to which humans are inevitably exposed.[20] Governments must be compelled (legally if need be) to divert funds away from animal toxicity programs and redistribute them towards these forms of research. Money should also be allocated towards the simple validation of a handful of the over one hundred *in vitro* (mutagenicity) assay systems that exist.[21]

In Scenario B, complex and costly validation schemes would not be tolerated, in the realization that they are unduly bureaucratic, and unjust on several levels: (1) the majority currently use animal rather than human data as a standard for comparison when many scientists feel this is counterproductive to obtaining relevant data; (2) human toxicity data do not realistically exist for the over 75,000 chemicals now in commerce, and to obtain them in a timely fashion would be impossible; (3) industry has a lot of useful human data but will not release them for proprietary reasons;[22] (4) the criteria for the validation of *in vitro* methods are unduly rigorous when compared to the animal tests which have never been validated. The NTP has spent hundreds of millions of dollars on ineffective animal tests and fruitless validation programs, and it has never been held accountable for this enormous waste of public money.[23] In fact no one has successfully challenged federal regulatory policies which, despite decades of animal tests, have failed to protect human health and the environment.

Herman B. W. M. Koeter of the OECD advocates a 'learning-by-doing' approach: incorporating 'alternative' test methods in safety testing programs before they have been validated.[24] Federal regulatory agencies should be challenged to accept this approach sooner rather than later. After all, dramatic advances in technology, cost and time considerations, and the need to test a steady stream of chemicals, will make the adoption of non-animal methods inevitable, so why postpone the inevitable? Similarly, if uncertainty exists in one test system, why not accept the comparable uncertainty of an alternative test system that is faster, cheaper and more humane?

A reliance on better technology is not enough, however; ultimately we need fewer pesticides, fewer food additives, and fewer toxic ingredients in industrial, household, and personal care products.

Chemical bans

'The task of safeguarding human health from man made carcinogens seems a hopeless one, unless there is a complete ban on economically essential but hazardous chemicals.' Hans Falk of the National Cancer Institute, in Edith Efron (1984), p. 393

'Nothing less than a global ban on the production and use of all persistent toxic chemicals ... will protect our oceans and human health.' Tim Birch, Greenpeace International Toxics Campaign, *Greenpeace Quarterly*, Washington, DC (Summer 1996), p. 11

No technological fix can address the growing problem of mounting industrial pollution. Environmentalists like Erik Olsen of the Natural Resources Defense Council and Ellen Silbergeld, a toxicologist with the Environmental Defense Fund, believe that risk assessment research is a waste of time and resources, and the answer is to limit the use of toxic materials from the outset.[25]

This is not an irrational idea. The total amount of both organic and inorganic chemicals produced in 1988 was 609.55 billion pounds.[26] The fear of cancer and other illnesses caused by the intentional and unintentional releases of such vast quantities of chemicals into the environment is the reason why millions of animals are being sacrificed, and hundreds of millions of dollars are being spent on risk assessment research which has failed to protect human health. In addition, as discussed, the US Office of Technology Assessment (1993) reported that the cost of treating chemically induced illnesses has been estimated to reach well into the billions of dollars.[27]

Irrespective of whether chemicals significantly contribute or not to the onset of cancer, it cannot be denied that there are too many chemicals on the market whose effects on humans are unknown.[28] Instead of assuming that chemicals are innocent until proven guilty, and instead of asking, 'how do we better anticipate the development of new industries which introduce new chemicals into the environment?'[29] the US Congress, for example, should authorize federal agencies like the EPA to pass a moratorium on the development and/or production of new synthetic chemicals until we (if ever) learn to understand the health and environmental effects of the 75,000 or more chemicals already on the market. Sweeping federal legislation, akin to the US Clean Water Act, such as The Chemical Production Moratorium Act, could be passed with potentially more far-reaching effects and introduced on an international scale. For existing chemicals, federal labelling schemes could do much to help consumers distinguish between toxic and non-toxic products in stores. Unlike in the US, where the decision about how to warn consumers about a product's risk is left largely to the manufacturer's discretion, in Japan and some European and Scandinavian countries toxic products are made clearly recognizable by the application of symbols—such as a black X inside an orange box—which must by law appear on a product label.[30]

For a decade now, citizen groups have demanded bans and restrictions on deadly chemicals. Several campaigns to ban entire categories of noxious chemicals (including persistent organic compounds and chlorine-based compounds) are already under way. According to Erika Rosenthal and Monica Moore of the San Francisco-based Pesticide Action Network, 'bans have been catalysts for increased public participation in national decision making. Demands for such decisive action help to focus attention on sluggish governments and agencies.'[31]

American scientist/author Barry Commoner suggests that environmental programs have succeeded only where government has prohibited the production of pollutants (pollution prevention) and have generally failed whenever government has sought to regulate the allowable level of discharges (pollution control).[32] Again, the obvious dichotomy between simple solutions (bans) and complex bureaucratic schemes (regulations) reappears here. A model for progressive federal regulatory reform which substantiates Commoner's hypothesis and has resulted in undeniably positive changes in the area of waste prevention, is the German Waste and Packaging Law (or The German Federal Ordinance Concerning Avoidance of Packaging Waste). This straightforward and courageous initiative, enacted in December 1991 with little cost–benefit analysis, forces manufacturers to account for the consequences of their production processes; it should be seen as a model for what would be possible in the US and elsewhere in the area of pollution prevention given visionary political leadership. The fundamental philosophy behind the German law is that manufacturers and distributors are responsible for the packaging they create and use (in the same way that chemical companies should be held accountable for the pollution they create), and heavy fines punish those who break the law.[33] Such mechanisms are supposed to be in place in countries like the US, but as I have shown in Chapter 4, enforcement of existing pollution prevention laws is severely deficient.

Currently, animal-based risk assessment is used as a form of pollution *control* rather than prevention, as it is used as an alibi for weak environmental regulations which allow for the continued release of pollutants into the environment.[34] In essence, honest regulatory policies, which truly seek to *prevent* rather than control releases of potentially health-destroying chemicals into the environment should be the norm

rather than the exception. Companies can no longer be rewarded for
polluting, or for manufacturing toxic chemicals which must then undergo costly testing schemes. Policies should be forged which give companies the incentive *not* to pollute; pollution prevention must become a
part of product design, and government should give huge economic
rewards to companies that already manufacture 'green' (or non-toxic)
products.[35]

Health and environmental advocates should demand that there be a
demonstrated need for any new chemical that is marketed. Currently,
products are manufactured in response to artificial market pressures,
designed to perpetuate consumerism, rather than in response to real
human needs. This has led to the creation of the existing market, one
that is flooded with hundreds if not thousands of drugs and consumer
products—many of which are totally unnecessary and are essentially
'improved' versions of previous products. Such an irresponsible approach to chemicals in our environment should not be tolerated.

Scientists and various advocacy groups have recommended phasing
out industrial carcinogens altogether and replacing them with safer
substitutes.[36] While the EPA has begun to seek funding for research
into the design of 'safer chemicals' that are less hazardous,[37] this
program does not address the underlying problem of overproduction,
and the fact that 'safer' chemicals would probably also have to be
subjected to toxicity testing. Furthermore, an emphasis should be placed
on the use of natural as opposed to synthetic ingredients, and non-
chemical farming practices. Education about, and support for implementation of alternatives to hazardous products should be a priority
for researchers and environmentalists. Under a new paradigm, for
example, a license would have to be issued based on a *demonstrated* need
for a new pesticide. As Neal Barnard, Director of the Physicians
Committee for Responsible Medicine in Washington, DC stated, 'the
criteria for necessity would have to be left to persons other than
regulatory bureaucrats who rotate from industry to government and
back again, and should be delegated to an independent agency for
which health interests are paramount.'[38]

In 1980, Gio Batta Gori, then Deputy Director of the Division of
Cancer Cause and Prevention at the NCI, suggested a regulatory
paradigm based on this idea. Gori envisaged the creation of an independent court which would rule on the allowable uses of chemicals
based on need, utility and hazard. In this context he said, 'the ethical
and operational incompetence of intransigent statutes might come to
be viewed as an embarrassment to be rectified, and as inconsistent with
the safeguards of due process that are at the philosophical core of a

free society … The future of manufacturing could well be characterized by restraints and solutions unthinkable a decade ago.' Gori's plan
attempts to come to terms with the failings of the current animal-based
testing system, and of the inevitable depletion of raw commodities.[39]
His is one of many ideas that could be implemented in the context of
a plan to replace animals in toxicity testing (and simultaneously preserve
the environment); but no strategic stone must be left unturned to achieve
that goal. Some ideas about how this may be accomplished will be
discussed below.

The path to revolution: forms of public protest

Several tactics have been used for decades by advocacy groups to achieve
desired goals (or at the very least to obtain concessions). These include
the staging of demonstrations, performing acts of civil disobedience,
holding press conferences, using stockholder resolutions, introducing
legislation, lobbying, conducting public education and outreach, letter
writing (and now E-mail) campaigns to newspapers, legislators, and
specific companies and individuals that are the targets of protest.

One animal advocacy group in Norfolk, Virginia has developed its
own agenda in the fight against animal testing which may serve as a
model for other groups. The organization is doing several things including:

1. Pressuring companies which continue to test products on animals by
   faxing them petitions, staging protests in their offices, encouraging
   their members to write the companies and return their products
   directly to them; in some cases, CEOs' homes have been picketed.
2. Helping compassionate companies develop cruelty-free logos.[40]
3. Providing documentation and expert opinions to federal agencies to
   keep the issue of animal testing at the top of the government's
   agenda.
4. Urging all companies regulated by those agencies to use non-animal
   testing methods.
5. Offering consumers practical information such as cruelty-free shopping guides, factsheets, and flyers by distributing them at street fairs,
   tabling and (other events), and placing them in cosmetics and retail
   outlets. (Others have urged consumers to ask their local markets to
   carry 'cruelty-free' products.)
6. Using celebrity endorsements in videotapes, and distributing these to
   the media and others who may want them, to expose companies that
   still test on animals and to illustrate the alternatives to animal testing.

7. Working with activists internationally to ensure that 'no animal testing' becomes a worldwide policy, and organizing international efforts to agitate against companies that continue animal tests.
8. Educating the public about animal tests to explain why they're outdated, unnecessary, useless and cruel.
9. Promoting *in vitro* and other non-animal toxicity testing methods in radio and television interviews, newspapers and classroom lectures.[41]

Several animal advocacy organizations, including the American Anti-Vivisection Society (AAVS) in Pennsylvania, through its Alternative Research and Development Foundation, and The American Fund for Alternatives to Animal Research (AFAAR) in New York City, have taken it upon themselves to offer financial support in the form of grants to scientists pursuing research on non-animal testing methods.

The Coalition for Consumer Information on Cosmetics (composed of nine international animal advocacy groups, including PETA and AAVS)[42] is evaluating the potential for an industry-wide move away from animal testing through the use of a questionnaire which it is sending out to myriad different companies. The Coalition's wish is to become recognized, by industry, government, and consumers, as the definitive source for information about this issue.[43] The fact that these groups have been able to come together to collaborate is significant since the animal advocacy movement has historically been marked by infighting. Because there is political power in numbers, the building of coalitions among organizations and interest groups will prove increasingly important in advocacy groups' future struggles against corporate interests.

Whether advocacy groups form coalitions or work independently, they must remember that we are living in a society whose primary concern is 'the bottom line;' in this time of shrinking federal (and global) resources, the development of comprehensive economic arguments against animal testing is of paramount importance; I have shown that corporations are concerned with cutting costs and often abandon animal testing for those reasons. Government agencies are motivated by the same concerns. Irwin Bross wrote, '[The US] Congress may suddenly discover that it can save many billions of dollars simply by eliminating waste and scientific fraud in the federal health and science agencies ... Nowadays there [are] ... no state or federal funds to cover budget deficits.'[44] Activists would do well to collaborate with economists and accountants to make sure all bases of this argument are covered when the issue is presented to governmental bodies and the general public.

The activist struggle in the face of economic globalization

'The mechanisms by which TNCs [transnational corporations] exercise control and manipulation over the political life of nation states are mind boggling. They involve multi-billion dollar political advertising campaigns and governmental lobby operations. They include business oriented think-tanks on public policy and the organization of citizen front groups. These mechanisms, in turn, are reinforced by an elaborate system of campaign funding for political parties plus government patronage operations in many countries. At the same time, the CEOs of the major corporations have worked their way into the drivers seat of public policy-making in regards to key sectors of the economy. If social movements are going to advance the cause for taking democratic control, then strategies need to be developed for dismantling these and related mechanisms of corporate politics.' Tony Clarke, *Dismantling Corporate Rule* (San Francisco: International Forum on Globalization, 1995), p. 29

Many social activist groups are pointing out that the concentration of power in the world today is no longer held by nation states or democratically elected governments, but by large transnational corporations (TNCs). Governments have reorganized their national economic, social and political systems to ensure profitable returns for these corporate entities, whose rights and freedoms are protected above and beyond those of the average citizen.

Tony Clarke, of the Council of Canadians in Ontario, is urging social movements to develop a new form of politics in response to the realities of corporate domination. He states that activists today must 'put more strategic priority on the task of exposing and dismantling corporate rule,' so that people can regain democratic control over the levers of public policy making. This does not simply mean trying to persuade individual corporations to become 'socially responsible' by adopting green labelling practices for example. Conventional strategies and tactics such as these are no longer adequate for tackling today's corporate domination, for they are 'piecemeal approaches to what has become a *systemic* problem.'[45]

Given that the basic powers of corporations are legally protected, Clarke believes that social movement activists must reexamine the ways in which they analyze problems, and adopt a set of multi-level strategies to achieve their goals. Clarke suggests a number of strategies to this end in a paper entitled *Dismantling Corporate Rule*, published by the International Forum on Globalization in San Francisco.[46]

At a time when economic globalization is affecting every facet of our lives, and international trade accords like the General Agreement on Tariffs and Trade (GATT) are ravaging animal and environmental protection laws,[47] activists will have to think about strategies systemically and in a global context. Currently 128 countries adhere to GATT, accounting for 90 percent of world merchandise trade. GATT cannot directly alter any law of one of its member nations, but a GATT challenge can be enough to prompt a government to change or repeal previous laws.[48] Although GATT cannot dictate the actions of individual corporations (for example it cannot prevent The Body Shop from selling 'cruelty-free' cosmetics), any GATT member nation can protest the laws and policies of another member nation if they are deemed to interfere with the free flow of markets. For example, EEC regulations governing the use of animals in research and testing (such as 86/609/EEC of 24 November 1986) are already written and designed 'to avoid affecting the establishment and functioning of the common market, in particular by distortions of competition or barriers to trade.'

In effect, nations can no longer express their citizens' wishes if those wishes conflict with free trade, as in the UK's Department of Trade and Industry and the US National Consumer's League's attempts to do away with 'cruelty-free' logos and labels.[49] Because it was determined under GATT that labels affect consumer behavior, and this in turn affects the market, labelling schemes (such as 'eco' and 'cruelty-free' labelling) have come under fire. Government laws or initiatives requiring companies like Procter & Gamble to label their products as having been tested on animals could be overturned under GATT. Laws which prohibited the use of animals in toxicity testing, or favored *in vitro* methods over the use of animals, could be challenged on the basis that they closed off market options to the use of live animals. State or local laws which sought to prohibit the sale of animal-tested products would also be challenged, and probably overturned.[50] The goal to end animal testing will have to be viewed within the context of these new threats to global democracy and progress. It is imperative that activists become knowledgeable about GATT and learn to understand the impact that such international agreements have on their issues.

Environmentalists and animal advocates: a necessary union

'The great convergence between animal and environmental protectionists is an important new development in the global effort to build a more humane and sustainable civilization. It is occurring because society is coming to understand that all things ... are profoundly interdependent.' Jan Hartke, President, Earthkind, a division of the Humane Society of the United States, quoted in *E Magazine*, January/February 1996, p. 39

'Animal activists should begin to build bridges to grassroots environmentalists and other activists to present a united opposition to these powerful establishments. Activists should be prepared to testify, well armed with facts and figures, that it could actually enhance the public health and safety if the wasteful or fraudulent [animal-based testing] programs were eliminated. Few would weep if these establishments died and the animals lived.' Irwin D. Bross, 'A Formula to Make Animal Activists More Effective,' unpublished paper, 1990

A union between animal and environmental (and health) advocates would build an enormous political power base and would seem inevitable in the face of the looming global threat to environmental and animal protection laws. But while animal advocates generally call themselves environmentalists, the reverse is not true; it is recognized that the environmental movement has resisted collaboration with animal advocacy groups. They are often embarrassed by the movement's tactics and agendas and see the concern for individual animal suffering as naive and overly sentimental.[51] It may therefore be up to animal advocacy groups to reach out to environmentalists and health advocates. The former may have to become more 'sophisticated' in the way they present their arguments. For example, in the tradition of their movement, which grew out of social crusades like the abolition of slavery, animal advocates could use specific campaigns to demonstrate that what happens to animals in toxicology laboratories affects human health and the earth, thus widening their philosophical angle to include environmental and health concerns. In addition, the use of a pragmatic rather than an emotional approach, including the presentation of solid scientific arguments against animal testing, may help to build the movement's credibility in the eyes of other interest groups.

By adopting a more holistic approach in their advocacy work, animal advocates may be able to reach people that would otherwise have been 'turned off' by a strictly 'animal-oriented' agenda. Environmentalists must also begin to understand that commonalities can and do exist between the two interest groups, particularly in the face of economic globalization.[52]

While some have written that environmentalism and animal advocacy are incompatible,[53] Murry Cohen, a physician and Co-Chair of the New York-based Medical Research Modernization Committee wrote in 1993 that, 'animal testing to assess human toxicity ... is unscientific. It is absurd for anyone, particularly an environmentalist, to advocate destroying some animals to benefit [humans or] other animals ... This approach only makes sense if animals are excluded from being considered part of the environment.'[54] Cohen believes this is an anthropocentric attitude which would result in the continuation of the planetary destruction environmentalists themselves oppose.

Legislation

'Legislation may not change the heart, but it can restrain the heartless.' Martin Luther King, Jr

While the animal advocacy community has historically protested against the testing of cosmetics/personal care products on animals, in reality the safety of cosmetics is no less important than that of any other kind of product which is legitimately made and marketed. If animal testing is to be abolished, present laws must be changed; progressive legislation, such as the proposed European Cosmetics Testing Ban, must be introduced (and passed) to this end. Laws could be passed requiring toxicologists to request literature searches on alternative technologies from a global databank, prior to beginning toxicological evaluations, and requiring them to use such technologies if and when they are available. For example, in The Netherlands, toxicologists are not only required, as part of their training, to learn about non-animal testing methods, but it is forbidden to use an animal for a purpose that could equally be achieved by an *in vitro* method, or a procedure which does not involve the use of animals.[55] In Germany, Article 7.5 of the Law on Animal Protection of 1987 prohibits animal experiments (on principle) for the development of laundry detergents and cosmetics.

The US-based Doris Day Animal League's main focus has been, and continues to be, legislation. While DDAL reintroduced The Consumer Products Safety Testing Act (HR 3173) in March 1996 with support from The Body Shop, John Paul Mitchell Systems, In Vitro International and Bic (a giant in the office and personal care sectors), the bill did not pass.[56] The proposed legislation would have (1) compelled each US regulatory agency to review and evaluate any and all regulations that encourage the use of animals in toxicity tests, (2) abolish the Draize and LD50 tests as quickly as possible, and (3) adopt non-animal technologies wherever feasible. Versions of this legislation have been introduced for ten consecutive years, but lack of interest in the bill and lobbying by industry groups, medical associations and proponents of biomedical research on animals have successfully blocked its passage.[57] Sara Amundson of DDAL believes that the effects of introducing legislation are cumulative, however; and so the Consumer Products Safety Testing Act will continue to be introduced until it passes, just as the Civil Rights Act of 1964 was finally passed after more than a decade of protest and lobbying. This is consistent with the idea that while participation in legislative politics by a minority is often futile, advocates must continue to bring suppressed facts to the surface; in the long run, these actions will benefit society as a whole.[58] Rudolf Bahro (1986) stated, 'laws come into being only after order has been fundamentally disturbed ... anyone who wants things to be different will have to live in a constant state of rebellion.'[59]

Herman Koeter of the OECD remains skeptical, believing that unless toxicologists begin to 'feel responsible for the well-being or even the lives of animals, nothing much will happen. No legislation, no regulation ... will change that.'[60]

The False Claims Act: a legal challenge to the US government

'A scientific fraud is actually a fraud against the US government. Therefore, a scientific fraud is actually a fraud against the people of the US. It's no longer then a mere unethical activity which will be settled by gentlemanly discourse amongst scientists.' Dr Eugene Dong of Stamford University, quoted in Robert Bell's *Impure Science: Fraud, Compromise, and Political Influence in Scientific Research* (New York: John Wiley & Sons, 1992), p. 265

Ninety-five percent of scientific activity in the US, including toxicity testing, is funded by the US government.[61] Biostatistician Irwin Bross and veterinarian/medical historian Brandon Reines have suggested that US activists and/or organizations take advantage of a 1986 amendment to a nineteenth-century law called the False Claims Act (sometimes referred to as 'The Abraham Lincoln Law') to expose what they believe is the scientific fraud of animal testing. Irwin Bross writes that:

> in one way or another, all the activities of establishments are paid for by ... taxpayer dollars. There is now overwhelming scientific evidence that the animal research on mutagenic diseases gives false or misleading findings ... Even ... [the journal] *Science* has recently admitted this in articles and editorials. Hence from now on, it should be much easier to prove in a court of law that taxpayer dollars are being spent on scientific fraud.[62]

The Act, which applies to all areas of federally supported science, allows ordinary citizens to file charges against institutions they believe have made fraudulent use of federal funds. Once a complaint is filed, the Justice Department must decide whether to enter the case. If it chooses not to, citizens can pursue a case on their own.[63] Because defendants are fined *treble* (triple) damages, if a case is won, plaintiffs can reap sizeable financial rewards: 10–25 percent of total damages awarded plus $5,000–$10,000 for each of the defendant's offenses.[64]

In the last several years, defense contractors have been the primary targets of most False Claims Act cases; but lawsuits can be filed against federally funded scientists, and federal officials who may have helped to cover up improper behavior. All you have to show, states Eugene Dong of Stamford University, is that the defendant knew the consequences of his or her actions even if he or she did not intend them. The burden of proof is 'the preponderance of the evidence.' Though they are not perfect, specific provisions in the False Claims Act protect plaintiffs against retaliation by the defendants. Robert Bell, author and professor of economics at the City University of New York, says that the False Claims Act is unique in that it may force scientists to 'live up to the strictures of the scientific method.'[65] In this vein, Gio Batta Gori (1993) wrote this about animal-based risk assessment:

> agencies should be required to regulate on the basis of scientific evidence— not conjectural assumptions and hypotheses—and to observe the same basic standards of scientific evidence and ethical conduct that are expected from any academic scientist. Regulation ... should not be permitted to become a bully pulpit for the promotion and profit of special interests under pretext of the public good.[66]

While an effort to prove that federal animal testing programs are fraudulent would require extensive historical and scientific research (some of which has been presented here), not to mention time, and resources to pay qualified lawyers, the potential for success could be worth it. The opportunity to expose the fallaciousness of animal testing to the courts, governments, and more importantly to the people, as a result of the publicity such a case could garner, would be immense. It should not be forgotten that, aside from the False Claims Act, more traditional legal means may be used to expose government waste, fraud and incompetence *vis-à-vis* animal testing. For example, if and when federal agencies do not comply with mandates to develop and implement non-animal toxicity testing methods (or are being sluggish in changing outdated and inhumane laws and guidelines), legal means may be used to force compliance. Results of polls showing lack of public support for animal testing may be used to make the people's case. Environmental groups have used lawsuits successfully for over two decades to force compliance with environmental laws, and it may be increasingly necessary for animal advocacy groups to adopt these tactics since resistance to the adoption of alternatives is bound to endure.

The future of toxicity testing without animals

'For education to be translated into voluntary action that will make a difference to the quality of life, people must make the connection between abstract research and their personal lives. They must be confronted with the fact that the choices they make directly affect the survival of life on this planet.' Andrée Collard, *Rape of the Wild* (Indiana: Indiana University Press, 1989), p. 148

'Whistleblowing should become part of the scientist's ethos.' Dr Joseph Rotblat, physicist and anti-nuclear activist, quoted in *The New York Times*, 21 May 1996, p. CI

Realistically, Scenario B described earlier *is* radical; it demands a break with tradition; and it asks for the abandonment of a method of research that, however bad, is a known quantity and has become incorporated into our scientific and regulatory institutions, and into our cultural psyche. But given the failings of the current animal-based system, compromise is counterproductive in this case—radical solutions are needed; the slate needs to be cleaned. We have nothing to lose in trying something new, and perhaps much to gain. Given the bureaucracies and entrenched attitudes inherent in government and science, and given that, more often than not, compromises rather than fully-fledged victories are the norm in politics, it is imperative that revolutionary demands continue to be made by animal advocates and others, because they will inevitably be stripped down and diluted to the point of being neutralized. Too many groups have become used to negotiating compromises they think are 'realistic;' too few are involved in direct action; and too few make radical demands.

It will also be up to progressive scientists, industry employees and others to speak out and lead by example. Those involved in this struggle must remember that they are pioneers; they are advancing ideas that society, as we know it, is not ready for. Progress will probably be slow as the challenges are immense; this will be extremely frustrating to those with the stamina to persevere. But perseverance is essential if we are to reform science, and do away with bureaucratic, inhumane and ineffective environmental health science policies. It should be remembered that scientists throughout history have joined the ranks of those who oppose animal testing and experimentation, both on scientific and ethical grounds, and they continue to do so. Without the presence of animal, health, and anti-vivisection advocacy groups to point out the fallaciousness and inhumanity of such experimentation, such shifts in consciousness, in many cases, might not have occurred.[67]

The phenomenon of the growing ozone hole has educated millions of people everywhere that if we damage a single link in the ecological chain, we damage the whole. Ecologists have told us for decades that human health is dependent on the health of the earth, and all the life forms upon it.[68] It is only logical that if we keep defiling the earth, we will continue to suffer ill health and squander billions of dollars on inhumane and inconclusive research in an attempt to heal ourselves and undo our mistakes.

Indeed, as long as millions of non-human animals are needlessly killed in the most grotesque forms, on the pretext of protecting human and other life, while we simultaneously allow the manufacture, sale, and release of poisons into our environment, we can never hope to achieve the goal of physical, environmental and spiritual health we desire.

Notes

1. Gordon Graff, 'The Chlorine Controversy,' *Technology Review* (January 1995), p. 57.

2. Ibid., p. 59.

3. Alan M. Goldberg and John M. Frazier, 'Alternatives to Animals in Toxicity Testing,' *Scientific American* (August 1989), p. 30.

4. In this vein, there have been calls for an international chemical reference database to consolidate toxicity testing information from industry and the public domain, 'making the most of results from earlier live animal experiments so that unnecessary repetition can be avoided.' Anon, 'Message in a Bottle,' *The Economist*, 22 April 1995, p. 85. Others have voiced the need for databases linking alternative data with *in vivo* data. H. M. Van Looy, in *Alternatives to Animal Testing*, C. A. Reinhardt, ed. (New York: VCH/Weinheim, 1994), p. 18.

5. According to EPA toxicologist Carlton H. Nadolney, scientists should be the ones to coordinate large-scale validation efforts. Personal communication with Carlton H. Nadolney, EPA, 28 October 1995. However, it has been demonstrated that a majority of scientists do not embrace the concept of alternatives. Andrew Rowan, et al., *The Animal Research Controversy* (Massachusetts: Center for Animals and Public Policy, Tufts University School of Veterinary Medicine, 1995), p. 59.

6. ECVAM was set up to coordinate the validation of alternative test methods at the EC level. This involves specification of test protocols, choice of chemicals to be tested, and analysis and evaluation of test results. ECVAM set up and maintains a database on alternative procedures; it promotes dialogue between legislators, industrial companies, scientists, consumer groups and animal welfare groups, 'with a view to the development, validation and international recognition of non-animal testing methods.' Erminio Marafante and Michael Balls, 'The European Centre for the Validation of Alternative Methods (ECVAM),' in C. A. Reinhardt, ed. (1994), pp. 21–5. The Netherlands established The Netherlands Centre for Alternatives in Utrecht which plays a part in coordinating validation studies in cooperation with ECVAM. L. F. M. van Zutphen, 'Animal Use and Alternatives: Developments in The Netherlands,' in C. A. Reinhardt, ed. (1994), p. 60. According to William Stokes of the NIEHS, different countries are increasingly collaborating to harmonize international testing guidelines and methods, although animal testing is still deemed an

essential part of those guidelines. Personal communication with William Stokes, NIEHS, 1 November 1995.

7. Warren E. Leary, 'Four Percent (4%) Rise Sought in Science Budget,' *The New York Times*, 8 February 1994, p. C5.

8. Leonard Rack, Henry Spira, 'Animal Rights and Modern Toxicology,' *Toxic. & Ind. Health* 5, no. 1 (1989): 133–43. Spira's recent call to challenge 'creeping routinism' in institutions who 'tend to do tomorrow what they did yesterday,' may signify a change in his position. Leslie Pardue, 'Testing for Toxins,' *E Magazine*, January/February 1994, p. 15.

9. Coenraad F. M. Hendriksen, in C. A. Reinhardt, ed. (1994), p. 68.

10. For example, the US Inter Regulatory Alternatives Group (IRAG) (comprising EPA, FDA, OSHA, CPSC) is involved in a worldwide validation study, in cooperation with ECVAM and the German Alternatives Center ZEBET, to establish criteria for the evaluation of *in vitro* eye irritancy tests which could potentially replace the Draize test. What, if any, progress has been made since the early 1990s? Horst Spielmann, et al., in C. A. Reinhardt, ed. (1994), p. 83.

11. 'Validation and Regulatory Acceptance of Toxicological Test Methods,' a report of the *ad hoc* Interagency Coordinating Committee on the Validation of Alternative Methods (Draft) (North Carolina: NIEHS, 16 October 1995).

12. William Stokes, 'Alternative Test Method Development at the National Toxicology Program,' in Proceedings of the Toxicology Forum, Winter meeting 1994, Washington, DC: CASET pub., pp. 302–12.

13. Personal communication with Pam Logemann, Director, In Vitro Lab Technology Sales, Advanced Tissue Sciences, La Jolla, California, 14 August 1996.

14. Ironically, the term 'alternatives' is hardly used in the NIH Revitalization Act, indicating the NIH's continued aversion to the concept. Andrew Rowan, et al. (1995), p. 60.

15. Personal communication with William Stokes, NIEHS, North Carolina, 1 November 1995.

16. Anon, 'Ban on Cosmetic Testing Looks Unlikely,' *BUAV Parliamentary Bulletin* 11 (November 1995), published by the British Union for the Abolition of Vivisection, London.

17. See note 15. In this regard, activists should be aware of the threats to progress posed by the General Agreement on Tariffs and Trade (GATT); see this chapter.

18. There is hope that the EPA and FDA will begin using both the Corrositex and Irritection assays by 1997. Personal communication with Diane Birely, Marketing Services Manager, In Vitro International, Irvine, California, 2 October 1995.

19. Personal communication with Tracy Donnelly, Applications Coordinator, In Vitro Lab Technology, Advanced Tissue Sciences, La Jolla, California, 24 October 1995.

20. Dennis V. Parke, 'Clinical Pharmacokinetics in Drug Safety Evaluation,' *ATLA* 22 (1994): 207–9.

21. Curtis C. Travis, et al., 'Quantitative Correlation of Carcinogenic Potency With Four Different Classes of Short-term Test Data,' *Mutagenesis* 6, no. 5 (1991): 353–60.

22. According to EPA toxicologist Carlton H. Nadolney, this barrier may never be overcome. Personal communication with Carlton H. Nadolney, Division of Chemical Screening and Risk Assessment, EPA, Washington, DC, 28 October 1995.

23. According to Peter Aldhous, 'the support received by private and non-profit groups dedicated to validation efforts from governments has historically been trivial

in the context of government expenditure.' Peter Aldhous, 'UK Government Funds Humane Research,' *Nature* 349 (24 January 1991): 272.

24. Herman B. W. M. Koeter, 'Test Guideline Development and Animal Welfare: Regulatory Acceptance of In Vitro Studies,' *Reproductive Toxicology* 7 (Suppl.) (1993): 117–23.

25. Jan Ziegler, 'Health Risk Assessment Research: The OTA Report,' *Env. Health Persp.* 101, no. 5 (October 1993): 406.

26. Marc Lappé, *Chemical Deception* (San Francisco: Sierra Club Books, 1991), p. 36.

27. Jan Ziegler (October 1993): 404.

28. Ironically, if Doll and Peto (1981) are correct, and if the majority of human cancers are caused by 'lifestyle factors' such as smoking and bad eating habits, then the majority of cancers would be preventable through behavior changes, and the hundreds of millions of dollars that are spent each year testing chemicals on animals should instead be used to fund anti-smoking and health education programs.

29. Anon, 'National Toxicology Program Final Report of the Advisory Review by the NTP Board of Scientific Counselors,' in the *Federal Register* (17 July 1992) Vol. 57, No. 138, p. 31724.

30. Personal communication with Phil Casterton, Amway, Michigan, 16 August 1996.

31. Monica Moore and Erika Rosenthal, 'The First Word,' and 'The Dirty Dozen – Banned But Rarely Banished,' *Global Pesticide Campaigner*, newsletter published by Pesticide Action Network, San Francisco, California (September 1995): pp. 2 and 11.

32. Barry Commoner cited in Eric A. Goldstein, et al., 'NY Air,' *The Amicus Journal*, published by the Natural Resources Defense Council, New York (Summer 1990): 28.

33. The German law redefines the concept of corporate responsibility, requires recycling on a massive scale and prohibits incineration. The law asks little of consumers but requires that companies take back and recycle used packaging. As a result of the law, which if violated results in considerable fines to manufacturers, industry moved quickly to establish packaging collection schemes. The government has also proposed manufacturer take-back and recycle laws for automobiles, electronic goods and other durables, which has already stimulated auto and computer companies to redesign cars and computers to facilitate recovery and recycling of components and materials. Since the 1970s, emission standards for oil and gas heating appliances have improved by over 30 percent. In 1989, under the National Environmental Policy Plan, the Dutch government decided to eliminate toxics like cadmium and chlorine from every stage of the production process. Sweden banned 'in principle' the use of cadmium in many products over a decade ago, and the idea of 'sunsetting' or phasing out the use of various toxic chemicals is popular there. Ten states in the United States have banned heavy metals from packaging.

A number of 'eco-labelling' schemes, which identify non-toxic products, have been successful in Germany, Japan, Sweden, Norway and Denmark. (The US and Canada also have such schemes: Green Seal (a private effort) and Environmental Choice, respectively.) In Germany, paints, lacquers, and varnishes that are low in solvents and other hazardous substances now make up 50 percent of the German do-it-yourself market, compared with just 1 percent in the 1970s. Japan's Eco-Mark program covers more than 850 products in 31 categories. Office of Technology Assessment, *Green Products by Design: Choices for a Cleaner Environment* (Washington DC: US Government Printing Office, September 1992).

34. The dioxin problem is a case in point. Given the apparent lack of consensus in the scientific community on the health effects of dioxin, and given that we cannot afford to study all 11,000 chlorinated hydrocarbons one at a time to learn about their effects, Greenpeace advocates a ban on all chlorinated hydrocarbons. This would entail a ban on the bleaching of paper with chlorine compounds; less toxic oxygen or hydrogen peroxide processes pioneered in Sweden could be used instead. *Greenpeace* magazine, Vol. 15, No. 5, September/October 1990, p. 26. Incineration should be banned or greatly curtailed in favor of waste reduction and recycling at the national level.

35. Office of Technology Assessment (September 1992).

36. Jeffrey A. Foran, 'The Sunset Chemicals Proposal,' *International Environmental Affairs* 2, no. 4 (Fall 1990): 303.

37. Faye Flam, 'EPA Campaigns for Safer Chemicals,' *Science* 265 (9 September 1994): 1519.

38. Neal Barnard, 'Getting Chemicals Out of Our Environment,' *PCRM Update*, newsletter of the Physicians Committee for Responsible Medicine, Washington, DC (January–February 1990): 5. Organizations could lobby to amend the Federal Insecticide, Fungicide and Rodenticide Act—which gives EPA authority to regulate pesticides—and press the agency to ban groups of chemicals, such as those in the chlorine family which produce dioxin. Such proposals have surfaced many times, but have never become law because they are unpalatable to industry. Germany, Italy and The Netherlands have shown leadership in limiting the use of atrazine (a weed killer widely used in the US) because of suspected damage to wildlife. Gordon Graff (January 1995), p. 58.

39. Gio Batta Gori, 'The Regulation of Carcinogenic Hazards,' *Science* 208 (18 April 1980), pp. 256–61.

40. Benetton, an international clothing and personal care products company, is now seeking People for the Ethical Treatment of Animal's (PETA's) help to promote its new cruelty-free logo for products not tested on animals; Prevail and Taiyoyushi, two Japanese cosmetics manufacturers, recently began putting 'no animal testing' labels on their products. *JAVA News* (Spring/Summer 1996), published by the Japanese Anti-Vivisection Association, Tokyo, p. 3.

41. Caring Consumer Campaign fact sheet, People for the Ethical Treatment of Animals, Washington, DC, October 1995.

42. The Coalition includes PETA, The Doris Day Animal League, The Humane Society of the United States, the American Humane Association, Beauty Without Cruelty, Animal Protection Institute, In Defense of Animals, New England Anti-Vivisection Society, American Anti-Vivisection Society.

43. Personal communication with Amy Morgan, Caring Consumer Campaign coordinator, People for the Ethical Treatment of Animals, Washington, DC, 28 October 1995.

44. Irwin D. Bross, 'A Formula to Make Animal Activists More Effective,' Unpublished paper, 1990, p. 19, courtesy of the author, Buffalo, New York.

45. Tony Clarke, *Dismantling Corporate Rule: Towards a New Form of Politics in an Age of Globalization—A Set of Working Instruments for Social Movements* (draft) (San Francisco: International Forum on Globalization, 1995): 1–49.

46. Ibid. Clarke's suggestions include (1) mounting non-violent resistance campaigns on a massive scale, similar to the US Civil Rights Movement and the Anti-Apartheid Movement in South Africa; (2) initiating legal measures to amend or revoke the charters of transnational corporations, thereby challenging the corporation's right

to exist. At least 49 states in the US provide people with a legal base from which to challenge the charters or certificates of authority granted to corporations on the grounds that they have misused or abused their power; (3) generating economic leverage through strikes and boycotts; (4) lobbying the government demanding an end to the government–corporate alliance; (5) building popular resistance at the community and regional levels. This step includes educating the public to find points of corporate vulnerability, design alternative policies and programs and make creative use of the media; (6) developing global solidarity with activists and resistance movements in different countries; and (7) developing a common strategy for aggressive legislative action aimed at dismantling corporate monopolies, mergers, and cartels.

47. Patricia A. Forkam and Leesteffy Jenkins, 'Good Laws Doomed?,' *HSUS News*, magazine of the Humane Society of the United States, Washington, DC (Fall 1995): 32–4.

48. Ibid. The most controversial element of GATT is the creation of the World Trade Organization (WTO), a permanent body in Geneva with considerable power to force member nations to comply with the agreements reached under GATT. Currently, humane, environmental and other non-governmental organizations (NGOs) do not have access to WTO deliberations or decision-making processes when laws are challenged. US NGOs are actively lobbying government trade representatives to remedy this situation, though it is unclear how open the WTO intends to be.

49. Holly Hazard, 'Progress in Product Testing,' *The Animals' Agenda* (July/August 1996), pp. 29–30.

50. Personal communication with Leesteffy Jenkins, attorney specializing in international and environmental law, Washington, DC, 15 November 1995. Although more of concern to welfarists and not those seeking the total abolition of animal testing, animal welfare laws which dictate the way animals are treated in laboratories could come under scrutiny for being too rigorous, as humane slaughter laws already have.

51. Jim Motavalli, 'Our Agony Over Animals: Achieving Empathy for the Non-human Animal World is a Slow, Painful Process, and One the Environmental Movement Has So Far Resisted,' *E Magazine*, September/October 1995, pp. 28–41. A majority of humans use non-human animals every day as food, clothing, in scientific study and so on, without questioning this utilitarian relationship, or questioning why wild species are any more deserving than domestic species of consideration.

52. See Rik Scarce, *Eco-Warriors* (Chicago: Noble Press, 1990); David Day, *The Environmental Wars* (New York: St Martin's Press, 1989).

53. Bill Breen, 'Why We Need Animal Testing,' *Garbage*, April/May 1993, p. 42.

54. Murry J. Cohen, Editorial to *Garbage* magazine, in response to Bill Breen's article cited in note 53, courtesy of Murry J. Cohen, Virginia.

55. L. F. M. van Zutphen, in C. A. Reinhardt, ed. (1994), p. 58.

56. Personal communication with Sara Amundson, DDAL, Washington, DC, 25 July 1996 and 20 September 1996.

57. Heidi J. Welsh, *Animal Testing and Consumer Products* (Washington, DC: Investor Responsibility Research Center, 1990), p. 36.

58. Rudolf Bahro, *Building the Green Movement* (Philadelphia: New Society Publishers, 1986), p. 207.

59. Ibid., p. 209.

60. Herman B. W. M. Koeter (1993): 117–23.

61. Robert Bell, *Impure Science* (New York: John Wiley & Sons, 1992), p. 265.

62. Irwin D. Bross (1990).

63. Joseph Palca, 'Old Law Puts New Wrinkle in Fraud Probes,' *Science* 247 (16 February 1990): 802.

64. Robert Bell (1992), pp. 264–7.

65. Ibid., pp. 266–7.

66. Gio Batta Gori, 'Whither Risk Assessment,' *Regul. Toxicol. Pharmacol.* 17 (1993): 228.

67. Roger E. Ulrich, *Rites of Life: A Book About the Use and Misuse of Animals and Earth* (Michigan: LifeGiving Enterprises, Inc, 1989). Ulrich was a former animal experimenter. See also Hans Ruesch, *1000 Doctors Against Vivisection* (Switzerland: CIVIS, 1991). Membership in organizations like the Physicians Committee for Responsible Medicine in Washington, DC and the London-based Doctors and Lawyers for Responsible Medicine continues to grow.

68. See for example Edward O. Wilson, *The Diversity of Life* (Cambridge: Harvard University Press, 1992).

Index

1,2,3-trichloropropane, 111

2-acetylminofiuorene, 47
2-naphthylamine, 58

5-desaturase enzyme system, 51

Abelson, Philip H., 151
Acceptable Daily Intake (ADI), 30–2, 36, 106
acid rain, 46
Adams, Carol, 83
adjuncts, use of term, 174
Advanced Tissue Sciences (ATS) company, 73, 156, 176, 183, 184, 211, 212
Agency for Toxic Substances and Disease Registry (ATSDR) (US), 30, 35
Agent Orange, 117
agricultural chemicals, dangers of, 113
agriculture, organic, 108
Aids, 170
air quality, 107; in New York, 107
Alar, 112; study of, 75
Alden, C.L., 161
aluminum, dangers of, 111
Alzheimer's disease, 111
American Anti-Vivisection Society (AAVS), 218
American Association of Poison Control Centers (AAPCC), 87
American Cancer Society (ACS), 8
American Dental Association (ADA), 187
American Fund for Alternatives to Animal Research (AFAAR), 218
American Public Health Association, 118
Ames, Bruce, 9, 75, 154
Ames *Salmonella* test, 152, 154, 159, 168, 187

Amundson, Sara, 127, 222
Amway company, 116, 163, 183, 185, 187, 191
Anderegg, Christopher, 168
Andersen, Melvin, 160
animal advocacy, 4, 156, 173, 174, 189, 209, 212, 217, 218, 221, 222, 225
Animal and Plant Health Inspection Service (APHIS) (US), 23
Animal Enterprise Protection Act (1992) (US), 174
animal research ethics committees, 135
animal tests, functions of, 33–4
Animal Type Culture Collection, 173
Animal Welfare Act (1966) (US), 23, 80, 170
animal-tested products, sale of, 220
animals: data, use of, 28–37; debate about nature of, 137; disposal of carcasses of, 85; experience of pain, 80; feelings of, 78, 79; multiple use of, in tests, 81; reduced use of, 176; research, sale of, 134; testing on *see* tests, animal-based *and* animals used in testing
Animals (Scientific Procedures) Act (1986) (UK), 80, 81
animals used in testing, 21–4; axenic *see* axenic animals; baboons, 13; birds, 22; cats, 22, 51, 74; chickens, 22, 58, 79, 81, 88, 117, 170; cows, 29; dogs, 13, 22, 23, 45, 51, 74, 130, 210; fish, 22; frogs, 22, 170, 171, 172 (packing of, 171); geese, 79; guinea pigs, 22, 26, 46, 58, 74, 80, 83, 117, 126, 134, 173, 177; hamsters, 51, 58, 112, 114, 117, 118, 119, 126, 134 (Syrian golden, 58); hens, 22, 23, 27; marmosets, 79; mice *see* mice; mink, 34, 117; monkeys, 13, 45, 57, 63, 74, 79, 81, 112, 117, 210; pigeons, 22;

Center for the Evaluation of Risks to
Human Reproduction, 133
Chanel company, 156, 186
Charles River Laboratories, 37, 68, 82,
134, 169, 170, 178
Charles River Research Primates, 134
Chemical Industry Institute of
Toxicology (US), 171
Chemical Manufacturers' Association
(CMA) (US), 84, 131
Chemical Production Moratorium Act,
proposed, 214
chemicals: absorption of, 63; allowable
uses of, 216; banning of, 133, 214–17;
classified by toxicity, 183–4; growing
usage of, 19, 207; market for, 216;
overload with, 104; pollution by, 113,
208; prevention of releases of, 102;
reduction of dependency on, 87; test-
ing of, 207; total production of, 214
Cheminova company, 113
CHEMLINE database, 33
China, 164
chlordane, 103, 109
chlorinated naphthalenes, 12
chloroform, 58
cinnamyl anthranilate, 112
citronella oil, 116
civil disobedience, 217
Clarke, Tony, 219
Clean Air Act (US), 10, 106, 107
Clean Water Act (US), 214
Clemedsen, Cecilia, 55, 155, 209
Clemmensen, Johannes, 87
Clinton, Bill, 173
Clonetics Corporation, 136
coal tar, used in testing, 11, 12
Coalition for Consumer Information on
Cosmetics, 188, 218
Code of Federal Regulations (US), 211,
212
coffee, 62, 75
Cohen, Murry, 221
Colgate-Palmolive company, 169
Collard, Andrée, 64, 78, 83, 101, 112,
206, 225
Commission on Risk Assessment and
Risk Management (US), 104
Commoner, Barry, 215
COMPACT program, 154, 159
Comprehensive Environmental
Response Compensation and
Liability Act (CERCLA) (US), 30

computerized modelling, 136
Conning, D.M., 103
consumer lawsuits, 191
Consumer Product Safety Commission
(CPSC) (US), 20, 122, 125–7, 130
Consumer Products Safety Testing Act,
222
Cooper, Mary H., 107
Corrositex assay, 157, 158, 167, 176, 212
Cortese, Anthony, 105
Cosmetic, Toiletry and Fragrance
Association (CTFA) (US), 176, 178
cosmetics, 83, 122, 124, 156; testing of,
13, 24, 180, 188
Coulston Foundation, 134
Coulston International Corporation, 88
Croce, Pietro, 48, 66, 83, 173
cruelty-free claims and labelling, 188,
189, 217, 220
culture assay, 153–6
Cummings, Tim, 21
Cunninghamella elegans, 166
cyclamate, 75

daminozide, 112
DDT (Dichloro-Diphenyl-Trichloro-
Ethane), 58, 102, 118–22, 164;
banning of, 119, 120
decaffeination, 112
Delaney Clause, 14, 107, 108
Department of Trade and Industry
(DTI) (UK), 220
DES growth promotant, 109
diagnostic techniques, non-invasive,
161–2, 167
diazinon, 108, 113
dieldrin, 109
dimethyl-benzo-alpha-anthracene, 58
dimethylnitrosamine (DMNA), 119
Diner, Jeff, 151
dioxins, 109, 117–18
Diptorex, 59
DNA, 153, 154; damage to, 8, 154, 161,
162, 165, 209
Doll, Richard, 9, 50
Dong, Eugene, 223, 224
Donnelly, Tracy, 212
Doris Day Animal League (DDAL), 127,
128, 222
dose-response estimates, 30–2
dosing strategies, 11
DOW Chemical company, 164, 177